THE
MARRIAGE
OF
SPIRIT

Enlightened Living in Today's World

LESLIE TEMPLE-THURSTON
with Brad Laughlin

CoreLight Publishing
Santa Fe, New Mexico

For information:
CoreLight Publications
223 North Guadalupe Street, PMB 275
Santa Fe, NM 87501-1850
(888) 989-3552
Website: www.corelight.org
email: info@corelight.org

Distributed by:
Blessingway Books, Inc.
(800) 716-2953

Cover design: Christinea Johnson
Cover photograph: Brad Laughlin, Old Jerusalem, 1998
Book design & typography: Kathleen Sparkes, White Hart Design, Albuquerque
Editors: Diana C. Douglas, John Lyons-Gould & Brad Laughlin

The illustrations opening each chapter are *yantras* by artist James Emery.
Yantras are ancient mystical symbols for
transforming consciousness in gazing meditation.

Publisher's Cataloging-in-Publication Data:
Temple-Thurston, Leslie.
The marriage of spirit : enlightened living in today's world /
Leslie Temple-Thurston with Brad Laughlin. —1st ed.
p. cm.
Includes bibliographical references and index.
LCCN: 00-102305
ISBN: 0-9660182-0-6
1. Spiritual life. 2. Self-actualization (Psychology)
3. Spiritual journals—Authorship.
I. Laughlin, Brad. II. Title.

BL624.T46 2000   291.4'4
                                                  I00-426

ACKNOWLEDGEMENTS

Although neither of my two former teachers, Frances Stearns and Frederick Lenz, would have wanted to feel bound by a formal lineage, each has seeded me with different aspects of the information birthing into fruition with this book. *The Marriage of Spirit* is a synthesis of what they both impressed upon the soft clay of my awareness.

They each expressed their devotion to the perennial philosophy and to humanity in different ways, and it was left to me to meld their different viewpoints of truth into the one, coherent form that was my destiny to find. They validated the truth that was trying to birth in me, gave me a vocabulary, a sense of structure and much more. What they asked of me in no way equaled what they each gave. I thank and bless you both.

To my inner guides, the many masters who were midwives to truth—I bless you and thank you—we live together eternally, as One.

To birth the Marriage of Spirit and to teach it with my own voice has taken more than three decades, yet it is something I feel sure all my teachers wanted. I have no words for the depth of gratitude that I feel toward them all.

Nothing happens in a vacuum, and the making of this book is no exception. So many wonderful individuals contributed their expertise. Brad Laughlin, my dear friend and partner in writing the book, whose voice stands alongside my own—thank you for your unshakable support, selflessness and endless endurance. I love you and bless you. My love and deepest gratitude to my children, who can take much of the credit for motivating me and who constantly impacted me with Generation-X viewpoints. Also my love and gratitude to the CoreLight staff who work faithfully as a team to hold the work of spreading the *dharma* and who helped move the book project forward in so many important ways.

The editors for *The Marriage of Spirit*, Diana C. Douglas, John Lyons-Gould and Brad Laughlin, deserve special praise. Editing what I gave them was not an easy task and they all rose to the occasion.

To all the others who helped in the many phases of the book production—designing; illustrating, critiquing; reading; proofing; researching; writing testimonials; donating time, energy and money—especially James Emery, Cyndi Laughlin, Christine Arundell, Linda Garcia, Tanya Sydney, Christinea Johnson, Kathy Sparkes, Holli Duggan, Judith Baker Miller, Raymond Diaz and Celeste Magers—we could not have done without you—thank you.

To all the blessed souls who have shared darshan and Marriage of Spirit classes with me, lending their own unique processes to the birthing of this material—thank you for being the final inspiration for this book

My love and blessings to you. You are all amazing grace.

*This book is dedicated to the divine essence
at the core of each one of us.*

THE MANY NAMES OF GOD —
DESCRIBING THE INDESCRIBABLE

The Absolute
All That Is
Allah
The Atman
Beingness
The Beloved
Brahman
The Clear Light of Reality
The Cosmic State
Deity
The Divine
Divine Mother-Father-God
The Divine Presence
Energy
The Enlightened State
Essence
Eternity
God
Goddess
Grace
The Ground of Being
Higher Self

Light
The Lord
Love
Nirvana
Omnipresence
Oneness
Presence
Pure Awareness
Seamless Awareness
The Self
The Shining Void
Spirit
The Source
Sunyata
The Superconscious
The Supreme
That
The Unified Field
Unity
Unity Consciousness
Yahweh

For the sake of readability, *God*, *the Self* and *the Divine* are the only names capitalized throughout the book, but many others are referenced throughout the book interchangeably. Out of respect for the varied traditions that are seeking to describe the same indescribable fact, we have listed them here, capitalized.

Table of Contents

PREFACE

Softer than the flower where kindness is concerned;
and stronger than the thunder where principles are at stake.

—Paramahansa Yogananda

When Leslie asked me to help her write *The Marriage of Spirit*, I was deeply honored. I feel very privileged and excited to assist in bringing forward these amazingly simple, powerful, and life-changing principles and techniques. Having worked with them for over ten years, using them myself and teaching them to others in workshops, I have watched them help to illuminate, balance, and transform the lives of thousands of people—including my own—very quickly.

The Marriage of Spirit principles and techniques serve a wide spectrum of purposes: from helping people move beyond apparent limitations; to healing past mental, emotional, and physical traumas; to achieving success and excellence in the material world; to assisting with spiritual growth. They help us transcend the swinging pendulum of consciousness—seemingly uncontrollable patterns of feeling off-balance and trapped in cycles of negativity, anger, pain, and fear which prevent us from living a fulfilled life.

For example, people use the techniques in a concrete and practical way to manifest more fulfilling relationships and careers, to reach higher creative potentials, and to create more abundance and happiness in their lives. Spiritually, the Marriage of Spirit assists us in living in a paradigm of higher consciousness, more in a flow of love, truth, joy, wisdom, compassion and true connectedness to all things. It becomes possible to bring the soul's full expression into the world, to know more of who we truly are, to touch the Divine.

Based on the metaphysical principle of the unity of all things, the roots of the Marriage of Spirit teachings are at least as ancient as recorded history. These specific teachings resonate with the core of all major truth teachings, traditions, and religions—such as Buddhism; Hinduism; Christian, Jewish and Islamic mysticism; Taoism; Tantra; and the ancient Egyptian mystery schools, just to name some of the more familiar.

Formerly shrouded in mystery and reserved for the select few who dedicated their lives to isolation and monastic discipline, the ancient wisdom teachings have been revamped and made simple and practical for the modern world. As the evolution of human consciousness accelerates, many are finding that the old methods of achieving spiritual awakening are inadequate for life in the modern, fast-paced, material world. New tools, like the Marriage of Spirit techniques, are being brought forward now to help us.

The Marriage of Spirit also bridges the ancient metaphysical principles and modern psychology, as much of the teachings are about actively bringing balance into our lives by clearing the ego, or releasing inner limitations. The distinction between the Marriage of Spirit and modern psychology, however, is that the Marriage of Spirit relies not only on our untying the knots of the mind, but also on the gift of grace—on giving-up the whole lesson to spirit's mysterious healing power in order to effect transformation in our lives.

Another important distinction is that the purpose of the Marriage of Spirit techniques is not about rearranging the ego into a more congenial, healthier form—as modern psychology can be. Rather, their purpose is to transform and to clear the ego so that the clear light of reality shines through it and so that we can live a truer expression of our own inherent divine nature. As Ram Dass once said, the ego is a prison, and so in order to know the truth of our spiritual nature, we are not concerned with rearranging the furniture inside the prison, but with breaking down the prison walls to let in the light that is always present. The Marriage of Spirit brings down the walls of our own inner limitations by making the unconscious conscious, by bringing the shadow into light, and by marrying spirit with matter. It is a course in awakening, in becoming conscious of the luminous core of enlightenment that is within each one of us.

Leslie's own magical story of awakening is unique and inspiring. Chapter One gives us a brief glimpse of her journey as a Western woman embracing the life of a mystic. She shares how she was taught the Marriage of Spirit principles by spiritual guides (both inner and outer), the insights and awakenings that this led to, and how it eventually culminated for her in the late 1980s in the full realization of the Self.

It was my good fortune to meet Leslie in 1990, during a time of intense soul-searching. She is the wisest, most compassionate and illumined soul it has ever been my pleasure to know. Her life, an embodiment of humility, generosity, grace, and unconditional love, is fully dedicated to the service of God and humanity. My respect for her continues to deepen over the years as I am graced daily with her living example of purity, heart, trust in the Divine, and unshakable dedication to truth.

It is a blessing beyond words for me to be able to participate in the creation of this book, and I am so very grateful for the miraculous transformations and soul-stirring awakenings that have come to me throughout the process of writing and working with Leslie. My role here has been to help compile this book from Leslie's writings and transcripts of her talks, and by summarizing our conversations over the years about key concepts.

With love and respect, I present this aspect of Leslie's life's work—a modern version of ancient spiritual and metaphysical truths—to people who are truly hungry for nourishment, fulfillment and spiritual awakening in the busy, technological, modern world. May every reader receive as much from this book as I have.

— Brad Laughlin
January 15, 2000, Santa Fe, New Mexico

How to Use this Book

*T*he *Marriage of Spirit* is divided into two sections. Section One presents the spiritual and metaphysical principles and details a progressive understanding of the nature of human consciousness and of spiritual awakening. It includes at the end of each chapter practical suggestions for putting theory into practice. Section Two presents the techniques and is devoted to concrete exercises for readers. It includes at the end of each chapter: 1) suggestions on how to maximize the results of the exercises, as well as 2) inspiring testimonials from people who have applied *The Marriage of Spirit* to their daily lives. If you ever need a boost while reading the book, you might try reading one of these extraordinary stories at the end of the chapters in Section Two, which will give you an idea of the kind of changes you might experience as a result of using *The Marriage of Spirit*.

As with any endeavor, learning is different for different people. Feel free to dive into the exercises in Section Two whenever you feel you are ready, or when you think that it would help your understanding of the esoteric concepts in Section One. There is no right or wrong way to approach this material. The important thing is to make a commitment of time, patience, and willingness to change. The rest will come.

Throughout the book, it is a good idea to read and digest each chapter slowly before moving on. Each chapter contains esoteric and fairly concentrated information, and so it is preferable not to rush through any of it. By taking your time with this book, you will deepen your self-knowledge. Of course, the time that this takes is quite subjective. Some people can do two months' work in a week; and so it all depends on you.

In Section Two, it is especially important to get a good grounding in the first technique, *polarity processing*, which is presented in Chapter Nine—Polarities, before moving on to the intermediate methods, Chapter Ten—Triangles and Chapter Eleven—Squares. By waiting and giving yourself time to really digest and practice the polarity processing technique, you will have time to see your own personality patterns emerging and to see yourself repeating your patterns quite regularly. It is invaluable to see this. Even if it is somewhat painful to discover some of the ego's limitations, you are on your way with the transformation. You can accomplish a lot of change just by doing the polarity processing technique.

I have included a list of book references in the back of the book for those who would like to take their research and understanding of the ancient spiritual principles presented here a step further. However, in the end the spiritual principles must be experienced and cannot be completely comprehended with the mind. Also, like the physical laws of the universe, such as gravity, the spiritual laws and principles work and affect our lives whether or not we can prove them with research and fact and whether or not we believe in them.

The Marriage of Spirit is not intended to replace other ways of progressing on the path of transformation and Self-discovery. Rather, it is an adjunct to other spiritual disciplines. To wake up it is essential to practice other disciplines, such as meditation, or other forms of clearing work.

As you are reading, you may find many words with which you are unfamiliar. There is a glossary at the back of this book that includes definitions of esoteric terms, including all Sanskrit words and phrases.

Finally, as you work through this program, try to observe actual changes taking place in yourself, in your life and in your way of viewing reality. Personality patterns, which are repeated over and over, begin to shift. Understanding the principles helps to create a new mind-set for you in a fairly short time, giving you a depth of vision about the structure of human behavior. Not only will transformation take place as you read through the book and do the exercises, but you will have a lasting set of tools to take with you on the rest of the journey.

SECTION ONE

THE MARRIAGE OF SPIRIT PRINCIPLES

Lead me from the unreal to the real,
Lead me from darkness to light,
Lead me from death to immortality.

—The Upanishads

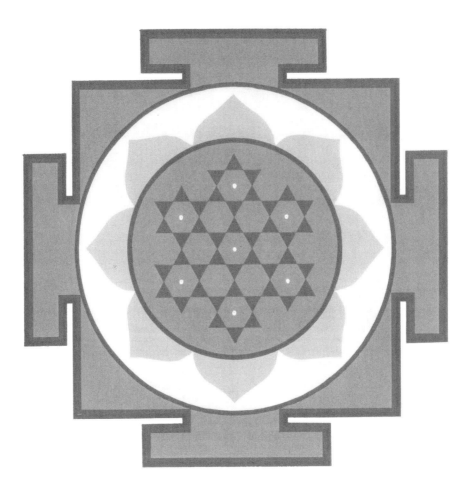

When by the flood of your tears the inner and the outer have fused into one, you will find Her whom you sought with such anguish, nearer than the nearest, the very breath of life, the very core of every heart.

—Sri Anandamayi Ma

THE STORY OF A RELUCTANT MYSTIC

In 1971, I had an experience of such significance that understanding it became my life's work. During the course of a week that year, I was deluged by a transmission of insight and of access to higher realms of knowledge. In the process I received a gift of spiritual awakening and clairaudience, which I had no way to integrate or understand when the experience was over. Hesitant at first, scared of what people would think and facing possible alienation from my family because of the voice I began to hear in my head—I finally made the only decision I could make. I decided to devote my life to interpreting this voice and to using the knowledge it imparted to assist people in their own enlightenment.

I invite you to consider my story as a frame of reference for the teachings in subsequent chapters of this book, and not as an indication of what you might experience or should be experiencing as a result of reading and using the Marriage of Spirit techniques. My journey was a product of the times and circumstances in which I lived. Chances are, your journey along the continuum of enlightenment will not be the same as mine, and that is as it should be.

A BREAKTHROUGH MYSTICAL EXPERIENCE

I grew up in South Africa—a country ravaged by apartheid. After graduating from the University of the Witwatersrand in Johannesburg with a bachelor's degree in fine arts, I assumed a career as a painter. Painting was my passion and was something that had always come easily to me. Since my childhood, art had served as a vehicle for expressing the inexpressible. Even as a child I experienced altered states, visions, and perceptions whose only acceptable outlet seemed to be through my hand and onto canvas.

It was only later with hindsight, that I came into the conscious understanding of how each vision and subsequent painting was a gift given from my unconscious, a learning experience that would help prepare me for my life as a mystic. Altered states often happened while I was painting or even while I was contemplating painting. This weaving of art and mysticism fostered in me an expanding desire to find a greater understanding of the nature of consciousness itself.

While painting in my art studio one morning in 1971, I went into an altered state. It seemed to have been brought on by my extreme response to an argument with some friends at dinner the night before. We had just finished eating and had stumbled into a thorny discussion about art and science. The two men at the table, one of them my husband, considered themselves scientists; my girlfriend and I were artists. At the time, it seemed like a stupid argument about the merits of art versus science, yet it had struck a chord deep inside me. I had unusual clarity that night, and I could see there was no intrinsic difference between the two. They sprang from the same source, expressed the same essence. At the core they were the same.

Seeing two seemingly opposed means of perceiving the universe, one based in intuition and one based in empirical logic, as one and the same thing was an extremely radical idea to all of us then. Yet the truth of this was crystal clear to me in that moment. It was my absolute certainty about this *sameness* that was so fascinating to me at the time. However, no matter how hard I tried, I could not begin to explain to the others what I was seeing. Suddenly I was painfully aware that all of us, by arguing about the supremacy of art or science, were not just missing the point, we were also involved in several polarized struggles. Male-female, right-wrong, real vs. imagined. For some reason, that night, this dualism was more than I could bear. I became very agitated and then quite disconsolate.

The next morning in my studio, after having been awake most of the night grappling with what I had *seen*, my mental state suddenly shifted. My mind broke open and became crystalline and vast. Time seemed to stand still. Understandings about the previous night's discussion flooded my awareness. I had the clear realization that my knowings of the evening were the truth. This sensing of truth was so profound, it made my heart race, and I experienced emotions I had never before felt. I was in what I now know to be a state of unity consciousness, a state for which I had no reference point at the time.

That morning, as the insights continued to pour through my consciousness, I knew that I needed to write. I was seeing the resolutions to all my frustrations from the night before, gaining a very clear mental understanding of them, which allowed me to verbalize them in my journal. As the pages accumulated, the innate unity which underlies all of the dualities that we know in this world became clearer and clearer. This initiated in my mind the understanding of the fundamental concepts behind the Marriage of Spirit teachings. I had always felt a mystical presence in my life, even as a child, and particularly in conjunction with my painting—but this intense and direct transmission of information about unity was something new, and it grabbed my full attention. I was compelled to be completely present with the experience.

During a week of accessing this state of higher consciousness, I wrote about thirty pages of notes and created two paintings. One painting was of a flying angel, painted as though I was looking up at it. The other was of a mother holding a child. Both were subjects that I had never used before. The two paintings emerged effortlessly, almost as though someone else was using my body to paint them. I know now that the paintings were another gift from my higher self, messages from the state of unity. The paintings would play a significant part in a later drama.

Each morning during this particular week I woke to find that the altered state was still present, and when it finally abated, I was overwhelmed with grief at the loss. However, I was still left with the legacy of the experience. Not only did I have the thirty or so pages of writing and the two paintings, but this breakthrough experience left me with clear but intermittent inner guidance—guidance which stayed with me in my everyday awareness.

Three difficult weeks passed as I tried to make sense of what had happened during this extraordinary event. I vacillated between elation and depression, wondering at times if I was going crazy, wondering why this was happening to me. Then I learned that I was pregnant with my first child. Caught up in the excitement of that, I put the precious pages into a closet, pushed the events which they recorded to the back of my mind, and temporarily forgot all about my experience. At the time, there was no place for it in my life and no time to make one. A month later, curiosity got the best of me, and I tried to re-read them. To my dismay, the writings were all but unintelligible. The concepts that had been obvious to me at the time, I was now unable to relate to. Because of the loss of the unity state, I had no context into which to fit them. They might as well have been written in Greek. The world stood still for a moment, and then it began to spin as my sense of reality tilted. My thoughts raced out of control as I fell prey to the belief that I had spent a week writing nothing but gibberish. My mind gave in to the fear that perhaps I was going crazy. Becoming increasingly embarrassed and paranoid, and to my later regret, I threw the whole dissertation away.

BECOMING A CLOSET MYSTIC

Much of the paranoia and fear that made me destroy the writings describing the mystical experience were related to a sense of apprehension about how my conservative husband would react. Initially, although I was relatively comfortable with the idea of receiving inner guidance, there were times when I questioned my own sanity. In 1972, shortly after the birth of my daughter, when I finally told my husband about the mystical experiences that were now commonplace in my daily life, his reaction reinforced my worst fears. He had recently done a medical elective in a mental hospital, and he assured me that the only people who heard voices in their heads were those who were mentally ill.

Neither one of us had ever heard of channeling or of other forms of divine communication back then, and when I saw the look of fear on his face, I thought he would have me committed to a mental institution if I persisted. Out of fear, I never mentioned my experience to him or anyone else in our circle of acquaintances again. For a long period of time, I lived a kind of double life—the one in my head, and the one in my body. My body continued to live the life of a doctor's wife, driving the car pool, going to social functions and taking care of the family. Eventually the discomfort of denying my inner self became so great and my confidence in the fact that I was not crazy was so strong, that I finally decided to come out of the closet. This was a gradual and painful process that spanned a time of many outward changes in my life as well.

A COUNTRY STEEPED IN POLARITY

I became an adult under the oppressive regime of apartheid—at a time when its ideology of separating black and white had reached a point of critical mass and when it was clear to most people that something monumental was going to happen soon. Stifling censorship and strict rules about how people—both white and black—should live their lives had for a very long time been an integral part of the nation's collective consciousness. In the summer of 1975, when I awoke from a dream and told my husband that we had to leave the country, we both knew instinctively that a time of great transition and upheaval was beginning.

I cannot imagine a more perfect example of extreme polarization into which a mystic could be born. My life-long feelings of depression and helplessness surrounding the injustices of the apartheid system in my country—feelings shared by many of my countrymen—would have to be replaced by hope, compassion and love if things were ever going to change. But how? The *how* came to me directly through divine intervention in a way that challenged head-on my notion that one person cannot make a difference. The voice that had come to me in 1971 was guiding me to hold the intention, hope and belief for the possibility for peace in South Africa. I understood that others were being asked to do the same, and that the individual and unified intentions of even a small number of people would be enough to bring about significant changes. Much later I came to understand that at a point of critical mass, when a certain number of individuals are holding the same intention, change is manifested in the whole of human consciousness. That is eventually what I saw happen in South Africa as the end of apartheid gave way to a new regime.

Two weeks after my prophetic dream, my husband was handed a solicitation for a research fellowship at the University of California Los Angeles (UCLA) Medical School. A week after he accepted the position, rioting broke out in Soweto, where my husband was completing his residency. It was the beginning of the revolution. Suppressed at first by the press was the fact that many of the first riots were staged by children, ages 8 to 18. The police opened fire on some of the groups, and many children were killed or severely wounded. It was a frightening and brutal time for all people in South Africa. I would have felt extremely guilty for leaving had it not been for the voices of my guides. They urged me to come to the United States to further my spiritual growth so that my prayers for peace in South Africa could grow in strength and meld with those of many others in South Africa and around the world who also prayed for the end of apartheid. It would be those united, individual voices that would eventually help shift the balance of energy, the magnetic charge of experience, in favor of dissolution of the old regime. Through this experience, I began to see that if enough people awaken to their true, inner, divine nature, the whole of human consciousness can undergo the kind of evolution of consciousness that seems to be what is required of us if we are to survive as a species on this planet. Since that time, the destiny behind my teaching the Marriage of Spirit principles has been to help raise consciousness.

COMING OUT OF THE CLOSET

After the birth of my daughter in 1972, a deep restlessness came over me. I knew I was looking for something but did not quite know what it was or where to find it. The clarity of the unity experience in 1971 was gone. I knew also that what I was looking for was connected to her arrival and in some way connected with what I was to give her. On the strength of that small knowing, I became available to inner change, and the spiritual seeker in me was born. The birth of my son followed three years later. His conception came at a time when I had just become initiated into formal meditation, and this time my expected baby announced his arrival in the form of a dream. I realized that a tremendous sensitizing of my awareness and my seeing was taking place as I observed the dream. I was beginning to attune to a more subtle level. Hence I perceived the meaning conveyed in the dream of my unborn son—a perception that would have been too subtle for my awareness to register in the past.

My marriage did not survive the coming out process—a process increasingly punctuated by periods of intense meditation, study, and inner work. My husband and I drifted further and further apart. After the unity experience in 1971, and during the later separation and divorce process, I found myself drawn to the writings of authors who were on the cutting edge of a new spiritual psychology. The writings of authors such as Carl Jung, Roberto Assagioli (*Psychosynthesis*), Arthur Janov (*The Primal Scream*), Fritz Perls (*In and*

Out of the Garbage Pail), and Erich Fromm (*The Art of Loving*), resonated with the inner teachings that I was experiencing at the time. Their work helped to ground me in thought and practice, and it helped motivate me to continue with my own spiritual growth.

In the early 1980s I was guided to work with two teachers of transformation for a period of about four years. My children went to live with their father, and in 1986, after becoming increasingly aware that I was growing in spiritual connectedness, I entered a period that was, in its conception and form, rather like a Himalayan cave experience. Many people are familiar with this concept—of Indian and Tibetan yogis, such as the great Tibetan ascetic saint, Milarepa, who retreat to distant caves, to live reclusive lives of meditation and austerity in their quest for enlightenment. Yet my cave experience took place in one of the most densely populated areas of west Los Angeles. I have often wondered why I was guided to go into seclusion in such an odd place and finally decided that, if for no other reason, my guides had a great sense of humor. In fact it was probably because I had several very rigid concepts about big cities. I believed that a large, densely populated area was the last place that I, or anyone else, could wake up.

During a two-year period in a small apartment near the confluence of two major freeways, on the west side of Los Angeles, I began an extended and solitary spiritual practice of complete seclusion and deep meditation. For two years I worked through a step-by-step unfolding of an awakening into the same state that I had held so briefly in 1971. It moved my awareness from the memory of a temporary, altered state, held at the dawning of my quest, to the solidly grounded, natural state in which I now permanently live.

Also during the inward-turning time of 1986-88, I came to see one of the amazing and intricate pieces of my own unfolding destiny. I realized that the experience in 1971 had also been a connecting with the soul of my as yet unborn daughter. The paintings of the angel and the mother and child that had emerged during that week were telling me of her imminent arrival in my life and most importantly that the state I was experiencing was her message to me. As amazing as it seemed, we had made an arrangement to awaken one another. I saw and understood clearly that she was the angelic being who at that time was helping me to remember the state of unity consciousness.

This notion of divine assistance is common in mystical teachings, especially amongst the Tibetans. The arrangement between my daughter and me was this: when I was caught in the forgetfulness of this life and she was out of the body, she was to remind me of who I really am—in a much larger and more essential way than I had been aware of up to that time. And when she took manifestation and was caught in the limitations of world and body and had forgotten her origins, I would be free enough to show her the way and to help her to awaken. She was born in February 1972, exactly nine months after my seven days of initial unity consciousness.

SORTING IT ALL OUT

We all have remarkable mystical experiences, whether or not we are fully aware of them or choose to admit to them. Unfortunately, our altered states are often quickly buried in forgetfulness or pushed aside when they threaten our existing sense of reality—which they do when we don't have a way to integrate them into our current awareness. However, in this instance, I could not escape mine easily because I had written it all down, making it real and concrete, even though those writings were now gone. I had tried to get rid of the experience by throwing the pages away, but I could still see them clearly in my mind. They had been branded into my awareness. As fate would have it, the basic premise of unifying opposites and a return to unity never left my conscious mind again.

I have since come to know that all human beings are inherently capable of accessing vastly different states of consciousness. It is part of our capacity for multi-dimensional awareness. However, it is not usually possible for someone in one paradigm of awareness to have the remotest understanding of another paradigm concurrently. It is possible to flip in and out of different modes of perception overnight, but much harder to cross-reference them—which would require a mental, emotional and physical integration of often paradoxical elements. For the most part, we understand certain states of awareness when we are in them, and we don't when we are not. It is a fairly basic metaphysical concept that helps explain why my thirty pages of writing suddenly appeared indecipherable to me once I was back in this worldly reality.

Although as an artist I used images that came to me through dream states, I did not have any formal understanding of metaphysics as a discipline until later in my life. What was present for me earlier, however, was a feeling of connectedness to nature and a more poetical sense of my inner self. Early on, I identified with ways of understanding that were outside of the sense of reality and conditioning that my family gave me. This is one reason that my life as a mystic was eventually so easily assimilated into my conscious being. Another reason that the mystic life agreed with me relates to the fact that I was caught in a relationship of dominance and submission with my father. While being submissive to the will of others is a behavior that I have had to unlearn and process quite a bit throughout my adult life, early on it allowed me to completely give myself to the voices and teachers I encountered. Their transmissions required total commitment and selfless absorption on my part—something that would have been hard for a stronger-willed person to accomplish. And so it often is with certain aspects of our personality and specific events in our lives—they are there for reasons we rarely understand at the time. In the true spirit of polarity, what seems to be cast in negative energy one moment is shown to be making a positive impact the next, and vice versa.

Knowing now that there is an inherent perfection to all events in our lives, I realize that it was fine that I threw the whole essay away. Although I regretted not saving it, I did not feel that the information was lost. Key pieces stuck with me, including the essay's very last sentence about *the unity of all things*. I also vividly remembered the central theme of the writings—that a process of bringing together or unifying all the polar opposites inherent in this dualistic life, brings us into the vast oneness of consciousness that is the true source of life. It was the memory of this oneness, which I had experienced directly for one week and which I know now as the unified state, that became my motivation for understanding the altered state I had experienced.

Finding the fundamental unity of consciousness underlying all of life's dualities is enlightenment—our *real* state of consciousness. It is the theme of this book. We can all experience this enlightened state by integrating the dualistic, or polarized, schisms in our personality. In other words what my unconscious was showing me that week was:

> *If we integrate the dualistic and polarized schisms in our personality, we can know directly and palpably the unity which we truly are, beyond the limited personality.*

These teachings, given over time, became the primary methods of integration which I used on myself and which have led to my ever-growing experience of the unity of all things. This unity is our true eternal nature. And the desire to know it is the source of the yearning inside every human being.

Unity consciousness allows us to bring the events of our lives full-circle. We yearn for closure in our lives, for events and thoughts to come around to completion and to reveal some aspect of truth about the structure of this reality and our place in it. Western culture in particular, with its heavy reliance on logical, linear progression, finds little solace in a life's apparent linear progression toward death and into the eternal void of purposelessness. We see ourselves living within the limited confines of space-time, and we often conceive of life as a form of suffering due to the perception of its nature as a random progression toward an unknown end. In contrast to this view, seeing larger circles of meaning at work in the structure of human life enables us to bring closure and spiritual significance to the journey of life. Digging into the subconscious mind, tying up the loose ends of forgotten lessons and significances, and releasing destructive patterns of behavior are practices that lie at the heart of the Marriage of Spirit teachings.

SUGGESTIONS FOR PUTTING THEORY INTO PRACTICE

1. Get a journal and keep it specifically for writing down all your mystical and spiritual experiences. By grounding these precious gifts in writing, you bring them from the realm of ideas and formlessness into form. You not only make them more tangible for yourself, but they often become fuller and more expanded. You begin to see much more of the experience and to absorb deeper levels of the gift spirit is offering you. Journaling helps preserve these treasures, rather than allowing them to be covered over by the sands of time and lost in the mists of memory.

2. Try to remember past mystical and spiritual experiences, even from childhood. Recapitulate the experiences and write about them in as much detail as possible in the very beginning of your journal. Make sure to date them, even if approximate. Dating them helps later on with understanding larger cycles of change. History has a way of repeating itself, and perception changes that happened years ago will be revisited in the future. Life is a spiral; we return to where we once were but at a higher level of vibration.

Because clarity and enlightenment are within your own nature,
they are regained without moving an inch.

—Lao Tsu

TWO

THE ALCHEMY OF
THE MARRIAGE OF SPIRIT

This chapter is essentially an overview of the basic Marriage of Spirit principles to give readers a context for understanding some of the more esoteric concepts which are expanded upon throughout Section One. Here we take a look at: the principle of the unification of opposites and its historical context; the roots of the Marriage of Spirit; the nature of enlightenment; the potential for the new paradigm of spiritual awakening; the practical benefits of what we call *processing*, which is how we apply the principles to our daily lives; and inviting grace into our lives.

UNIFYING OPPOSITES

The Marriage of Spirit is the name that I gave to a seminar which I have taught many times since 1988. It encompasses a set of principles and techniques which have their roots in the ancient teachings of the *reconciliation and unification of opposites*. The teachings are based on information that was initially given to me over a period of several decades by out-of-body teachers. In reading ancient scriptures and modern psychology texts, in studying with two teachers in the early 1980s, and through my own experiences, I have since validated the truth of these ancient principles.

The Marriage of Spirit is a course to assist your spiritual awakening. The teachings are a way to re-create balance and harmony in the midst of ordinary, everyday consciousness. They are a deceptively simple way of addressing and clearing conditioned egoic patterns. The techniques have the potential to create an immediate easing of the problems arising in our lives from the knotted, limited and unconscious places in our patterning. Taking the time to clear these mental-emotional patterns allows us to experience our spiritual essence more directly. In the past when I first began to use the techniques on myself, I was awed by their power to create immediate and permanent change. I have used them for years and still do, and I continue to marvel at their effectiveness.

The three techniques, presented in Section Two, are new and original, emerging here in a very different form than any way the principles were used in ancient times. They emerge in a form designed especially for the more mentally oriented Western world and are mainly, though not entirely, mental techniques, which are simple to do. The idea is that since Westerners are so developed mentally, we use the mind to help balance and clear the mind. Sri Ramakrishna, an Indian saint who lived in the 1800s, referred to this principle when he said that if you have a thorn in your foot, you take another thorn to remove the first thorn, and then you throw both thorns away. With the simple techniques of the unification of opposites, we can unravel the knots of the mind and completely let them go, allowing in the clear light of reality.

The primary principle is this—by unifying all opposites held in our awareness,
we will return to our original state of unity.

Consciousness in this world is polarized into pairs of opposites. We see opposites all around us, and we hold states of mind which are polarized opposites. Some examples of the more obvious pairs of opposites that most people hold are: good-bad, right-wrong, pain-pleasure and win-lose. There are many more, as you will see in later chapters. It is possible to find the underlying unity inherent in all the pairs of opposites within us. Finding this unity is an awakening to a more expanded state of consciousness and to our spiritual essence. And that, with its many ramifications for our awareness, is what the techniques are about.

ORIGIN OF THE UNIFICATION OF OPPOSITES

The historic origin of this principle is still evident in various forms in a great number of different religions and traditions—although it is more conspicuous in some than in others. Let's take a look at a few:

In the ancient Chinese Taoist tradition, the principle of opposites inherent in the teachings is revealed very clearly in the diagram of the yin-yang symbol (Fig. 2-1). In this wonderfully explicit symbol, the black and white sides wrap around each other in perfect balance, conveying the feeling of the opposites belonging together as one unified whole contained within the circle of eternity. As Carl Jung said, "When yang has reached its greatest strength, the dark power of yin is born within its depths. For night begins at midday when yang breaks up and begins to change to yin."

In *Tantra*, which means the balancing of opposites, the ideal of unity is symbolically expressed in the union of Shiva and Shakti, being and manifestation, and masculine and feminine. In the traditional practice of Tantric yoga, the unification of opposites is usually lived out in a physical way. Figure 2-2 symbolizes the manner in which the separations that exist within the physical realm are able to reunify in gesture and action.

In the *Bhagavad Gita*, which is the primary scripture of Hinduism, Krishna speaks of the unification of opposites to Arjuna. He says, "You must be free from the pairs of opposites. Poise your mind in tranquility."

In Buddhism, one of the principle tenets is that of the *Middle Path*. The Buddha advocated that walking between the extremes of the pairs of opposites is the path to enlightenment, or *Nirvana*.

An example from Christian literature is in the Gnostic text, the *Gospel According to Thomas*, discovered in 1945 in Nag Hamadi, Egypt, which is believed to have been produced in about AD 140. "Jesus said to them: When you make the two one, and when you make the inner as the outer and the outer as the inner and the above as the below, and when you make the male and the female into a single one, so that the male will not be male and the female not be female … then shall you enter [the Kingdom]."

Although the teachings of the Christian Bible do not emphasize the principle of the unification of opposites, there are still references to it. One of the more explicit references is in Isaiah 11:6-10, which implies that the knowledge of God comes when opposites are unified. "The wolf also shall dwell with the lamb, and the leopard shall lie down with the young goat; and the calf and the young lion and the fatling together; and a little child shall lead them. The cow and the bear shall graze; their young ones shall lie down together; and the lion shall eat straw like the ox.

Fig. 2-1. *The Taoist yin-yang*

Fig. 2-2. *Masculine and feminine unity is a Tantric symbol of the unification of opposites.*

The nursing child shall play by the cobra's hole, and the weaned child shall put his hand in the viper's den....For the earth shall be full of the knowledge of the Lord, as the waters cover the sea."

In fact, although all three major monotheistic religions—Christianity, Judaism and Islam—do not emphasize the reconciliation of opposites, their belief in the one God over the many is in itself an acknowledgement of God as the absolute state of unity.

The teaching of the unification of opposites is also clear in Islamic mysticism, or Sufism, and in Jewish mysticism, or Kabbalah. As Sufi master Hazrat Inayat Khan is quoted in *Universal Sufism*: "Mental purification means that impressions such as good and bad, wrong and right, gain and loss, and pleasure and pain, these opposites which block the mind, must be cleared out by seeing the opposite of these things. Then one can see the enemy in the friend and the friend in the enemy. When one can recognize poison in nectar and nectar in the poison, that is the time when death and life become one, too. Opposites no more remain opposites before one."

As Daniel C. Matt states in *The Essential Kabbalah* in his discussion of absolute undifferentiation: "At the deepest levels of divinity, all opposites and distinctions vanish, overwhelmed by oneness."

In the context of modern psychology, Carl Jung wrote extensively about the unification of opposites. For example: "Nothing can exist without its opposite; the two were one in the beginning and will be one again in the end." Also: "Therefore the perfected sage liberates himself from the opposites, having seen through their connection with one another and their alternation." Also: "The *Ramayana* says, 'This world must suffer under pairs of opposites for ever.' Not to allow oneself to be influenced by the pairs of opposites but...to raise oneself above them, is an essentially ethical task, because deliverance from the opposites leads to redemption."

If you find that you are getting curious about how this esoteric principle works in a practical sense, you can begin reading the introduction to Section Two and Chapter Nine—Polarities, the first chapter of Section Two, at any time. They present the first technique of the Marriage of Spirit teachings and offer simple instruction in applying the unification of opposites to your daily life. I do recommend, however, that you come back to Section One, the principles, to gain an understanding of how the spiritual laws that support the techniques work.

WHY IS IT CALLED THE MARRIAGE OF SPIRIT?

Marriage is the mystical and sacred blending of two different and seemingly opposite elements. The principles contained in this book teach us about the underlying unity of spirit inherent in all of life. Traditionally we think of marriage as an outward joining of two people, a man and a woman. In fact during the marriage ceremony, the energies of the two partners are blended into one energy. Although each of the individuals retains uniqueness as well, this creates at one level of the two individual people, a new unified energy. This paradox of unity versus uniqueness is the great mystery of our spiritual nature. The fusing of opposites is the alchemy of transformation.

The term *marriage* is also used with regard to the principles of this book to convey the full depth of possibilities available for the unifying of our own inner masculine and feminine aspects. On the path to awakening, this is what we must do. It is not just an integration, but an alchemic fusing together of all the opposites that we hold in our minds. Focusing on creating unity and equality between the masculine, feminine and all the other opposites within us is an essential part of the transformational work.

In enlightenment, too, this marriage happens. Our awareness is held in unity, and yet we retain our individual uniqueness. Unity does not mean uniformity; the awakened mind has the ability to see unity and yet also to live within the diversity of life. This paradigm is known as unity in diversity. The principle of *the whole being greater than the sum of its parts* is a profound aspect of the mystery of the spiritual life. It implies that as we reconcile all the opposites in our awareness, something new—a third element, the background presence of unity—is born in us, beyond the dual states that we held when we started the work. This is our awakening to the presence of unity. Paradoxically, unity is always present with us; we are just too distracted by the complexity of life to see it. As we revisit this unified state, we return to wholeness while living here in this amazing world.

THE MARRIAGE OF SPIRIT IN CONTEXT

The roots of the Marriage of Spirit lie in the important practice of self-inquiry, of looking within in order to understand and to know ourselves. Self-inquiry is one of the many tools essential for true transformation and enlightenment.

The Marriage of Spirit is a method born out of a synthesis of several disciplines, known for their different ways of practicing self-inquiry, yet it has a completely different manifestation from its roots. The method is born in many ways out of a mixture of: 1) Tantric yoga, the yoga of balancing opposites; 2) Jnana yoga, the yoga of the mind, or making the mind one with God; and 3) modern psychology.

The Marriage of Spirit's connection to Tantric yoga is that both use the principle of the unification of opposites to create balance, harmony and unity. However, unlike traditional Tantric yoga, which usually involves physically living out the polarities in order to find the unity, the Marriage of Spirit is a mostly mental approach to balancing opposites.

The Marriage of Spirit teachings and techniques are also closely aligned with Jnana yoga, or self-inquiry. Its resemblance to Jnana yoga has to do with finding out who we are at the source rather than at the surface and with continuing to inquire into our perceptions until we find the unity inherent in the mind.

The resemblance to modern psychology lies in our willingness to delve into and see our own unconscious personality patterns and also in our allowing those patterns to reorganize. As stated in the preface of this book, the distinction between the Marriage of Spirit and modern psychology is that the Marriage of Spirit relies not only on our untying the knots of the mind, but also on the gift of grace. Doing the inner exploration is important, but at some point we have to surrender the whole lesson to spirit in order to effect transformation in our lives. Through grace, spirit provides the changes we seek.

The Marriage of Spirit is about making the unconscious conscious, bringing the shadow into light, and marrying spirit with matter. It is about becoming conscious of the luminous core of enlightenment that is within each one of us.

WHAT IS ENLIGHTENMENT?

Enlightenment has been known by many different names—*cosmic consciousness, Self-realization, God-realization, liberation* or *awakening*. It could be described as a mystical state because it seems to be emanating from the mystery of being, beyond our everyday awareness. It is so rare in this world, yet it is a very sane and grounded way to be in the world.

Everyone holds an inner core of enlightened consciousness, but in general, most are unaware of it. Those who have attained conscious awareness of their enlightenment are often put on a pedestal, as though they are beyond life. It is certainly a state quite different from any other state experienced by most people. Yet it is only apparently beyond this world. In fact those that hold this way of perceiving are bonded with the world and dedicated to life far more deeply than most. What the state does give someone is a depth, a penetration into the soul of all of humankind. This is why enlightened individuals are often humanitarians or teachers. They have found a deeper perspective on life and are acquainted with its deeper meaning. The state of enlightenment is humanity's future. It is what we will become as we grow and evolve into the fullness of our soul awareness and beyond.

The enlightened state is experienced as an all-encompassing perception of the oneness of all of life. It is the awareness that we, humanity, are all one, interconnected on a mental, emotional, physical, and spiritual level, held and contained by the essence of being. An enlightened person perceives cohesive essence-as-oneness as the source that gives rise to the existence of the universe as we know it. The enlightened state shows itself as a state of naturalness and ease on many levels. It is a state where the inner turmoil has ceased, where knowing the truth of existence is always present. It is a deep caring and an absence of fear. It is a visceral knowing of oneself as an embodiment of unified presence. Ultimately, enlightenment cannot be described in words, only experienced.

THE TIME IS NOW—A NEW PARADIGM

It used to be that people seeking enlightenment would separate themselves from worldly life. This meant that there were extraordinary enlightened beings living mostly in isolation from society, often in monasteries or on mountaintops. This is no longer necessarily what spirit is asking of us.

We have arrived at a new and different time;
we are here to enlighten the physical plane, the body, and the personality
while living and working in the world.

At this time we are to open up the physical plane and to receive the enlightened consciousness right into the personality and the body. Although I did retreat from the world during my pseudo-cave experience in Los Angeles in 1986-88, it was not the decades-long isolation of the traditional Himalayan cave experience. It was in a big city and was for a relatively short period of time. I consider this was a step toward bridging the old way and the new. Furthermore, my guides told me that the inner exploration that had taken me ten years in the 1970s and 1980s would take others two years in the future.

We are being invited to open up and clear the personality, to rework it into a freer state, visibly woven into the fabric of the world. This expression of enlightenment integrated with worldly life will most likely catalyze changes in the environment and in institutions, like government, education, social structures, and so forth.

Currently we are seeing an unprecedented spiritual awakening of many souls, since so many are now focused on this process of transformation and Self-discovery. We see evidence of this focus almost everywhere, from the increasing number of self-help and spiritually themed books on the *New York Times* bestseller list, to the increasing number of people learning to meditate, and to a proliferation of spiritual communities thriving in every corner of the world. There is a great, quiet revolution underway in a segment of the population. A growing number of people are trying to find their *real* selves amidst the dehumanizing and mechanistic worldview of Western culture. There is a palpable sense of spiritual urgency—a yearning for many of us to reconnect with spirit, with the all-encompassing energy that creates and flows through life on this planet.

As more and more people wake up to their own enlightenment, it also becomes obvious how the oneness is able to express its unique perfection differently through each soul. For each individual who wakes up, there is a different expression of enlightened awareness in the world. As a result of this mass raising of consciousness, a new way of living is emerging. The emergence is the birth of a new paradigm.

This is the paradigm known as unity in diversity.

Unity is an energy presence which is seen to flow through all things, through all the diversity of life—people, plants, rocks, the earth, the sky, anything one can name. It is a different paradigm from the paradigm in which we now live, in that it is the flow of life coming from the oneness, and the oneness is the inner authority within each person. In this paradigm we each become our own authority, our own source of knowing in that we are directly connected to source. Some people call it *going God-direct*. The implementation of this new paradigm will result in a complete equality and respect for the differences found in this world, *giving a complete validity to all diverse forms*.

The system in which we now live is the authority of one person pitted against another, an authority of domination versus submission, based on human will and lived in separation. It is this old way that is the paradigm of polarities seen as oppositions—matter versus spirit, superiority versus inferiority, strong versus weak.

Living in the new paradigm is being able to live both within polarity and outside of it—at the same time. The new paradigm of consciousness is our ability to see that all opposites can also be perceived as *complements*, each enhancing the other. Seeing them this way allows us to penetrate the unity which underlies all polarity, and this is the dawning of enlightenment.

After centuries of being disguised in poetical, mysterious terms for the select few, the teachings of enlightenment are no longer shrouded by the privacy of monasteries and mountaintops. Currently the information is more available and accessible than ever before. The teachings emerge simplified, more straightforward, more easily understood and practical for the modern world.

Perhaps the reason for this is because it is an unprecedented time of critical mass in our world. Collectively, our degree of ignorance of our connectedness to spirit seems to be at its zenith. Our technological society appears to teeter precariously on the brink of global crises such as nuclear accidents, nuclear warfare, overpopulation, ozone depletion, global warming, deforestation, eradication of species, other ecological disasters and epidemics like AIDS.

In times like these, there is a heightened potential for and even an imperative need for a great number of souls to wake up to a new, more balanced, human consciousness. For those that are disturbed by these global crises, the most profound way to make a contribution is by practicing self-inquiry and clearing one's own ego. As our awareness becomes more empowered and as we hold an intention along with others for global transformation, our intention joined with others' begins to affect collective consciousness. Some may know this as the *hundredth monkey* principle. I like to call this principle *the power of one* because it reflects the power inherent in the one mind—the universal, unified mind that is common to all of us at some level. *The Power of One*, originally a novel by South African, Bryce Courtenay, and later a movie, is about how the power of one individual really can make a difference.

Throughout history there have been many predictions that the times in which we now live would come. Sages and seers of many traditions, including Incan, Mayan and Native American, have prophesied the loss of divine knowledge and the rise of the rational, technological mind, steeped in the belief in our disconnection from spirit, as the prevailing state for our current time. Humanity's journey in consciousness is always cycling from light to dark and back to light—from ignorance back to the knowledge of the Divine. I, too, see that we are currently at a turning point in the ignorance cycle. Its completion is heralding the return journey to wisdom and connectedness. This is the time we are now entering.

Traditionally, it is during times of darkness and ignorance that we are most likely to be visited by enlightened beings. It follows, too, that during times of darkness there is the greatest impetus toward awakening. Enormous numbers of people all over the world, especially in the West, are currently on a spiritual path, and their return journey to truth, love and inner integrity has begun. It is time now for the many to wake up.

WHAT IS PROCESSING AND WHY DO IT?

Processing is a form of self-inquiry. The term *to process* means to examine and to inquire deeply into the nature of our conditioned and unbalanced egoic patterning with the intention of finding the truth. We process our consciousness in order to become clear and to find our wholeness.

Why would we choose to examine and process our consciousness at certain points during the course of our lives? What is it about life that would make us feel the need to add this particular activity to our already overburdened schedules? In addition to practicing the *power of one* for the sake of the world, the truth is that we have a strong and inherent desire to find ourselves, to find out who we are. We yearn to find more of ourselves since we feel so limited and want to increase our resources. It is *because* our lives are overextended and over-stretched that we most need to do the work. We must let go of all extraneous baggage and streamline the system of mind, body and emotions to make the maximum use of our time and energy. To function to the best of our ability in this world, we must be willing to do some letting go and some clearing work to make space for the pace of life.

The energies moving into the world and through all of us at the moment reflect an enormously speeded up evolution. We have to learn to cope whether we like the pace or not. Things have changed so much in the last few decades that what we were taught in childhood is already loaded with obsolescence. Processing allows us a more fluid consciousness and an ability to flow with the changes in daily life. It frees us from being stuck in the past and from struggling with our goals for the future. A cleared consciousness is the most valuable asset in this life. It allows us to cope really effectively with life's challenges. It means our awareness is more flexible and free. We have the resources of insight, creativity, enormously increased energy and an intensity of purpose to take us into success in whatever life situation we seek. Being rigid, blocked, and without inspiration and energy is a dead-end street in the modern world.

Processing is about creating balance in the mind, emotions and body. On the journey from ignorance to knowledge, all are of equal importance. The Western mind, especially, is extremely busy and undisciplined. The consciousness of the mind must be clear and quiet if we are to see truth and gain wisdom. Processing and clearing emotional turmoil means a letting go of all the old reactivity and stored emotional memories. This leads to a refining of the consciousness of the heart and allows the higher emotions to be expressed—states such as gratitude, unconditional love, generosity, humility, compassion and forgiveness. (In Chapter Ten—Triangles, we will take a more in-depth look at these higher emotional states and will offer some easy and practical ways of bringing them into our daily lives. For a quick preview of a longer list of higher emotional states, turn to page 174 in Chapter Ten.) With processing, the physical body also changes, because the mental-emotional overlays which cloud the physical body are melted away. Clearing the consciousness of the body reveals its original state of balance and harmony and helps us to let go of attachment to the transitory physical body.

Processing is a very unique way of letting go. We are not making something new with processing; we are melting away the old. Over time, processing is powerfully effective to reveal the deeper states of inner and outer quiescence, giving rise to what is known in the East as the state of *samadhi*, a state of unity consciousness, which we will discuss in great detail further into the book.

Processing is also a way of seeing into the unconscious, which helps us to let go of imbalances in the mind. Traditionally there have been a number of ways of seeing into the unconscious—for example, dream analysis, rebirthing and past-life regression. These are all popular and valid ways of expanding awareness. The Marriage of Spirit methods in Section Two are an unusual and different way of viewing the unconscious.

Processing is a very fast path to spiritual awakening. When spirit gave it to me, I was told that it would be much needed for these accelerated times we are living in. Because the techniques are mainly mental exercises, they allow us to shift consciousness quickly—in the mind. We actively engage the imbalances in the mind and clear them away. When we don't do this kind of inner clearing work, we generally have to live out in the physical world the lessons that we took incarnation to learn. This is a more passive approach and is slower. By doing the clearing work mentally (by writing in a journal) and proactively, we learn the lesson without having to live out the experience physically, which means we save enormous amounts of time in the process of waking up. This is especially beneficial if we want to awaken more quickly.

Processing is about becoming capable of increasing our flow of energy. As we clear entrenched patterns, a tremendous liberation of trapped energies takes place in us physically, mentally and emotionally. We also find, through the clearing process, the freedom to express this renewed energy level in our lives. So much becomes possible when we have abundant energy.

In terms of our spiritual growth, this abundant energy raises our level of attention, allowing access to the deeper insight and wisdom that are naturally present in us. Wisdom and insight *already exist* in us. We do not have to learn them. But it takes abundant energy to retrieve those less accessible, higher vibratory levels of consciousness. We need the energy to get a lift off, to gain some *altitude* in life. In doing the clearing work our overall vibration becomes faster and our attention is raised into a more refined level of perceiving. Abundant, liberated energy brings joy into life, and it is fun to share with others. It invites creativity and inspiration.

HOW FAR DO YOU WANT TO GO WITH PROCESSING?

How far you want to go with this clearing work is a matter of choice and depends on the commitments you are ready to make. The clearing takes place gradually, gaining more momentum with time and creating mini-awakenings along the way. Partial clearing introduces more awakeness into your consciousness and will improve life's circumstances. Everyone must choose for themselves which areas of personality to focus on and how much clearing to do. As people clear, they begin to succeed in whatever they apply themselves to. In other words, before awakening to the enlightened or cosmic state, you first become very creative, inspired, energized by life, and impeccable. These are the qualities which make for success in the material world *and* on the path to enlightenment.

Many people who have practiced the Marriage of Spirit techniques have blossomed and developed highly successful careers because that was what they were seeking. However, their success is a success generated by a flow of light, which comes from their center of inner inspiration and fullness. It is not a success driven by outer goals and ambition, which come from a sense of inner emptiness and which are seldom fulfilling or fully satisfying. At some point with doing this work, one must choose whether to go on to the direct, conscious experience of union with omnipresent being, which is full awakeness or enlightenment.

It was the nineteenth-century Indian Saint, Sri Ramakrishna, who said that no stone may remain unturned in the course of fully waking up, and in my perception this includes the full examination of the personality. However, processing the personality works just as well for the individual who simply wants to overturn a few problematical stones. Because the Marriage of Spirit techniques evolve through different levels, from a simple, beginner level to a more complex and advanced one, they can be used to whatever end you choose. If you are seeking full awakening, in time you will have to look at every minute aspect of the personality.

THE BENEFITS OF PROCESSING

There are many benefits to processing, which range from the concrete and worldly to the spiritual. As you move through the book and learn to process, try to notice what improvements are manifesting in your life. The following list names a few of the benefits of processing.

Worldly benefits:
- Having fewer personality clashes with others
- Healing of physical, mental or emotional traumas—past or present
- Increased ability to deal gracefully with anger and volatile emotions (yours and others)
- Greater harmony and equanimity inside and out
- More energy to use for things that bring you joy
- Feeling less drained
- Higher level of productivity
- More creativity
- Better communication skills
- Increased vocabulary
- Ability to resolve conflicts more easily
- Ability to let go of counter-productive, obsessive and self-destructive behavior patterns
- Greater tolerance, love, compassion and appreciation for other people and for the world around you
- More fulfilling work
- More fulfilling relationships
- Ability to let go of negativity and fear
- Increased flow of abundance
- Increased spirit of generosity
- Greater focus, mindfulness, awareness and insight

Spiritual benefits:
- Ability to live with an open heart
- A more tangible connection to the soul
- Greater alignment with your highest path
- Wisdom
- Psychic ability
- Purity of mind and heart
- Knowledge and experience of the connectedness of all things

- Experience of the peace that passeth all understanding (known in the East as *samadhi*)
- Experience of the magic healing power of grace
- Greater devotion to spirit
- Bliss states (known in the East as *ananda*)
- Greater and greater levels of spiritual awakening, or enlightenment

ASKING FOR GRACE

In the processing work grace has a powerful and essential part to play. The fusing and unifying of opposites takes place because of the subtle mystery of grace. As you do the integrative work and surrender it to grace, she comes in and assists in the reorganizing process. In the processing methods presented in Section Two, you and grace each play a role.

Grace is an aspect of the unfathomable intelligence of the universe. It is the expression of your higher self, which orchestrates for you the circumstances that you in your limited state cannot. Receiving grace is like getting a surprise bonus, supporting your situation in life. Grace comes to you in enormous quantities when the heart is open. Receiving grace can be a consequence of selflessness, humility, good works—or as it is known in the East, *good karma*—and acts of faith. Grace is yours for the asking and is a gift—if you are willing to see it.

Many people live most of their lives thinking there is nothing else beyond what they can touch and see. They play the games and take the falls. Then suddenly, it becomes time for them to consider that there is something more to life, and they begin to seek. What they seek as they begin asking for change is grace. Nobody changes without it. Transformation takes place when we ask for grace to enter our lives and to help us change our limiting situations.

UNITY IS A SIMPLE STATE

Knowing unity is essentially what everyone is looking for. It sounds simple, and it is. It is so simple that the mind, which is actively engaged in complexity and churning thoughts, does not find it. If you turn off your thoughts for a moment, it is there. To the untrained awareness it is seemingly nothing, a vacancy. But that is it—seemingly *nothing*. And yet it is also *everything*, a complete contradiction apparently. This spiritual journey is, almost more than anything, about becoming comfortable with paradox. The unified state contains everything and is in itself nothing.

The Marriage of Spirit methods are a way of permanently creating the emptiness of thought that allows the discernment of the unified presence, so subtle when you first contact it, but becoming so strong as you find it more and more. Most thoughts arise from stored baggage in the mind. The mind is cluttered like an old hall closet that has not been cleaned out for years. Every experience, every trauma, every hope, wish, dream, desire and more, is locked up as a thought form in the mind. Most of it is not needed, used, or even useful.

Humans are like pack rats when it comes to holding onto things in the mind. This old and excess baggage tends to replay in the mind, often consciously and mostly subconsciously, just below your surface awareness. When you try to find your spiritual self by becoming quiet and meditating, you find that these thoughts just beep and beep constantly. Try as you might, you cannot shut them off. They will not shut off until you have taken the time to clear out the old stored stuff that is the source of the thought forms. These methods do that. They help clear the clutter and make way for the presence of oneness and unity to be felt—so palpably that eventually you will feel it right down into your body.

CHAPTER SUMMARY

Here are some of the main points we have introduced so far:

- The Marriage of Spirit is based in the ancient principle of the unification of opposites.
- The teachings are about the sacred and alchemic fusing of two different elements, creating a new, unified energy, which reflects the underlying unity of spirit.
- The Marriage of Spirit is born out of a mixture of modern psychology, Jnana yoga and Tantric yoga.
- Everyone holds an enlightened core of consciousness, which ultimately cannot be described, only experienced.
- We are in a new and different time. We are here to enlighten the physical plane, the body and the personality while living and working in the world.
- This is a new paradigm known as unity in diversity.
- Processing is a form of self-inquiry. We process our consciousness to become clear and to find our wholeness.
- Processing is a fast path to spiritual awakening.
- You can take the processing along the continuum of enlightenment as far as you like—from achieving success in the material world, to directly, consciously experiencing your own awakened, divine nature.
- There are numerous worldly and spiritual benefits of processing (see list on pages 26 and 27).
- The unification of opposites takes place through the healing power of grace.
- Unity is the simple state that everyone is looking for.

SUGGESTIONS FOR PUTTING THEORY INTO PRACTICE

1. If you are curious about how the principle of the unification of opposites works in a practical sense, try reading the introduction to Section Two and Chapter Nine—Polarities, and then return to Section One later.
2. When opposites are unified, we move into states of higher emotion. To get an idea of where the processing work will take you, meditate on the list of higher emotional states on page 174 of Chapter Ten—Triangles.
3. As you learn to process, be aware of the changes manifesting in your inner and outer life as a result. Write about what you notice in your journal.
4. Make daily affirmations in your journal or say some prayers to invite grace into your life in a more profound and conscious way.

It is only in the act of contemplation when words and even personality are transcended that the pure state of the Perennial Philosophy can actually be known. The records left by those who have known it in this way make it abundantly clear that all of them, whether Hindu, Buddhist, Hebrew, Taoist, Christian or Muslim, were attempting to describe the same essentially indescribable Fact.

—Aldous Huxley

THREE

KNOWING
GOD

There is a state of awareness which at some time during our lives most of us have aspired to know. We may call it *God* or *knowing God*. What we call it does not matter; there are many names for it. We may not think of God specifically as a *state of awareness*, because that implies that this state is an intrinsic part of our own consciousness. Our tendency in this life is to mistakenly see God as some *thing* outside of us. When the state of awareness is recognized and understood as an inner state, God becomes a visceral experience, is no longer outside or distant, and there is no sense of separation at all.

Knowing God can mean many different things to different people. God can be an idea held in the mind. It can be an emotional belief held in the heart, as love for God. It can be a life lived in service to God. It can also be the desire to be good in order to be redeemed. Perhaps we vaguely associate it with a more formless, connected and open time from childhood and yearn for its return. Yet in each of these possibilities, there is usually an intrinsic experience of God as outside of us and as existing somewhere else. Most of us have fallen into denying that God is inside us, accepting the training which life gives us, to turn away from this truth, and choosing instead to identify ourselves with the limited personality.

Re-experiencing the palpable, direct connection to that inner state of divine awareness is a very real possibility. Throughout history humanity has sought to understand its relationship to God. We have sought to return to the experience of connectedness with the Divine, to deepen our knowing of this unfathomable mystery. It has intrigued us and called to us for eons. What is knowledge of and connectedness to the Divine? What does it mean in our daily lives? What will we be when we have it? Is there something to be gained through this divine experience, something that will enhance our lives? Who are we in relation to God?

While the whole of this book addresses these questions, in this chapter we will take a look at some of the basic principles involved in answering them. First, we discuss when, why and how we experience separation from the Divine. Second, we look at the paradox inherent in this, since all the mystical philosophies in their purest form tell us that there actually is no separation. Third, we briefly explore the historical context for the mystical journey. Fourth, we will discuss how the Marriage of Spirit principles are a pathway to reunification.

THE JOURNEY FROM SEPARATION TO UNITY— A BRIEF HISTORY

Our sense of separation has been with us as long as we can remember, and the teachings of the return journey also reach back in time, beyond our memory.

We can be certain that for at least the past five thousand years, roughly all of recorded history, most of humanity has been living in a state of feeling separate from God. When and where did our original separation happen? One possible answer is that it happened at some point in time before this cycle of civilization. To explore the mystery further, let's take a look at one of the oldest and most familiar records of the story of our origin—the story of humanity's fall from grace and loss of Eden as told in the book of Genesis. The legend implies that at some point in our history we fell deeply into a sense of separation from God. It suggests that Eden may possibly have been an earlier form of civilization where this was not so. If this is true, we have no conclusive record of it.

You may wonder at the relevance of this legend to modern Western humanity. Yet whether the story is literal or is even an accurate allegorical description of our origin, the influence which the story has had on human consciousness in its repeated tellings over millennia has left its mark in shaping our perception. Accurate or inaccurate, literal or allegorical, we have heard it so many times that it has become an archetype passed down through generations, and therefore it in itself holds the power to affect our mindset.

If the story of Adam and Eve is an allegory of our evolution into human form, then it is also the description of our apparent *fall* into separation. While the story implies many aspects of loss to humanity, the one we want to examine here is the idea that we became autonomous. We look at this in the context of our discussion because separation implies autonomy. After the fall God's support vanished, or at least that was the impression that was created. Adam and Eve could no longer enjoy the pleasures of Eden that God freely supplied unless they worked for them. They became separate from God's counsel and God's support and in effect became cursed. Adam and all his descendants, due to their separation and autonomy, had to labor for their survival and to take care of themselves. At some level of our awareness we have imprinted this story as a loss of our divine connectedness. It describes metaphorically the condition to which humanity is now subject—that of having to seemingly support itself—as well as how the veils of separation came about. These are the veils that obscure the divine spark within us that is our true nature.

It is interesting to note here, though, that the story also implies that there was a gain for humanity, too, in its becoming separate and autonomous. Separation and autonomy also created the effect of our being in control, or of seemingly getting *to play God in the world*. Genesis 3:22-23 says, "And the Lord God said, Behold, *the man is become as one of us*, to know good and evil. Therefore the Lord God sent him forth from the garden of Eden, to till the ground from whence he was taken." And so, paradoxically, this experience of separation and autonomy also gives us the experience of getting to be like a god and to play at being a god in relation to the world, rather than to be one with God, which is the enlightened state. Autonomy is the apparent ability to be in control of our own lives, to be the *do-er*. It also makes us subject to polarity—good and evil.

At whatever date this legend began, the belief in separation and autonomy—in both its loss and its gain for humanity—has persisted in our world right down to present times. It is the prevailing belief humanity in the West holds today of its relationship to God.

Prior to the dissolution of the older goddess civilizations and prior to the dawn of the patriarchal age, which began about 3000 BC, the mindset was more rooted in nature and thus more connected to the earth spirit. In the earlier goddess cultures, a cosmology of many different energy forms and nature deities was venerated and celebrated in its prescribed and proper place in everyday life. Although the people of the goddess cultures lived in a way that allowed for something of a mystical union with the invisible realms, they were still experiencing some degree of separation between themselves and God. Separation, while less than our current time, was still present in the human mind.

As our modern era dawned with the birth of patriarchy around 5,000 years ago, what little sense of connection there was began to be lost. With the exception of many indigenous cultures, which still hold remnants of aspects of the earlier goddess cultures and whose relationship with nature and spirit has been more integrated, the modern, technological human has tended to slip into a philosophy of deep separation from spirit. We have progressively come to live this separation, barely remembering that there is any other way to be. As each millennium has crept by, humanity has been evolving a program in consciousness, leading it deeper and deeper into a state of ignorance about its true nature.

In his fascinating book *Art and Physics*, Leonard Shlain points out that "Beginning in the 5th century BC Parmenides divided the world into being and not being. His pupil Democritas soon followed with the strict separation of atoms and the void. Both Plato and Aristotle endorsed either-or logic, and Christianity incorporated a Manichean duality into the doctrine of good and evil and heaven and hell. Later Descartes divided the in here from the out there, and in so doing strongly influenced all subsequent philosophers and scientists."

For generations modern humanity has been conditioned to hold God outside of itself. Despite the preaching of Jesus, who told us quite clearly 2,000 years ago that "the kingdom of God is within you," (Luke 17:20, KJV) we are still looking outside ourselves for truth. We still hold the belief that the outside is separate and disconnected from who we intrinsically are in our bodies and in our limited identities.

It seems it has been humanity's destiny to experience its separation and its disconnect from source and that like the journey of the prodigal son, life's purpose is to grow back toward unity. The study of this journey is what we call metaphysics. *Why* we take this journey in the first place is one of the most basic and yet most complex of all metaphysical questions.

THE RETURN — MYSTERY SCHOOLS AND ANCIENT TRADITIONS

The mystical truth of who we really are and of how we are divinely connected within ourselves is the discovery that there never was a "fall" and that there are, in fact, no separation and no veils between each one of us and source, no matter how it may look. We have been deluded by a belief in separation, which has been passed down through the generations since at least the legend of Adam and Eve. If this story of our fall only appears to be true, then you might ask, "Why do we have to live in this deluded state?" And the answer is that truly, we do not. When it is our time to make the conscious journey back to unity, something deep within the soul calls to us to let go of our old reality. Life changes in that we will begin to see glimpses of unity, to recognize it as home and to consciously seek it. We become initiates into the journey and privy to a whole new realm of awareness.

We feel the yearning to uncover the divine spark within us in different ways. In the East this is known as uncovering our larger Self, or undertaking a path of Self-discovery. Sometimes it is born of an intuitive flash, a *satori* experience, which so lifts us beyond our old reality that it inspires us to reach for that again. Sometimes the hunger is born of pain, of feeling so frustrated, blocked and corralled by our limitations and by life's hardships that we know there must be another way to live, that there must be more to life. Often it is a mixture of the two, seeping into the awareness slowly and permanently, like a stream of honey leaking in, yet punctuated with bursts of insight and spiritual awakening.

In the various ancient cultures that were some of the generators of our current civilization, such as the Egyptian, Indian, Celtic and Greek, just to name some of the more familiar, there were two levels of religion. One was a popular religious practice for the masses. The other was a secret mystery school for more developed souls. In these cultures, the religious cosmology was a pantheon of gods and goddesses, expressing the many vibratory essences of life in its transcendent form. The majority of the people saw the gods and goddesses as a focal point for their worship, because their human sense of separation required that they have a form outside themselves to focus on.

It was only in the mystery schools that the truth was taught about separation being erroneous. They gave initiations and instruction in the science and art of integration back to unity. This led initiates and adepts to an eventual realization of the truth of the most blasphemous idea in the human experience—that of complete union with the godhead. Over time, these extremely durable mystery teachings have come to be known as the Perennial Philosophy.

Remnants of the mystery teachings describing the separate state and how to achieve conscious union with the godhead have come down to us in the form of colorful stories and in scriptures, some of which are still alive and very much in use today. Let's take a look at a few examples.

One is the story of Isis, Osiris and Horus from the mystery schools of ancient Egypt. The story is impossible to date since it was kept secret by the priesthood and was only for initiates in the mystery school. It later became known to the public about the time the Greeks entered Egypt. It is the symbolic story of Osiris' fall into separation and his fragmentation into many parts. Through the passion of Isis, who represents the love of the divine feminine, he experiences reunification. It is the union of the divine feminine and masculine that produces Horus, their offspring. Horus is known as the great unifier and has come to symbolize union with the godhead.

Some other examples are in the literature of the Vedas, the oldest parts of which most scholars and yogis say were written anywhere from 4000 BC to 12,000 BC, if not before that. Expressions of parts of the Vedas—the *Ramayana* and the *Mahabarata*—are ancient epic Sanskrit poems of India. They depict the Vedic age, at a time when warrior kings ruled the world, guided by spiritually aware mystics and saints. In these reputedly true works, the stories are told of awakened beings—fully aware of their own divinity—such as Rama and Krishna who lived thousands of years ago.

Krishna Dharma, a scholar of the ancient Sanskrit writings of India and part of an unbroken disciplic line from the spiritual master who wrote the *Ramayana*, talks about it in his introduction to his translation of the *Ramayana*. "It was an age when men lived in the understanding that they were eternal souls, passing from life to life, towards a state of final emancipation. Thus the pursuit of virtue and truth was considered paramount, and human life was seen as an opportunity to attain spiritual liberation...." In the *Mahabarata*, the God-man Krishna, at the first glimmering dawn of civilization, guides "the families of the sons of God" in a battle against their relatives, "the sons of man", implying humanity's struggle with the separation between God and human existence.

From the *Mahabarata* come the passages known today as the *Bhagavad-gita*, India's primary Hindu scripture. They are a precise description of the four major yogic paths to awakening given by Krishna to his warrior/devotee Arjuna. Today, this work forms the basis of the teachings of the four major yogas and is studied by millions. The modern practice of yoga still holds the teachings of the return from separation to unity. According to W.F. Evans-Wentz in his book, *Tibetan Yoga and Secret Doctrines*, "Yoga implies a joining, or yoking, of the unenlightened human nature to the enlightened divine nature in such a manner as to allow the higher to guide and transmute the lower."

There are also remnants of these mystery teachings in some Christian literature. In the Gnostic text, the *Gospel According to Thomas*, Jesus said, "If those who lead you say to you: See, the Kingdom is in heaven, then the birds of the heaven will precede you. If they say to you: It is in the sea, then the fish will precede you. But the Kingdom is within you and it is without you. If you will know yourselves, then you will be known and you will know that you are the sons of the Living Father. But if you do not know yourselves, then you are in poverty and you are poverty."

ENLIGHTENED BEINGS

Where did the knowing that it was possible to attain this state, to return to the source, first take form? Where did the pathways that led back to truth come from and who devised the rigorous training that taking the path engendered? We can only speculate on the answers, since they reach back, fully fledged, into the mists of the past.

We do know, however, that throughout every era, most unusual persons—emissaries— described by those who knew them as awakened, have come to help the world by initiating and assisting those seeking to reconnect with their own inner divine nature. The Buddha, Jesus, Lao Tsu and Mohammed are the best known and are more recent. But there have been many others, some famous and remembered by name, some forgotten. There are even some reputed to have come at a more remote time than we can remember, yet who changed the world through the message of love that they brought and by their radically different viewpoints.

This mystical state, known for centuries in the East as enlightenment, has been a rare attainment in our world. Its well-documented occurrences in various cultures, such as the Vedic, Yogic and Buddhist traditions, as well as Christianity's Jesus and Islam's Mohammed, are enough proof for most that it exists. Yet some argue that the boundary between provable historical fact and legend is blurry in this area. As a way around this blurring, the Vedic, Yogic and Buddhist traditions have held to a system of lineages which has supported the passing down of the understandings of unity with Self, from enlightened teacher to student, for thousands of years. Many of these lineages exist today in religious practice throughout the East, especially in India and Tibet.

THE MESSAGE OF LOVE

In addition to sharing with others the understandings of the Perennial Philosophy, there are other reasons why these enlightened beings appear in the world at various times. Here is another excerpt from Krishna Dharma's introduction to his translation of the *Ramayana*:

> *If Rama is accepted as God, then a question arises: why does he appear? What is he doing as he moves about the earth, seeming to act exactly like an ordinary man? Such questions are answered in another of the Vedic literatures, the Bhagavad-gita. There it is stated that God appears in this world for different reasons. He comes to establish religion and to destroy demonic elements in society when they become too powerful. But he also appears in order to reciprocate the love of his devotees. It is this last fact which is most significant and which is said to be the primary reason for the Lord's appearance. The Bhagavad-gita explains that the Lord has no material purpose to fulfill when he appears. He is not acting in the same way as ordinary men who are interested in material gains such as profit, fame and adoration. Nor does the Lord have any political purpose. He is simply acting out of love.*

What is clear in all the teachings given in all the mystery schools, is that love is the force with the power to dissolve our erroneous sense of separation. And it is love that heals the aberrant and discordant behaviors arising from our mistaken identity with the separate self. Taking up the exploration of consciousness with the intention to create integrative transformation is, more than anything, a return to love. Love is an important component of awakening and of the unified state; it becomes one of our teachers as we seek union with the Divine. We must learn the lessons love teaches us; otherwise we will never find the unified state.

Love is the glue that binds the fragmented and unbalanced parts of us back together. It is a force with the power to dissolve all resistances and withholds. It joins all the seams, knits all the displaced faults, smoothes all the joints, and spackles over all the cracks. When it is present in its pure form, it is the melding, melting force that fuses awareness with the Divine. Love is, in the end, the force that draws us onto the path and keeps us going forward, by calling us back to its most pristine state, unity—over and over again.

WE ARE ALREADY ENLIGHTENED

Seers and teachers through the ages have stated categorically that we are already enlightened and that there is no way to *become* enlightened. This is true and is the great secret of our true nature. Like all issues of a metaphysical nature, however, it is also a paradoxical statement, because we do not see our enlightenment. The truth of this paradox startles the mind into awakeness. It becomes a kind of Zen *koan*, shattering the mind with its paradoxical logic and hopefully exposing to view the luminous presence beyond the surface mind. The koan reveals that the unified presence is always unfailingly present with us in a permanent, unbroken way, as the ground of our being if we could but see it. It is saying that we actually can see it if we know what to look for.

Why is it that we do not see this truth that the presence of God, or unity, is always with us as the ground of being? Why don't we always experience the unified presence in our lives as a tangible, immanent closeness? Or find the capability of consciously drawing on the intelligent resources of this presence? Why do our worldly preoccupations distract us so much that we don't notice it there? What happens in our awareness to block this knowing? These are the same questions that I asked back in 1971 during the experience described in Chapter One, in which my mind broke open to reveal the vast knowingness of unfettered consciousness. Exploring these questions is part of the purpose of this book. In the rest of this chapter and in the chapters to come, I will share some of the insights I have received over the passing years, which hopefully will shed some light on them.

The Personality Is a False Identification

What stops us from knowing our own enlightenment is our identification with the conditioned personality. This personality is made up of all the ways we see and describe ourselves based on what we were taught as children by our parents, the school system, the media and others who helped to mold us and to teach us who we are. For example a person may describe herself as a creative, intuitive, emotional, free-spirited artist, who is also usually messy, disorganized and chaotic. We take these traits, which are based on the conditioning we received from the world, and we identify with them. We think these traits are who we are. We call this personal identity in metaphysics *the false I* or *the separate self* because it is not the truth of who we are and because it keeps us locked into a limited, separate reality. Modern psychology refers to it as *the ego*.

This separate self is comprised of things such as: ideas in the mind which give rise to seemingly random thoughts, stored emotional baggage, emotional reactions to day-to-day situations, desires, fears, hopes, wishes, dreams, physical senses and our perception of our physical appearance. None of which is who we truly are. Our simple state of *I-am-ness* is overlaid by descriptive and egoic elements. For example, someone might say, "I am too fat, and I hate the way I look." Or, "I am tall, handsome, and I love the way I look." We think this is who we are. Gradually dissolving the tendency which we all have to identify with these elements comprising the separate self allows us to feel the pure, unconditioned *I-am-ness* of original awareness, which is our true Self. The unification of opposites techniques presented in Section Two assist with dissolving the veil of the separate self.

Paradoxically, letting go of identification with the separate self does not mean a loss of identity. Rather, we gain a new identity as the Self, and we experience ourselves as more expanded and more connected with spirit and with the world (Fig. 3-1).

Of course, it is impossible to represent the infinite quality of God/the Self in a diagram because of its limited nature. But here we have attempted to provide some visual framework for the concepts presented here, using the oval to represent God/the Self.

The egoic mind, with its polarizations, is like a maze. This is why it seems so impossibly difficult to get out of the separate system. Traversing a maze is an attempt to reach its center or its exit. Yet when you are in the maze, you can't see your way to the goal; finding it is haphazard at best. In ancient times mazes were built in physical form both for fun and to symbolize the journey of the soul back to the source (Fig. 3-2).

Unless there is someone who is willing to show you the way, or you remember being shown in another life, or you have some excellent tools to help you navigate the maze, you will never find the doorway out. Most individuals struggle, unable to find the openings alone. That is why knowledge has been handed down from teacher to student, generation after generation. Like a compass and a map, the unification of opposites techniques in Section Two are simple tools to help you escape the maze.

THE INVITATION TO CHANGE

Discovering and living in a more integrated state are an invitation offered by the soul at a certain point in our evolution. Learning to live in an even flow with events and change is a must. Should we choose to accept the invitation, we can expect major changes in perception and even changes in our lives. In fact we find ourselves facing many changes, and this can be unsettling. Yet we are

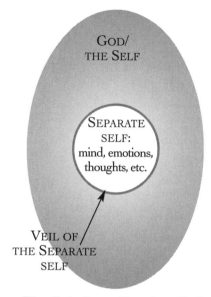

Fig. 3-1. *By making the veil of the separate self transparent, the light of the Self shines through.*

Fig. 3-2.

already living in a world where our experience of change is speeding up constantly. It may seem overwhelming to consider deliberately plunging into even more change. The growth that certain cultures are experiencing in electronic communications and the technology of the information age are undoubtedly pushing many of us through more and more change each year. Life is speeding up. When we are committed to spiritual transformation, learning to face change with equanimity is part of the training. With practice, it becomes easier and more comfortable to face change.

Preparation for the journey beyond the boundaries of the separate system takes place when we invite change. At the beginning of the journey, this can take the form of curiosity about life and its meaning, about God and oneself, or even just the feeling that there has to be *more*. Some sort of decision is made to find answers, or we make a commitment to spirit or to ourselves to face changes. Being in pain and/or or feeling stuck are motivators which drive us to seek change.

When we are frustrated or in distress, whether beginners or well-initiated souls, we are at a threshold of maximum potential for change. This is an excellent time to make the commitment to grow. Often there may be a feeling that *anything* is better than the situation we are in. Most of us can remember at least once when we have said to spirit that we would do anything, whatever it took, to break the cycle we were stuck in. Commitments made at times like that are hugely significant and could affect our life situation deeply. Let's take a moment to address the power of commitment.

The Power of Intention and Commitment

Transformation is instigated through commitment and intention. As you begin the spiritual path, you initiate change in the direction you wish it to go by making the commitment to have it begin. It is impossible to overestimate the power your commitments have to initiate change. If you are really serious when you make a commitment, it will start a cycle of change that will not complete until you have reached the change to which you committed. If you were not quite as serious but were wavering and half-hearted with the commitment, the process will be somewhat obstructed, although it will still try to fulfill itself.

The process of transformation becomes obstructed by contradictory commitments still held in the unconscious from the past. Much of your old reality and its patterned expression remain in place by intentions made long ago and of which you are no longer conscious. They may have been made so far back that they are long forgotten. Yet they still have the power to affect your mind and behaviors in the present. For example, as a child you may have vowed to the universe in a moment of frustration and anger that you would *never* be like your mother, or that you would *never* put yourself in a subservient position, or that you were going to become rich *no matter what*. Often in the processing work, you will come upon these old commitments and intentions, and it is necessary to consciously rescind and dissolve them. Forming new ones changes the flow of energy into something that is more in line with your new purpose and intention for your life.

I suggest renewing your commitment to your growth in whatever way you feel to be in keeping with your spiritual desires every time you complete some piece of the transformational work. Sometimes people feel that the original commitment that they made when they first started on the path of spiritual awakening will take them all the way to enlightenment and that they do not have to worry about renewing it. For example, "I commit to waking up." Or sometimes people feel that a general commitment made long ago to heal an unbalanced issue in their consciousness is enough. For example, "I commit to stop blaming my parents for my problems." This is unfair to the process of transformation. When you make a commitment, you make it with the part of yourself that is conscious. As you progress, more of you moves up out of the unconscious, and those new parts of you need a new commitment. Each time you experience a resolution to a problem or the healing of a troubled situation, rededicate yourself to the next step. In this way things will keep moving.

FINDING THE SELF

When we wake up to our true identity, we have the ability to continuously hold the deep, core knowledge of who we are beyond the personality. We are one with the Self. In this state we are plugged into a knowingness of where we originate, because we feel the divine presence inside and outside as well. We have become the Self, the one, always aware of its eternal beingness, of its *I-am-ness*. The Self is self-knowing. It does not experience itself reflected back from *an other*. It feels complete and whole within itself, needing no other. The unified state, the Self, is called *the one without a second*, implying that it is not dual. Desiring nothing, it allows life to move through it completely in each present moment. As the melee of life unfolds all around in constant change, the unified state becomes the backdrop to life's activity, itself remaining changeless, constant, eternal. It is eternal presence, and it is our true nature. As we find the Self, we find the secret of our own spiritual immortality.

CHAPTER SUMMARY

Here are some of the main points we have introduced so far:
   - We are conditioned to believe we are separate from our true, inner, divine nature.
   - We can return to our true nature as the Self if we choose.
   - The feelings of separation have deepened in modern times.

- The mystery teachings tell us we are not really separate and that we are already enlightened.
- The Marriage of Spirit offers techniques for integration of and dissolution of the separate self.
- The techniques are based on the unification of opposites.
- To live in a state of beingness, saturated with divine presence, we must dissolve the learned separations which everyday life has forged in the personality.

SUGGESTIONS FOR PUTTING THEORY INTO PRACTICE

1. How comfortable are you with change? Consider making a daily affirmation for a period of a few weeks, whether mentally or in your journal, to invite more personal transformation into your life. Pray and ask inwardly for help with beginning a path of self-inquiry or with having your path of self-inquiry speeded up.
2. Examine some of your old commitments and intentions. Consider rescinding any that are limiting or are not in keeping with the path of transformation and self-inquiry. Renew any that you wish to keep. You can do this by simply writing in your journal or by saying inwardly to spirit that you rescind or renew them.
3. Make some new commitments; for example, "I want to experience spiritual awakening." Or "I want to take the next step on my path of spiritual awakening." Then, in the coming days be aware, mindful, and open to the possibility of the fulfillment of your commitment.

People are in bondage because they have not yet removed the idea of ego.... How much confusion of thought comes from our interest in self, and from our vanity when thinking, "I am so great", or "I have done this wonderful deed"? The thought of your ego stands between your reason and truth; banish it, and then you will see things as they are. He who thinks correctly will rid himself of ignorance and acquire wisdom.

—The Buddha

FOUR

THE NATURE OF THE SEPARATE SELF

The presence of unity, interconnected in and through everything in existence, is always with us. It waits for us to perceive it from the level of the personality. It is what we are. We do perceive the presence of unity with the deeper levels of our awareness but not usually with the conscious mind. The inner state of unity appears coated by the veils of personality. Because this veiling blinds our awareness to the authentic Self, the surface personality becomes our substitute sense of identity. As inauthentic as it is, we assume it is all we have. It is an identity made up of how we see ourselves physically, what our skills and attributes are, how we feel and think, and what we like and dislike, desire and fear. With it, we—the awareness of Self—have become deluded into thinking we are the personality. We have become locked into a rigid and fixated state of identity and bound by enormous limitations. This method of describing ourselves, taught to us from infancy, is a completely superficial and inadequate description of who we really are. It does not take into account our eternal Self, the luminous beingness behind the personality that animates all of the personality qualities into life.

However, the above description is a surface glance at the nature of the separate self. Deeper causes of our separateness and its worldly context lie in the basic design of the system—a system which I have come to call *the separate system*. Consciousness has a structure in this system—an architecture and engineering. Let's take a look at the design and engineering of the separate system and see how we ended up in the separate state.

There are four main features in the design of the separate system, which affect our consciousness in limiting ways. They are: duality, the spin of opposites, the unconscious, and negative and positive polarization.

OURS IS A DUALISTIC WORLD

This world is known as a world of duality. It is a world of opposites—of negative and positive, good and evil, right and wrong, pain and pleasure, war and peace, superior and inferior, night and day, and many more. The list of dualities in this world is a long one, as you will soon see, since working with opposites is what we will be doing. Almost everything you can think of has its opposite side. A moment of examination will reveal the truth of this. We will be exploring this in detail throughout the pages that follow. It is an integral part of the architectural design of the whole system. As a primary feature of consciousness here in this world, duality, more than anything, has the most impact on our awareness. Its impact is most felt in how we hold our self-identity and how we live our lives. Thus, in this world we appear to be bound by a system designed to incorporate duality into our consciousness. Another way of saying it is that:

Our original state, the unified energy, has been seemingly imprinted with duality.

Here is a very simple description of duality. Imagine that you have an apple before you. The apple represents pure, undifferentiated, unified consciousness. The whole apple represents *all that is*. It contains within itself everything as a potential. Consciousness, which is what we are beyond our human state, is like the apple. If you were to cut the apple in half, you would be creating two pieces of apple. It is split into two parts. It has become dual, or two. The architectural blueprint for dualistic consciousness in this world is a program overlaid onto original, non-dual, undifferentiated consciousness. And that makes the consciousness of this world similar to an apple cut in two. It is this division of unified consciousness into duality that gives rise to all the polarized states that we know in this world.

Imagine that you could join the two sides of the apple together again. If this were possible it would become the one unified apple or one unified consciousness again. This is the principle of the unification of opposites. It is about re-unifying all of the perceived dualities in our individual awareness, allowing us to return to a perception of the whole, original, unified state.

The separate system is held together and contained by an electromagnetic field. What this means to us is that at the moment of creation, when consciousness separates from the whole, three things happen. One: consciousness, held by the magnetic field, divides into two—duality. Two: it is magnetized into negative and positive. Three: it divides into a conscious and an unconscious.

Consciousness in the system of duality is split in two and becomes caught up in the dance of magnetism. One pole develops a positive charge, and the other pole develops a negative charge, binding the two sides tightly together. We call this polarization. All dualities in our awareness are now held in a magnetized attraction-repulsion with one another, a dynamic push-pull between negative and positive.

THE LAW OF OPPOSITES AND THE SPIN

Something obvious to all is that in this world we are subject to constant change. A notable but less obvious feature of these changes is that all the dualities of the world change sides too. The seasons reverse, night and day alternate. Humanity passes through times of peace and times of war, times of prosperity and times of scarcity. Drought comes and so do the rains or floods. So, too, do the dualities in our minds alternate their positions in our awareness. This happens because all the different dualities in this world are charged positively and negatively, and they spin around each other. This turning gives rise to a law that we all must live by, which is that:

> *Within the time-space continuum,*
> *everything will eventually turn into its opposite.*

We find everything in our lives eventually turning into its opposite, from our passing moods to life's circumstances. For example one day we may have success, and on another we have to face failure. This spiritual law is the law for everybody living in the separate system. The law of opposites does not specify how much time any duality will take to turn into its opposite. It just states that it will at some point. So we can rest assured that at some point our depression, self-confidence or boredom will turn into its opposite, maybe tomorrow, maybe next month, maybe next lifetime.

We gain a tremendous advantage once we realize that we are stuck with this law, because we can begin to work around it. There is a way to do this. In the normal course of events, however, most people are in denial about the law of opposites and the changes it brings. They struggle to stay on the positive side of the personality as much as possible, becoming devastated when they find themselves flip-flopping into the negative side.

In fact, learning to be comfortable with the continuous change that the spin creates is one of the important steps on the path to waking up. Just knowing about the inevitability of the spin of opposites helps in the initial stages. It guides us into an even-minded acceptance of the cyclical nature of life. Eventually, as one becomes aware of the presence of unity, the mind and emotions become very centered, balanced and detached from the spinning of the opposites.

ATTRACTION AND REPULSION

Attraction and repulsion cause the mind to divide all worldly phenomena into the different camps of negative and positive, giving everything a negative or positive value. This leads us into separating and compartmentalizing everything in our minds. Our conditioned tendency is to align with one side (attraction) and disown, reject or avoid the other (repulsion).

We have no choice in this; we are bound unrelentingly by this system of judgment. Life is seen through this filter of negative and positive—that is, until we agree to do the transformational work. The moment we decide there is more to life, and wish to explore other options, we have the potential for moving into another paradigm, one that exists beyond negative and positive.

Most people have a tendency to be attached to the positive. For example, we cling desperately to something like pleasure, shunning pain, and an attraction-repulsion is set up. Attraction-repulsion is a powerful dynamic, which puts a spin on our mental and emotional energy. While we cling to the pleasure, we abhor the idea of experiencing pain. Yet the two are linked, and because of the law of opposites, they revolve around one another. One follows upon the heels of the other. Because of our clinging to the positive, the cycle keeps moving and eventually flips the polarity around to pain. Finally it changes back to pleasure, and then, of course, we try to hold onto pleasure because it is what we favor, and the cycle repeats itself. Because of the favoring and attaching to the one side of the polarity, that tremendous attraction for pleasure, we pull it toward us, and the wheel of our desire keeps turning. This is what is known in the East as the *wheel of karma*, and it is what we so deeply seek to escape. By clinging to pleasure, we inevitably create the return of the pain and remain trapped.

The energies of attraction and repulsion are extremely powerful forces. They have the power to shape our consciousness and our outer world. The force of our desire is capable of pulling material things, and even people, to us. And the force of our repulsion is capable of pushing things and people away from us. The act of repulsion is a very subtle form of violence, not just to others but to ourselves. It has the effect of fracturing the wholeness of our awareness field. Through the power of its pushing away, it creates separation.

The way to move beyond this fragmentation is through the unification of opposites. By examining the polarized states of awareness we hold within the electromagnetic field of consciousness, we have the opportunity to fuse them together into unity, and our whole field eventually becomes less dense and more transparent. Awareness can then pass right through it into the wholeness of universal mind, which is also a way of saying that awareness can move beyond desire and fear, good and bad, liking and disliking, and beyond judgment. This happens when we detach from the attraction and repulsion and from the spin.

WE TEND TO DENY ONE SIDE OF A PAIR OF OPPOSITES

We are all bound by each of the polarized pairs of opposites whether or not we are consciously aware of this. What usually happens to an individual is that he or she, in the course of life's drama, will play out one side of the pair more consciously, while the other side lives hidden in the unconscious, unseen and often denied. For example someone's personality pattern may allow for a positive feeling of self-confidence in the conscious awareness but will bury deeply the negative opposite feelings of worthlessness in the hopes that they will never need to be felt or dealt with.

It is part of being human to deny the hidden opposite side of every pair of opposites. While choosing to live out the one side consciously, we push the other into the unconscious. This carves the consciousness into partialities and defines the personality. Referring to the example above, someone could identify with the positive state by saying something like, "I can do anything I decide to do." This is a definite statement of confidence. The person is defining himself or herself by the state of self-confidence. And the person really believes the statement, because that is the nature of self-confidence.

From the divided place of duality, the personality cannot see both its negative and positive sides simultaneously, because one side of the pair is hidden in the unconscious. This blindness is one of the major sources of limitation in the personality. When a polarized state flips into its opposite, which it inevitably does, we can only then see and experience the opposite side. Highly self-confident people may suddenly find that they have lost their confidence and are wallowing in insecurity. This could take them completely by surprise since they have built such an identity around being self-confident, and such denial about its opposite. It could leave them very lost, confused and ashamed—even pivot them into a full-blown identity crisis, disrupting their lives and taking months to heal. It was their long-term denial of the hidden side that made the fall so hard to deal with. It was such a complete surprise and so pulled the rug out from under them, that they not only went into worthlessness but into shock as well.

The balancing and healing of their spirit happens as they come to a place of acceptance within themselves that having a worthless opposite side at least some of the time is normal. While this sounds like a reversal of their previous optimism and like something that could bring them down, it is actually a step toward becoming more realistic, balanced and self-aware. You will see more why this would be an advantage rather than a disadvantage as we progress in our understanding of the principles and techniques. Also, if the person in the example knew in advance that all consciousness in life is divided into opposites and that everyone is subject to the spin of these opposites, the person would be a lot less surprised and a lot more accepting when the self-confidence reversed. And last but not least, if the person could see that both the negative and positive sides of the personality are not who he or she truly is, the person would be taking a big step to freedom. As we explore beyond the partialities and limitations of the personality, there is a pathway through the jungle here which leads to our awakening.

In the separate self, there is usually an attempt to bury any state with a negative value in the unconscious. Most people feel a real prejudice toward admitting its existence at all. The unconscious, which we will explore in the coming pages, was created by our desire to be in denial of so much of ourselves. Because it is supposedly much more comfortable to live in the positive side, most people are in adamant and unshakable denial of everything that they have pushed into the negative unconscious. This is a very limiting choice, and we will continue to look at the ramifications of this to the spiritual seeker as we go along.

OUR HUMAN BOUNDARIES

Within creation, we experience consciousness split into myriad different states by the system of duality. The effect of this is twofold: First, it gives us the gift of life and the beauty and astounding diversity of the world around us. Second, it gives rise to the limitations we must deal with from being part of this world—a world where we seem to have lost most of our more universal resources, where wholeness is broken up into its many parts and where we feel separate from God, other people and the rest of the world.

Our perception has become limited to five senses, and we have for the most part lost our transcendental faculties, such as intuition, psychic ability, telepathy and clairvoyance. Instead, we have come to trust and to rely mainly on logic and discursive reasoning. We are bound by the physical dimension and by duality and have become disconnected from our attunement to the cycles of nature and to the web of life.

Just below the conscious awareness, we see this limiting of resources and how it affects our state in the world by reducing our power. We learn to perceive from childhood as the ego develops that not only is our power polarized with powerlessness, but so too are creativity, inspiration, insight and physical stamina polarized with their opposites—being uncreative, uninspired, bored and lethargic, and that it seems as though the force is not always with us. All the while we find that we have many dreams to fulfill and a destiny to live, yet we often stumble on an inherently built-in doubt about having sufficient resources to accomplish them.

The challenge and the handicap of life is finding ways to feel fulfilled when we do not have the full complement of resources and all the tools we need. The challenge in dealing with limitations is what forges character. In an evolutionary sense people's lives are defined by how they choose to deal with this situation. Life offers all sorts of solutions, both subtle and extreme, both healthy and unhealthy. For example, due to the apparent lack of resources, someone may compensate subtly by over-eating or by accumulating material possessions. More extreme compensatory behaviors could be things like kleptomania or alcoholism. Meeting life's challenge of limitation also can bring forward the best side of human nature as well. The state we think of as heroism is made of this stuff. Take for example, people who have physical limitations and yet who cope, cheerfully making the most of their situation, when they could get angry or feel like victims. Years ago, I saw an exhibition of art by individuals who had no hands. They had learned how to hold their pencils and brushes in their mouths or with their toes. I remember trying to imagine, since I was a painter myself, what my life would be like without hands. Limitation is relative. Sometimes it takes a hero's consciousness just to get through the day. The *Bhagavad Gita* says, "A serene spirit accepts pleasure and pain with an even mind and is unmoved by either. He alone is worthy of immortality." This is the hero. We all have our own physical, emotional or mental challenges. We cannot know our own heroism, or grow into it without the limitations of life to push against.

One would suppose that the system was designed like this so that we would eventually turn away from limitation and from the separate self toward spirit to begin our return journey. But oh, how many lives it takes to tumble to this! Success for the ego is in making life work and in finding fulfillment with our limited resources within the separate system. Yet it does eventually dawn on us that there is another way to be other than the egoic way. This usually only happens after trying all the other permutations. As we let go of the separate self and its seemingly autonomous life and as we give up playing God for the actual experience of returning to the awareness that we are God, we recapitulate our universal power.

It is time now to define some of the boundaries in consciousness that we face in the separate system. It is important to begin making them recognizable so that we will know when we bump into them and feel how they constrain or expand us.

First study them visually on the page below, looking at them, relating to them and savoring their meaning. This is to give you a feeling for some of the major schisms that you will come to understand both in a personal and in a more general, archetypal way. They are intimately bound up with our lives, often in extremely dramatic ways. Take a moment to really study them. Especially take the time to associate them with your own life experiences. Let the breadth and depth of the dimensionality of life which they convey to you, really sink into your understanding.

Masculine—Feminine	Loss—Gain
Conscious—Unconscious	Worthy—Worthless
Negative—Positive	Abandoned—Cherished
Active—Passive	Approval—Disapproval
Good—Evil/Bad	Love—Hate
Life—Death	Power—Powerlessness
Inner Space—Outer Space	Rejected—Accepted
Pain—Pleasure	Form—Formlessness/Space
Tyrant—Victim	Time—Timelessness
Praise—Blame	Existence—Annihilation
Superior—Inferior	Chaos—Order
Attraction—Repulsion	Creative—Destructive
Like—Dislike	Heaven—Earth
Desire—Fear	Heaven—Hell
War—Peace	Matter—Spirit
Work—Play	Sacred—Secular

Each one is a source of separation and an experience of boundaries in our own consciousness. They are a mere fraction of the total number of states forming the boundaries to which humanity is subject in our current state of humanness. Remember, due to the laws of attraction and repulsion operating in this world, the two sides of a polarity are held inseparably in a dynamic tension with each other.

Also, they are all part of the range of states to which we have access. They form a blueprint or design of awareness held in our minds. They give awareness access to the diversity of life. If at first glance this may not be clear or obvious, remember that we are looking at the way that the dual nature of consciousness defines us and our limitations. Please be patient with yourself. Understanding will come as you begin to work with some of your own dualities. If you have not already begun working with Chapter Nine—Polarities, you may find it helpful to do that now. As you begin practicing polarity processing, you will soon see how the dualities seem to lock consciousness into limitation.

IN THE BEGINNING — CREATION AS SEPARATION

When we first took incarnation and experienced separation, consciousness *fell* out of the wholeness of the unified field in a very particular sequence. The apparent first dualistic split, the original separation, was an emerging out of the unified state or the whole. This resulted in a subject-object split between *all that is* and the soul. The soul contains all of the frequencies out of which awareness in this system is fashioned. I use the word *frequencies* because creation, at its most fundamental level, is vibrational, with the particularized frequencies emerging out of the unity, which contains them in latent form. This androgynous soul form includes both the masculine and feminine frequencies, both negative and positive, and both conscious and unconscious (Fig. 4-1).

The second schism is the splitting away of the individualized self, or separate self, from the soul. It institutes the division between conscious-unconscious, negative-positive and masculine-feminine. The individual is split into the masculine frequencies if in a male body or feminine frequencies if in a female body. The soul's awareness manifests a body in either gender, making a selection of frequencies suitable for matching the gender. It also matches

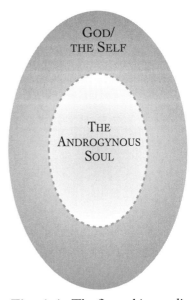

Fig. 4-1. *The first schism: split between subject-object*

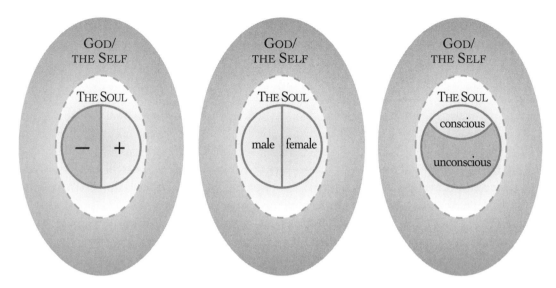

Fig. 4-2. *The second schism: split between soul and separate self. (The separate self is depicted as the innermost circle.) Simultaneous schisms happen between negative-positive, feminine-masculine, and conscious-unconscious.*

the relevant frequencies needed to support the particular personality pattern which is manifesting. In this way for example, someone in a male body could have a personality with many feminine qualities integral to its makeup, or vice versa. We use only a small portion of the available frequencies of creation for our limited and patterned life. The remaining, unused frequencies, which are in the majority, are projected into the unconscious. At death all frequencies return back into the soul (Fig. 4-2).

THE DIVISION BETWEEN CONSCIOUS AND UNCONSCIOUS

At the moment when the vast soul consciousness is seemingly squeezed into manifestation and limitation and becomes the individualized self, it is *imprinted* with duality. The memory of original wholeness is lost. This is the schism between conscious and unconscious. Our unconscious is our hidden side, the side of our awareness we do not see; it is unknown. We are, under normal circumstances, quite blind to it. Others can see our unconscious aspects at times, but we usually do not.

Since manifestation means that we are now divided in two and that most of our consciousness is locked up in unconsciousness, we cannot know everything as we did in our original state. Since the unconscious part of us is much larger than the conscious, we are left with a tiny, limited portion of our original Self.

Culturally, the conscious, surface aspect is generally what society chooses to acknowledge. There is even subtle pressure from society not to scratch below the surface too much, and so *surface* is what most people are aware of. Humanity chooses, for the most part, to keep the conscious awareness as shallow as possible. We even have a saying that *ignorance is bliss*, which very aptly describes this phenomenon. Some people experience pain associated with this superficiality, especially children. I vividly remember childhood pain around this issue.

I was always described as rather deep and serious as a child. And what bothered me was the way it was always said, by adults as well as childhood friends, as though it was an untouchable subject. The message I got was that I was not only different, but that I was somehow unknowable. And this translated to my young ears as unacceptable. I was accepted as long as I did not expose what was below the surface awareness. As a child, I seemed to have a fairly expanded awareness, and this they labeled deep. I suppose, relatively speaking, it was. So, I learned quickly, as many children do, to hide the depth and the ways I was different, trying to fit in more with the others and to conform.

However, the bright side of this is the fact that there is much more to us than our current world would have us believe. We are free to begin retrieving parts of our unconscious and expanding our awareness back to its original wholeness as soon as we desire it. Penetrating into the unconscious usually only takes place with a desire and commitment to enter.

We Tend To Fear the Unconscious

The division between conscious and unconscious awareness is one of our most fixed boundaries. The view is definitely veiled. The conscious personality is just the tip of the iceberg in relation to the unconscious.

We tend to fear our unconscious, projecting that it contains all manner of evils, including our own negative ego. Sometimes the unconscious is called the *dark side*, not because it is bad or negative but because it is hidden. Many people misconstrue the dark side to mean the bad or negative side. It sounds ominous, but this definition is not necessarily true. The hidden, unconscious side can be either positive or negative, good or bad, since the good-bad projection is subjective.

> *The unconscious mind has a positive as well as*
> *a negative aspect, just like the conscious mind.*

The unconscious is also known as the *shadow side* of humankind; and every person on the planet, without exception, has an unconscious, unless they have worked to make everything conscious (Fig. 4-3).

Entering the unconscious is also the path of returning to the knowledge of our universality and our multidimensionality. We must develop a willingness to unveil the unconscious if we are to return to *all that is*. Until we are willing to enter it, we do not discover that it contains all sorts of gems, including the soul's endowments and attributes from other lives. Most individuals do not think of themselves as having a vast reservoir of available consciousness which they can enter for information, understanding, wisdom and inspiration. Rather, they tend to feel that they are just composed of the surface personality and behaviors, feeling moreover that they don't have access to wisdom or inspiration at all. By way of an example: if perhaps we had had a past life where we distinguished ourselves in some way, say in the arts or sciences, the knowledge gained would be stored in the unconscious. We could access that soul wisdom to enhance our current life's resources.

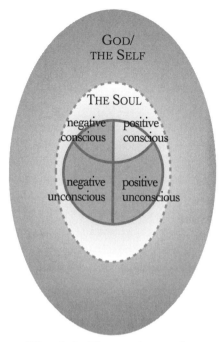

Fig. 4-3. *The conscious and unconscious mind.*

The unconscious contains the power stored from many lifetimes. Years ago, when I first began to move into advanced Self-discovery, I had a dream in which Anubis, a man with the head of a jackal, came to me and initiated me into my journey through the unconscious realms. When I woke from the dream, I did not know who Anubis was, nor did I understand its meaning. But the dream had been so vivid that I remembered his name and looked it up in a dictionary of mythology to find that he is the ancient Egyptian god of the underworld. The dictionary's definition of Anubis was rather limited as I later discovered. It associated the underworld with the dead and not with the living. This was terrifying to me. I found myself frozen with fear for several days until I told myself that it was just a dream and was not real.

When finally I mustered the courage to delve into the fear, I found that not only had I assumed the dream was about dying, but that I had had a knee-jerk reaction about the underworld being an undesirable place where demons and unbelievable horrors lurked. I thought I was lost for sure. My mind associated it with Hell in a Christian sense, even though I was no longer a practicing Christian. It took a while before I realized that this was not just a dream but a message from my unconscious, and that it was actually a blessing. A Jungian friend finally pointed out to me that it was a sign that I was going to recapitulate my spiritual power. Spiritual power lies in making the unconscious conscious.

The desire to be good is often a reason to suppress and deny the unconscious. Being good is not the way back into *all that is* in the sense that we have come to understand *good*. We have looked at how most people desire to emphasize the positive. We equate the positive with being good. We suppress the negative or bad parts and try to hide them from others, even deny them to ourselves. We do this because we believe that we must be good to be redeemed back into Heaven—something we desire more than anything else, at least unconsciously. This is an archetypal belief that conditioning has given us, especially in the West. The interpretation seems to have its origin in Western religious practices.

This belief creates a problem for you if you are trying to wake up because it is necessary to unveil the unconscious. When you try to get rid of parts of yourself which you dislike, there is nowhere for the disliked parts to go except into the unconscious. Since everything is consciousness, which is eternal, nothing can be lost or disposed of. Therefore your repressed parts remain present but become veiled.

Suppression might be a wonderful solution in theory, but in its practice the veiled parts still exert an influence on your life. They rearrange your world in ways that you just have to put up with, since you cannot see how your unconscious is doing the rearranging. In the dualistic state you have the luxury of an unconscious where you can sweep your garbage under the rug, but the downside is that you are passively subject to the effect of this.

In this process of Self-discovery, you have to account for all the missing pieces of yourself, even those you labeled negative. You can no longer choose to ignore these missing parts by creating a shadow over them. You must make another plan for the negative that does not involve suppression, avoidance or denial.

On the understanding that the polarities unify into a higher vibratory state, consider making a commitment to make the unconscious conscious, which will set the process of your growth in motion. This releases you from the need to stuff anything into the unconscious.

MAKING THE UNCONSCIOUS CONSCIOUS

We have a personal unconscious, relating to our individual selves, and an impersonal unconscious, common to everyone. Jung called the impersonal unconscious *the collective unconscious*, implying that this collective awareness of all humanity is one state common to all of us. In my own journeys into collective awareness during deep meditation, I have seen this to be true. The collective unconscious is a rich repository of all the archetypes, memories and wisdom of all humanity. As you explore it in the course of your transformation, you come into contact with the totality of all consciousness and you become capable of accessing it energetically. As you progress through the steps outlined in Section Two, you become acquainted with some new ways of looking into the unconscious. For now, it is necessary just to realize the importance of seeing into the unconscious. In other words, one must make the unconscious conscious.

In the end we come back to the realization of the absolute truth presented in the mystery teachings and postulated by modern physics, which is that all separations are an illusion. So although it appears that the original, one consciousness is now divided into a conscious and an unconscious side, this is only an appearance. It never really happened. One way of describing this truth is to say that our perception of separation is a program imposed on awareness. It could be compared to a computer program—the current program for life on planet earth. Our lives here are a kind of virtual reality created to give consciousness (us) an experience of life lived in limitation. However, when you are in it, and until you awaken to the truth, it seems very real.

In essence we are pure awareness. We think we are all sorts of other particularized things, like smart, athletic, educated, desirable, and so forth, but we are not those things. Our true nature is as energy, or light.

UNDERSTANDING AND DISSOLVING THE CONDITIONED PERSONALITY

The personality is a matrix of intertwined energy frequencies forming a design. It has a shape and a structure. Because of its structured organization and its density in the time-space continuum, it tends to play and replay like an old tape, giving few options to maneuver and locking personality into limitation. People living in and identifying with the personality find themselves running on automatic, becoming robotic in their behaviors and with little ability to flow with life.

Conditioning is the imprinting of patterns of behavior onto the soft clay, first of the infant and then of the child. Parents, family members, ancestors, the school system, the media and the world are responsible for the process of conditioning. They teach us to be *a person* in relation to *the world*. Our childhood conditioning structures the consciousness with our sense of who and what we are in a worldly sense. But this is our identification with *being the personality*—with all the conditioned states that make up the personality. It is the identification with the personality that forces us to live in the world as a personality, rather than having the deeper knowing of ourselves as pure consciousness.

As long as you identify yourself with the personality in this way, you are really stuck with your limited and unbalanced patterns. This stuckness is because it is really difficult to let go of something as long as you think it is you. You would be trying to let go of yourself, and that is unthinkable, because the ego has an imperative need to know it exists.

How can you change your way of identifying yourself? The first step toward letting go of your conditioned identity as you begin to process is to examine the ways in which you believe you are the personality. We will discuss this in great detail later in the book, but for now, it is enough to practice this first step. If you practice letting go of the sense that you are the patterning of the personality, you will see the patterns, but you won't feel that you need them as an identity. For example we all have a tendency, in keeping with defining ourselves by the qualities of the personality, to say things like, "I am angry." You are in effect saying, "I am the anger", which you are not. This means that you are defining yourself by your anger—an erroneous thought and the source of much of your limitation and emotional pain. When we stop using our states of mind and feelings to define ourselves, we would say something like, "I have anger at the moment" or "anger is passing through me." By doing that, you have differentiated yourself from the anger. It takes a bit of time, but the moment you really see that you are not dependent on the personality as a barometer of who you are, you can allow it to change.

What this means is that it is beneficial to try to detach from identifying with the personality. The personality, or the identity, which we think of as *I* is not our true *I* essence. You will gradually begin to see that:

> *We are not the conditioned personality, or ego.*
> *We are in fact pure, undivided, non-dual consciousness—*
> *energy, light and love.*

Some of these conditioned imprintings are obviously important and useful for getting us through the day, and we would not want to let go of them. For example, our parents conditioned us not to put our hands onto the stove or to play with fire. Other belief systems and conditionings, however, are a hindrance to waking up and need to be examined, processed, and released.

We also live with the idea that our interior world is our private domain, locking awareness into the vault of inner space. The imprint of autonomy, meaning we alone are in charge of our lives, gives rise to the *do-er*. In the interest of being in control, the personality is the one who is solely and often desperately responsible for making life work. The *do-er* has left its mark on the personality and on outer life; it places us in the most limited scheme of possibilities. Our sense of living separately from the whole makes us feel cut off from life and from other people. We often feel so disconnected inside that we feel alienated from the things of the world in subtle and even not so subtle ways. We think we have to work really hard at reconnecting to the things we presume to be disconnected from. For example, some of the aberrant ways we try to connect with other people are by doing things like talking too much or too loudly in order to get attention, acting out to get attention and approval, or sexual addiction, just to name a few. Sometimes if these things don't work, we may even resort to more extreme forms of negative connecting, because even that feels better to the ego than not connecting at all. This could look like rule-breaking to get attention, rebelling against authority or acts of violence. Really, in these instances of seeking to connect with people and things which we interpret as separate and as outside of us, we are simply looking for connection to the missing parts of ourselves. We are really looking to reconnect with *all that is*. It is not that connecting is right or good or bad or wrong. That is not the point here. But rather, on the path of Self-discovery, becoming conscious of the motivations behind the desire to connect is extremely beneficial. This is because our desire to connect sometimes comes from a place of deep alienation inside of us, where we are unable to see our place in life and our natural and intrinsic connection to everything. Uncovering our hidden motivations for behaviors helps us to unravel the conditioned and limited personality—which keeps us locked into the separate state—and therefore assists in the waking-up process.

PROCESSING THE EGO

It quickly becomes evident to anyone on the path who is really serious about enlightenment that one must practice self-inquiry and deal with the ego. Yet even with the strongest resolve, it is still one of the hardest things to do. Why is this? Most people do not see themselves clearly. All of us have an idealized version of who we would like to be and another version which is a compromise of this ideal.

We do not understand who we truly are, and so we have to make up stories about ourselves, often not even recognizing that they are stories. It is because we feel so fragmented and confused inside about our true identity, that most of us have a really potent resistance to facing ourselves. We are afraid of what we will find inside ourselves. We are afraid of looking at the fragmentation, afraid of finding out that we are not who we hope we are. Obstructed from within as well as from without, the ego resists change to itself. It has built-in survival mechanisms to block change—and transformation is about change. Processing the ego makes it possible to create change, overcoming the shadows in which we have wrapped ourselves, along with the confusion that the shadows create in our minds. Among the benefits that we receive from actually doing the processing are that the changes are permanent, our energy increases, and the personality becomes wonderfully smoothed out.

Long before you get to the point where you can actually feel unity consciousness on a continuous basis, you pass through a number of stages in which you experience the ironing out of all the hard knots and wrinkles that are in the personality. All of the things that make you uncomfortable with yourself will begin to drop away. Change happens. You become someone you actually like. It is possible to really like yourself, to love yourself. Many people do not. Many people have a hard time living with themselves. There are aspects which they defensively and proudly support as being extremely worthy. And there are also little things which they try to hide because living with them is very uncomfortable. In fact, feeling worthy is ego, and feeling unworthy, or worthless, is also ego. We are as much in ego when we feel that we are the worst as when we feel that we are the best.

Eventually we come to see that we are neither worthy nor unworthy. In fact, in time we will see that our whole identity is an assumed role. It is something that is given to us at birth and in childhood when we were conditioned to a certain way of being.

LETTING GO OF THE PERSONALITY

When I lived in California, I was at the beach one day, grappling with my process, which would not yield. I wished that I could just unzip, peel, and step out of the conditioned self, dropping it away, the way that I saw the surfers doing with their wetsuits, after they had finished their play. Within the context of this processing work, the personality is like these wet suits—a thick, black skin, which un-zips down the front. Since then, I have seen that the analogy is fairly accurate. Transformation is a wonderful emergence, like a snake sloughing its constricting skin, or a butterfly emerging from a chrysalis.

In bringing about this metamorphosis, you become capable of seeing yourself *doing* your limited personality routines, and you surprise yourself. You catch yourself in the act, so to speak, as you play out your conditioned stuff. Eventually, you may peel the separate self away from your divinely illumined Self and step out into the light.

All the personality games you play, the stories and dramas to which you are addicted, block the awareness of divine presence. They have to be thoroughly and gently examined and released over time. They are the thick, black rubber of the wet suit, not the real Self at all.

All of existence is consciousness—and who you are is no exception. We are all purity itself in our essential, original state. In our human form the conditioning process means that we are imprinted, so to speak, with a personality. But that personality is rather like the role that an actor would assume in a play. It can also be likened to the clothes that we wear when we get dressed every day. The metaphor for our essential state would then be the naked body. As we process, we can learn to easily remove the costumes and masks, and when we are ready to do this, it becomes an inevitable part of our evolution. Even though we have spent decades wearing them, we can take them off, discover who we are in our naked state and adopt the raiment of a new paradigm. Our realness, our true identity, is as spirit. In time, it is possible to totally let go of the old identity and to know who we truly are.

On the path of Self-discovery, we are always searching for the missing pieces of ourselves. To find them we have to be able to see into the unconscious. One of the ways we can do this is through the simple exercise of asking the question, "What is the opposite of this?" when we feel stuck in believing we are the states of the personality, like anger for instance. We often get surprising results. We are so used to seeing only one side of the story that it takes our breath away when we see its opposite side. It is something of an epiphany when we simply ask, "What is the opposite of this?" When we see we are *love*, for example, and not just locked into *anger*, then we come another step closer to our wholeness.

It is extremely difficult to transform and to integrate the personality without seeing its polar opposite. This is because we have only half the story. It is essential to see the whole picture to create change and to grow.

SEEING CYCLES OF GROWTH AND DISSOLUTION

It is the nature of existence to run in cycles. They can be seen everywhere—in the seasons, the weather and in the birth, life and death of all living things. So too, it is the cycles of change which allow growth and evolution in your own being. If you slow down these cycles momentarily and take a magnifying glass to this natural process, you can see more specifically what is happening. As an old cycle completes itself, it halts its process of growth and goes into a process of the opposite. This is a cycle of dissolution or decay. The prevailing order is changed.

Every dissolution is followed by a renewal and a rebirth.

This is true of your awareness, too. It is important to allow the dissolution and not to hold onto the old. It must naturally flow away from you. Have faith that a new cycle will replace the old. So too, in this life your body goes through a process of birth, growth, maturation, decline, and death. These are natural cycles, which occur within the boundaries of life. It is possible to accept them with humor and grace as a natural and inevitable phase and not to be attached to that which has moved on. Rather look to the birth of the new and feel the flow of life all around you.

CHAPTER SUMMARY

Here are some of the main points we have introduced so far:
- We are examining the separate system's architecture and engineering of consciousness.
- This is a world of duality.
- It is magnetized into negative and positive.
- It is divided into conscious and unconscious.
- The dualities spin, and within time everything will eventually turn into its opposite.
- In the dual system, we are bound by attraction and repulsion of positive and negative—until we agree to do the transformational work.
- We tend to deny one side (usually the negative) of a pair of opposites and to push it into the unconscious.

- The system of duality gives rise to the beauty and diversity of the world and to its apparent limitations—including our loss of resources, wholeness and connectedness to God, other people and the rest of the world.
- Consciousness fell out of wholeness in a particular sequence of schisms.
- First is the subject-object split (between *all that is* and the androgynous soul).
- Next is the soul-individual split (which includes the splits between masculine-feminine, conscious-unconscious and negative-positive).
- We tend to fear the unconscious, which results in suppression, avoidance or denial.
- On the path of Self-discovery, it is important to make the unconscious conscious.
- It is important to understand, dissolve and let go of the conditioned personality, which is like peeling off a constricting wet suit.
- We are not the conditioned personality; we are pure, undivided, non-dual consciousness—energy, light and love.
- Every dissolution is followed by a renewal and a rebirth.

SUGGESTIONS FOR PUTTING THEORY INTO PRACTICE

1. Try to become aware of how you tend to deny, avoid or suppress one side of a pair of opposites. Write in your journal about what you see. (If you need help with this, you may consider trying the polarity processing technique in Chapter Nine if you have not already.)
2. Meditate on the list of polarities on page 51 of this chapter. How do they relate to your own life experience? Write in your journal about what you see.
3. Consider making a commitment to begin making the unconscious conscious.
4. Practice detaching from your identification with the personality. Begin with some daily affirmations, either by speaking them, saying them inwardly, or writing them in your journal. They can be things like:
   - "I am not my personality."
   - "I am pure awareness—the Self."
   - "I am whole, complete and unlimited."
5. When you find yourself in an uncomfortable situation or are running an unbalanced behavior pattern, for example an irrational burst of anger, ask yourself, "What is the opposite of this?" Try to find your wholeness by seeing both sides of the polarity. Ask inwardly for grace to come and assist with the changes. Write in your journal about what you see and experience.

Judge not, that ye be not judged.
(Matthew 7:1)

—Jesus

FIVE

JUDGMENT AND MIRRORS

As we have seen, life is a dance of pushing and pulling, of attracting and repelling as we make our way through experiences. We attach labels of *good* and *bad* to the negative-positive dynamic at work in most of our experiences, and thus our repulsion or attraction to one or the other side of a polarity keeps our consciousness spinning. Most of this happens on an unconscious level, and so what we notice—physically, mentally, and emotionally—is a sense of being uncomfortable and unstable in our environment. The trick, then, is to not identify with positive or negative aspects of experiences, to see the whole picture, which brings more balance into our lives, and to know that we are pure awareness.

In this chapter we will further examine the architecture and engineering of the separate system—specifically, how its design incorporates judgment and mirrors. We will look at four main aspects: first, how our negative and positive judgments affect our world and our consciousness; second, how judgments lead to projections which create our outer reality; third, how the hidden unconscious side of our judgments holds the key to our liberation from the separate system; and fourth, how the outer world mirrors our own unconscious.

THE EITHER-OR MIND

By taking up a position on one side of a pair of opposites, we put ourselves in an *either-or* state of perception. It is usually difficult to synthesize and be aware of both sides at the same time. For example, we can usually be only happy or sad at any one moment. It is unusual to feel both happy and sad at the same time. We can be only a winner or a loser, not usually both. We can be right, or we must be wrong.

Or, more common and more dangerous, we are right, and the other person is wrong. Polarization within ourselves and with others can lead to separations and suspicions caused by differences, even mushrooming easily into alienation and spiraling down into a full-blown war. Polarization leads to enmity. We might say something like, "You are either with me or against me." Being on one side or the other is what the either-or mind does with polarization. Because we have taken a position on one side of a polarity, we have lost the all-encompassing, over-arching state, which connects both sides.

Of course there are many shades of gray between the black and white of this world. We are not always in extreme polarization. Some people have the ability to move in and out of the gray areas more easily than others and also to see both sides of a polarized situation. This is the trait of diplomacy, and it helps in creating compatible relationships. But if you examine the gray areas closely, they also include degrees of polarization, albeit to a less extreme degree than black and white. For example, at one extreme we may have love-hate. A less extreme polarity is like-dislike. A less extreme polarity than that is tolerance-intolerance. So, there are gross and subtle levels of polarity. But when we are in any kind of polarized consciousness, we are still in the either-or mind and have apparently lost the connection between the two sides. Because of this, polarization is what keeps us trapped in limited awareness and in a limited persona.

We have become programmed into limitation because this negative-positive judgment now blocks us from knowing the true and intrinsic nature of everything in this world, of being able to look deeply into the mystery of life and to see that which is— its quality of *is-ness*.

In fact as we take up positions of judgment about both sides of a polarity, we develop a very defined position for ourselves—the beginning of a completely fixed identity held in limitation. We now define ourselves by positive, which equals right and what we like, and negative, which equals wrong and what we don't like. Our language perfectly describes us. Look at the makeup of the word:

INDIVIDUAL = (IN-DIVIDED-DUAL)
A human being is consciousness divided and in duality. Divided in two.

And how different the meaning of the word *individuality* has become to us now. The current usage of the word describes our uniqueness, something we value. It must be said at this point that we do value our dualistic state too, otherwise we would not be here in this world. It offers us an amazing experience of diversity, of apparent autonomy and control, of beauty and ugliness, of love and war, of life's roller coaster with all its ups and downs. But we have the potential in us *to be it all* as well; we can retain the ability to live in the dualities and know and experience the unity as well. We can retain our individuality in the sense that we currently use the word, meaning uniqueness, even as we move into enlightenment. There is an inherent guarantee given by grace that each individual will not lose his or her uniqueness. We have the potential to know ourselves as a reflection of the divine spirit, at one with everything, yet also expressing our uniqueness in the world. Paradoxical, but true.

Most people do not realize that the conscious return to original wholeness—or health (same meaning, same root in the English language)—is our birthright. Not only that, but most people do not see that it is up to them to claim it. In a sense it is a return or a reawakening to the inner and outer Eden, our original state. It is a return to the perception of connectedness with everything, to the all-knowing state of our universal nature, our greater body of consciousness, beyond and yet including all negative and positive polarities.

LIVING IN A SYSTEM OF JUDGMENT

Because of the either-or mind, we do not see anything with true eyes. This is why this world can be described as *a system of negative-and-positive judgment*, which is part of the separate system's engineering. Since we are taught from birth to hold a value for everything, we see things either as positive or as negative. We like them, or we dislike them. We are attracted and desire them, or we are repulsed and fear them. With this kind of good-bad seeing, we are projecting a judgment onto everything. This seeing and judging everything as having a specific value is firmly ingrained, and it often happens so instantaneously that we tend to take it completely for granted. We simply do not see ourselves doing it. The fact is that this knee-jerk reaction of judging everything has a profound effect on our lives, trapping us in limited perception and denying us the ability to see the actual nature of everything. When we are in judgment, we are left with the idea of things being only either good or bad, and the intrinsic wonder of life's gift of diversity, the unique and intrinsic nature of each object, including our own intrinsic nature, the simple *is-ness* of everything, is missing

Judgment is not necessarily either a good thing or a bad thing. Discernment from a balanced place is an important and necessary aspect of life in a physical body. But judging unconsciously and by habit, without knowledge of its effects and repercussions, keeps us locked in limitation. This is what leads to suffering. Because of our soul's choice to enter the system of judgment, the separate system, our awareness is bound by agreements to stay separate. Therefore we must look away from the numinous web of connectedness; we must *ignore* it. Look at the makeup of the word *ignorance*:

IGNORE – ANCE
Ignorance is the practice of ignoring.

In fact in the East, the English word *evil* is often translated as *ignorance*, implying that judgments based on the dual system of good and evil are born of ignorance of the *all that is*. By ignoring our unconscious side, our connectedness and our own inner divinity, we become ignorant, and we look instead into the so-called *real world* of life in the separate state, which is all about judgment, hard edges and separations. We must then live with the fact that generally somewhere inside us we feel alone, disconnected and with limited resources.

Born of our sense of isolation and of the sketchy and superficial knowledge of how we are made up, it seems to be human nature to imagine that we alone are the way we are—that no one else is like us. So, people feeling the negative side tend to be so ashamed of these feelings that they try hide them. People project onto others that no one suffers as they do, that no one else has negative traits, that they must be the only ones who do. Really all they are seeing is that others may be doing a better job of hiding their negative judgments and issues. It is helpful to know that everyone, without exception, comes equipped with a fully active negative and a fully active positive side to their personality. It is part of the software of being human.

JUDGING THE OUTSIDE

Judging the things of the world and seeing them as separate from us, and as random occurrences, is something that we do without thinking about it; it seems so natural to do. Like fish in water, we are not even aware of the water most of the time. And living in an unaware state, with our positive and negative judgments, we help to hold in place our world of limitation and duality. By placing values on the apparently separate things outside of us and by not seeing our connectedness, we perpetuate the problems of the world and are unable to manifest our hearts' desires. This leads to blaming the outside, when in reality the root of the issue is actually within us.

In general, we tend to evaluate diversity and all the perceived differences in the physical world, projecting hierarchy onto them. Apart from the obvious visual differences between the forms of the physical world, we see, for example, the differences between species very clearly. We do not necessarily perceive our kinship and our sameness, let alone our direct connectedness, for example with the animal kingdom—even less so with the plant and mineral kingdoms. In general we respond to these diverse forms from a place of separation, with judgments of our superiority and their inferiority. Usually their value to us is in how we may use them to satisfy our needs. Usually we do not respect them as a part of the great oneness, nor do we have appreciation for their intrinsic nature. How can we see their intrinsic nature since we do not see our own? The way the world is set up at the moment, we often do not even see other racial or cultural groups as part of the same circle which we ourselves inhabit. We see differences with the eyes of superiority and inferiority.

We have made diversity unequal, and we seem to feel instinctively that equality should be uniformity.

Yet in many ways we are seduced by all the diversity in this world. It tempts us with what seems to be a wide array of personal choices. Especially in the West, our material world abounds with choice and diversity. Just surf the Internet or the hundreds of cable television channels, and you will see that the world appears to be our oyster, where we feel that we can taste and experience the diversity. And we can to some extent; yet for most people this opportunity to experience diversity often turns out to be very limited, in the actual experiences unfolding in life. Because of our patterns and limitation, much of the potential joy to be found in diversity escapes us. People desire many things but are seldom able to manifest even a fraction of their desires, despite their best efforts. And if they can manifest them, often the result is not fulfilling. Why is this?

It takes great effort for most individuals just to keep their lives together, never manifesting most personal dreams—to say nothing of ideals such as peace between nations, food and education for everyone, or ecological stability. No matter how hard we desire these things, both the personal and impersonal, we do not seem capable of creating them for ourselves. Why is this so? Why can we not even solve our most critical problems, the ones that seem to threaten the survival of our own species—to say nothing of other species?

We are stuck in patterned thinking, because we do not understand how to dissolve the patterns of behavior in which we live or how to move beyond judgment. We recognize that change is needed, but we do not understand how to bring it about. We see the need to eliminate the problems, but the ego is limited and resourceless at finding solutions from the same level where the problems were created. Often we end up, instead, eliminating the other species, even the *other people*, who *seem* to be creating the problems.

> *We are not able to, and will never, find win-win solutions with a win-lose mind.*

Actually all problems originate in consciousness rather than in the physical world, although we see them mirrored there. The sources of the problems are the knots held in our patterning. They create the obstacles we see manifesting in our outer life. The reality we are given as children does not teach us this.

By facing our patterns, we begin to see where we hold judgments, erroneous beliefs, tangled principles and unfulfilled needs. These sorts of patterns are knots in consciousness generally held in places where we have made choices to withhold our energy from life. They are withholdings lodged in our mental-emotional awareness, usually out of fear and pain imprinted from old, traumatic experiences. By unraveling and clearing the patterns, we become clearer and more able to manifest fuller expression in our lives.

Often our powerlessness to create needed change is due to our inability to see where the source of the problem lies. We are looking in the wrong place. The source of the problem is inside us, not outside in the world around us. Problem solving must begin with us—with processing of our own knotted issues. Instead what usually happens is an attempt to change the outside as a way of changing the inside—often with fruitless and heartbreaking results. The outside will change naturally and easily if we look into the inner cause of the obstacle and shift that.

One common way of solving problems is to try reshuffling the deck and changing the outer circumstances of our life, in the hopes that we will get a better combination. In our desperation for a solution we may change jobs, or partners in business or marriage. We may even emigrate to another country in the hopes that this will make us happier. This approach tends to be a rather hit-or-miss solution. When the real issue, which is in our patterning, has not shifted, we will most likely re-create the same situation again in the new circumstances. Ostensibly there is nothing wrong with changing the physical circumstances of one's life, but sometimes it is easier and less heartbreaking to all involved if we try to change the pattern that is causing the unhappiness first. Perhaps by processing the issues and clearing the problems at a deeper level, we will make decisions that are more life-supporting to everyone involved. And then the physical moves we make will be real steps forward in our growth.

For example, in every nation there is a leadership change from time to time. Each time a democratic nation chooses to hold a political election there is a re-arranging of the players in a wild game of musical chairs. The people are trying to find better leaders to solve their problems. We see this boldly exposed on the small screen, where our leaders grapple with their own limitations and our problems. In sitting by and watching passively, we have given up our personal power to those who try to lead, and what's more, we blame them when they fail on our behalf. We expect our politicians to solve our problems for us—yet they are no more resourceful than we are. We cannot solve problems by putting them outside ourselves onto others or blaming outer circumstances. At the root of every problem we experience is a knotted pattern in us.

Imagine what the world would be like if everyone willingly examined their issues, took responsibility for them and cleared them for themselves. It would be a very different place—politicians would be there to administer a nation's logistics, rather than trying, usually fruitlessly, to solve our problems.

Here we are, in a catch-22. In order to solve the problems of the world, we need to change our limited behavior patterns and to move beyond our inferior-superior judging. But like the fish that does not know it is even in the water, how do we transcend the inherent nature of the separate system in which we live when we are oblivious to it? How do we move beyond seeing things as separate and outside and beyond judging them when that is the very nature of the separate system? As each of us does the inner work of transformation and Self-discovery and reconnects to our own inner divinity, we will move beyond judgment. With enough individuals living from that place, we can create a new reality for this world.

As you process and create shifts, those with whom you interact act differently. Just because *you* process and clear something, they change. How is this possible? Because of the underlying interconnectedness of all things. Ultimately for everyone, there is always an amazed recognition of this hidden reality as they see the interconnectedness of their behaviors and the behaviors of those around them. The changes to the outer world are only possible if there is an energy connection between you and the world around you. It is necessary to be aligned in unity to see this principle.

Begin noticing, as you develop your processing practice, how others' attitudes and behaviors toward you change. Writing about it helps you to ground the experience and deepen the understanding of it.

RECLAIMING OUR UNCONSCIOUS SIDE

In reality unity and oneness is all there is, but in our limited state, we have a very partial view of the whole. The unconscious contains all the rest of the vibratory frequencies of existence that make up the whole. If we want to reclaim them and our wholeness, we must look around at everything that *appears* to be outside us as though it were inside us. This means we must allow in the notion that:

> *We are not just the body but are much more.*
> *We are also that which is outside the body.*

In our unbounded state of consciousness, theoretically we can be anywhere and every-where. Our consciousness is not bound by our bodies.

Examples of consciousness being more than the body are prevalent in all of the popular life-after-death-experience books. Many people have experienced their conscious awareness traveling far beyond the confines of the physical body and then returning to the body to tell about it. Also, many children experience the phenomenon of consciousness being more than the body. I recall experiencing this when my mother used to brush my hair. I had fine baby hair which became knotted during the night, and I hated having it brushed because it was painful. I remember as a six-year old watching the whole procedure from the other side of the room. Often if something is painful, the conscious awareness will leave the body. This is especially true for little children who have not yet become fully attached to their bodies. The doors of perception are still quite open for them.

Seeing the outside as not separate from you is very difficult at first. It actually takes quite a long time before you really do perceive it as being part of you. Only when you have reached states of unity can you actually experience the physical world that is outside and separate from your body as connected to you.

This is an experiential thing. As the ego clears, you are actually able to feel whatever people are thinking and feeling even if they are standing on the other side of the room. And, it is not as though you go out of your body and enter them to feel this. You actually feel it inside yourself because the inside of you is the cosmos.

We all contain everything, and we are much more than the body. As Ajit Mookerjee describes it in his book *Kundalini—The Arousal of the Inner Energy*: "...the microcosm parallels everything in the macrocosm. The complete drama of the universe is repeated here, in this very body. The whole body with its biological and psychological processes becomes an instrument through which the cosmic power reveals itself. According to Tantric principles, all that exists in the universe must also exist in the individual body." We are so identified in this world as being the body, that all we can see is the logic of, "This is my body, that is your body, and there is nothing but space between the two of us." On other levels there is a tremendous energy flow between two people. Once you begin opening up the unconscious, you become aware of that. We discuss the ability to be aware of and see these energy exchanges in more detail in Chapter Seven—Seeing the Light.

OUR UNSEEN PROJECTIONS

With our desires we create an energy field which pulls things from the outside toward us, and with repulsion or fear we push things away. These are actual energy flows, also known as projections. And, so, when you look at your friends or your parents or your siblings, you will see them clouded by your own projections. What you see in that person is what you are projecting on to them.

Have you ever noticed how you may see a certain individual a certain kind of way, but if you ask someone else how they see that individual, they see that person in a completely different way than you do? There may be some characteristics which you both see. There always are because we are very similar, and the things we project are often very similar, too. But you will see what you want to see in that person, and the other person will see what they want to. These are the subtle and subjective projections.

You may say, "Well, do those people we are projecting on have an objective life of their own?" Yes, of course they do. But you may never really see the truth of who they are. All you can see are your own projections. When you have recognized and brought in the projections, made them conscious and integrated them inside yourself, then you might see those people for the very first time. You might see who they are.

All of us have the choice to believe that the outside has nothing to do with us, is not connected. "Seeing is believing, and I do not see that my body is connected to the outside.

That is how I want it to be because I want to have a relationship with the outside world. I do not want the outside to be me. If it is me, there is nothing to relate to." So, that is our choice. We are choosing to live in the separate system. That is perfect for most of the people on this planet. That is the choice the majority of us are making. But if we want to wake up, we have to make another choice and be willing to own that we are much more than the body. We have to be willing to explore that vast and expanded unconscious and to open to the experience of feeling the vast unconscious inside of us. With the onset of enlightenment, we realize and experience that all of the cosmos is inside of us.

PROJECTIONS AND MIRRORS

Our thoughts, beliefs, judgments and knotted internal issues color our world. This we know to be true. The unseen dynamic is how the opposite side of our conscious awareness, which has been stuffed in the unconscious, affects the world around us. It is, in fact, the hidden side, the unconscious side, that truly holds the key to locking our outer reality in place and that leads to our liberation from the system of separation and limitation.

When we stuff something into the unconscious, we push it away from us, and we hold onto the conscious side. In fact, we push the unconscious so far away that it manifests outside of us and becomes part of our outer reality. The principle is this:

Everything outside the body and in the world around you
is a mirror of your own unconscious self.

Normally you are blind to your projecting the hidden side onto the outside world, onto people and things seemingly outside of you. It takes time to actually realize that the world around you is a projection of your own unconscious. This is truth in a more integrated paradigm, not the truth of this current world.

To illustrate the point, let's look at a very simplistic, but clear, example. Most people are given a value judgment about good and bad as soon as they are born. Most people love goodness and abhor badness. We try to hold onto goodness as much as possible and to make it our conscious reality. This means we try to be good by behaving in certain ways—by obeying the laws of the land and by keeping the company of law-abiding people. We identify ourselves as being good. We have pushed the opposite side, being bad, into the unconscious. At this point we have projected bad people outside and into the unconscious. As long as our inner consciousness is split into good and bad value judgments, our outer reality will reflect that. When we identify as good, badness is in the unconscious and therefore it will surface in the outside world. When we identify as being bad, then goodness is in the unconscious and is outside of us. Generally, we act out one side of the polarity, and the other side, the unconscious side is acted out by the outside world. When we reconcile and unify both sides of the polarity, we create balance and wholeness within us and in the world around us, too.

The polarity processing methods in Section Two help in very specific and grounded ways to awaken this awareness of our outer reality as our own unconscious, and this begins to create a more integrated and balanced life. If this metaphysical principle seems too esoteric to grasp right now, you will get some practical, hands-on experience with it as you work through Section Two.

ACT AS THOUGH THE OUTSIDE IS YOU

Being able to accept yourself as pure consciousness in a sense requires that you first enter into something of a contract with your higher self—albeit, accepting the terms of the contract intellectually at first. The contract says that in terms of your processing work:

> *You will own that everything you see outside of you*
> *is really a hidden part of you.*
> *If initially you have difficulty seeing this,*
> *you can act as though it is true.*

By acting as though the outside is you, even if you are not feeling it yet, you begin to allow the principle to register in the conscious mind. With agreeing to see life in this new way, you begin to recognize and reclaim the split off parts of your being from your unconscious, which are being reflected back to you from the outside world. As you recognize this and reclaim it, you begin to reassemble awareness back into wholeness with your processing work. Initially this agreement to alter your perception will not seem very real because you have been taught, as part of your separate state, that the outside is not connected to you. However, if you are willing to act *as though it is*, you become capable of seeing your world and yourself in startling new ways. This leads eventually to an experience of unity. For example if you tend to identify with being good, you might try to act as though the people outside of you that you judge as bad are actually part of you. Perhaps next time you watch the news and see a report about some criminal, make a mental affirmation or prayer that you wish to own the criminal as a part of your own unconscious. Or try it with someone you know whom you judge as bad. Besides using mental affirmations, you can also simply imagine what it might be like to be that person. Write in your journal about any shifts in awareness that come as a result. By doing this, your perception of life will become more integrated, whole and as a result, much more fulfilling and stimulating.

This contract of owning the outside as you is not so unusual. In fact in the Christian Bible, Jesus tells a parable which has a different slant to it, but which in effect contains the same principle. It is Matthew 25:34-40: "Then the King will say to those on His right hand, 'Come, you blessed of My Father, inherit the kingdom prepared for you from the foundation of the world: for I was hungry and you gave Me food; I was thirsty and you gave Me drink; I was a stranger and you took Me in; I was naked and you clothed Me; I was sick and you visited Me; I was in prison and you came to Me.' Then the righteous will answer Him, saying, 'Lord, when did we see You hungry and feed You, or thirsty and give You drink? When did we see You a stranger and take You in, or naked and clothe You? Or when did we see You sick, or in prison, and come to You?' And the King will answer and say to them, 'Assuredly, I say to you, inasmuch as you did it to one of the least of these My brethren, you did it to Me'." In the beginning as you do the processing work, the agreement to own the outside as you can be as simple as the religious teachings of seeing the face of Christ or the Buddha in everyone.

If you are able to remember the contract much of the time, the integration will be much fuller, more complete and more all-encompassing.

If you are to know yourself as one with everything,
which is the enlightened state,
then you must begin to own everything as you.

Initially you can make a commitment to seeing this way in prayers or affirmations, or by reminding yourself about your commitment simply as often as you feel necessary. Depending on how serious you are about transformation and waking up, you may find yourself wanting to commit very deeply to this contract. Whatever your level of commitment, you will find that it actually goes against the grain of all you have been taught, which is to see the outside world as separate from you. This old, conditioned, illusory way of viewing life continues in you—for quite awhile. So, you have to act as though there is no separation—for quite a while. Yet it is possible to gain so much ground in your integrative work if you can make the leap and go with this. Over years of working with people, I have seen that they really move quickly when they take on this commitment.

As you come to accept that your mode of perception is heavily bound up in projection onto the outside, you begin to understand yourself more. If you look at the world around you with this in mind, you are able to see the hidden parts of yourself, and you develop enormous compassion. As you let go of the projections more and more, you eventually begin to see the world as it is. You start becoming a seer of truth.

This will undoubtedly seem magical, yet it happens because it is higher truth that the inner and the outer are one. When one shifts, the other does too. In this seemingly miraculous way it is possible in time to change the entire dynamic which holds your world in place—and thereby change your world. You often can change the world around you in a much needed way, without doing the usual problem-solving things. For example, if you have had an argument with a friend which ended in an angry exchange, your first instinct may be to try to bury the resentful feelings and to try to patch things up as quickly as possible. Unless you get clear inside first and come into balance, equanimity and true forgiveness within yourself by doing the necessary processing of your own issues, picking up the phone to call the friend may result only in a tenuous and superficial mending of the friendship. Or you may even make the problem worse by saying the wrong things.

This does not mean that you may not in some instances try to talk things through with the other person. But experienced processors usually will try to do all the processing needed to clear the issue before they pick up the phone. They shift the consciousness beforehand in order to ensure that the call goes well. This is not manipulation or any sort of hocus-pocus. It is a natural consequence of your own inner-outer resolution.

> *By changing the organization of your own consciousness,*
> *it is possible to open a pathway*
> *and manifest the outer change you seek.*

The blocks and obstructions which we find in our outer lives are often the result of strange convolutions which exist inside our own minds and in our projections onto others. The convolutions are based on conditioned concepts, beliefs, and ideas of ourselves. The techniques in Section Two are about clearing and balancing the convolutions, and as a result the outer world reflects this clear, balanced place.

AN EXAMPLE OF ACTING AS THOUGH THE OUTSIDE IS YOU

I was processing with a man who felt as though his life was a mess, mainly financially and with his work, which was as a self-employed maker of fine furniture. He had been on a spiritual path for quite some time, had a fair amount of spiritual development, and had had experiences of seeing that the outside world is a mirror of his inner reality. But he complained that he felt especially stuck in the areas of work and money, that somehow his life just was not working in those arenas.

He said that people with whom he subcontracted for his business would often flake out and not deliver materials on time or just not show up. He also said that often the sub-contractors and clients were terrible petty tyrants, making unreasonable and harsh demands of him, getting angry at him, manipulating or dominating to get their way. He explained that people were very tight with their money toward him. He often had trouble getting people to pay on time, and he experienced that most people were always trying to cut corners by penny-pinching with him to get the price reduced.

He had become so frustrated over the years at having to deal constantly with this kind of behavior from the outside world that he had tried several times to quit and sell the business. He told me he was totally confused and bewildered by the whole situation because he thought that he was a very honest, hard-working, reliable craftsman and businessman. He felt that he treated all of his subcontractors and clients fairly and that they were treating him unfairly. He could not see and was not willing to own that this outside world was a part of him, that it was a mirror of his own unconscious. In desperation, he wanted to process to try to change things.

I asked him to pretend that the outside world—his subcontractors and clients—was actually him. I said, "If that were true, what would you do? How would you feel?" He said that he would feel terrible if he treated people that way and that he would want to change. So, the first step he took was to do the polarity processing technique (presented in Chapter Nine), which included writing a list of all of the bothersome behaviors and character traits of the subcontractors and clients. He used words like: flaky, not on time, not show up, tyrant, unreasonable, harsh, angry, manipulative, dominating, get their way, tight with money, late payments, cut corners, penny-pinching, prices reduced. When he had finished his list, he looked at me and said incredulously, "That list is me?!" It was a bitter pill to swallow, and he just could not own it as part of him. I assured him that it was all just ego anyway, that it was only half the picture, and that really none of it was who he really is.

The next step was that he made a prayer. He asked that he please be shown how the list of words was actually his own unconscious mirror, and he asked for help with acting as though the outside were part of him. Then he finished the next two simple steps in the technique, and we waited for the shifting to happen.

The insights that came to him in the next hour were amazing and life-changing. In re-examining his list, he started seeing aspects of his own life in which he behaved just like his subcontractors and clients, but it had never really occurred to him that there was a parallel situation happening between his inner and outer realities. He had never seen the mirror effect because it was all unconscious—until he had made the list and made it conscious. He told me that actually many of his girl friends had complained to him that they thought he was very flaky, non-committal and irresponsible, which are exactly the behaviors he complained about in his business relationships.

He saw areas of his life in which he was an enormous tyrant, too. Especially with his girl friends, he said he could be quite unreasonable, harsh and angry toward them. He also saw how he was just as angry and enraged with many of his business relationships as they were with him—except that he never expressed it because he was too afraid. Instead he preferred to suppress his anger and let it remain in the unconscious, which meant that he got angry subcontractors. They were acting out his unconscious anger for him.

As for the financial aspect, he saw a dynamic he played out with his clients in which he would manipulate the price quotes, raising the prices in a deceitful way with false information, because he was afraid they would somehow begrudge him his profit with manipulative negotiations. So, his behavior was actually just as manipulative as theirs, but in his mind he had somehow justified it and had not even realized he was doing it! He was deceitfully raising the prices of his products, just as he knew his subcontractors were doing to him. He also acknowledged his own penny-pinching nature came out in this way—and especially with the IRS. He confessed that his creative bookkeeping with his tax reports to the IRS was so extensive, contrived and devious that he did not even want to begin to explain it to me. He had never correlated his behavior with the IRS to his behavior with his business relationships. Somehow in his mind he had justified his behavior with the IRS by telling himself that the IRS did not count. Of course his own lack of generosity with the IRS and with his business dealings was the exact kind of stingy, miserly behavior that he was complaining about in other people.

He started to see how these parallel experiences between his own behavior and the outside world's behaviors toward him were somehow related. He was willing to concede that perhaps the outside actually was a mirror of some part of him and that his own behavior did feel somehow locked in a dynamic with the outside. It was in acting as though the outside was his own unconscious mirror and in praying for help to see it that he gained some profound insights into the truth of the situation.

For now, until you have had a chance to learn the methods presented in Section Two, here are some reminders of simple ways that you can begin to act as though the outside is you:

- Put yourself in the shoes of the person on the outside and write about what you observe and how it feels.
- Make a list of adjectives and other descriptive words from these observations and try to see aspects of yourself in the list.
- Pray for help acting like the outside is you and seeing how the outside is you.
- Put sticky notes in creative places around your house that say things like, "The outside is me."

CHAPTER SUMMARY

Here are some of the main points we have introduced so far:

- In the separate system we perceive from the either-or mind.
- An *individual* is consciousness divided in duality.
- The separate system is a system of negative and positive judgment.
- *Ignorance* is the practice of ignoring.
- Judging and blaming the outside comes very naturally to us.

- We can't find win-win solutions with a win-lose mind.
- We are not just the body but are much more. We are also that which is outside the body.
- Since everything is interconnected, when we shift our inner reality, the outer shifts, too.
- Being able to accept ourselves as pure consciousness requires that we enter into a contract with the higher self. We agree to own that everything we see outside of us is really a hidden part of us. If this is difficult at first, we can act as though it is true.
- If we are to know ourselves as one with everything, which is the enlightened state, then we must begin to own everything as us.
- By changing the organization of our own consciousness, it is possible to open a pathway and manifest the outer change we seek.

SUGGESTIONS FOR PUTTING THEORY INTO PRACTICE

1. Begin to look at how you judge the things of the world and see them as separate from you and as random occurrences. Can you discern some of your patterns and knots in consciousness where you withhold your energy from life? Write in your journal about what you see.
2. As you learn to process, notice how others' attitudes and behaviors toward you change. Write in your journal about what you see.
3. For one week, write a daily affirmation in your journal or make a daily prayer that you wish to act as though the outside is you. Write about the changes you notice.
4. Try the four simple suggestions of ways of acting as though the outside is you, on page 78.

Yoga is the restricting of the fluctuation of mind stuff....
Then the seer [that is, the Self] abideth in himself.

—Patanjali

SIX

THE
WITNESS

We have seen that the architecture and engineering of the separate system includes perceiving with an either-or mind and judging things outside of us as negative or positive. Although judging and blaming the outside comes very naturally to us, we can come more into equanimity with life when we learn to perceive ourselves as one with our outer reality. This new way of perceiving leads to balance and harmony and is what we call the witness. Developing the witness is an essential aspect of the path of Self-discovery.

Here we talk about: what the witness is; how and why it works; the importance of the witness; what the benefits of having a witness are; and what some of the obstacles to witnessing are, such as fear, doubt and blame. We introduce the Eastern concept of *samadhi*, an advanced stage of witnessing, which in the Christian religion would equate to *the peace which passeth all understanding*. We also introduce some basic, simple steps about how to develop a witness. (In Section Two, Chapter Fourteen—Developing the Witness, we will take a look at advanced stages of witnessing. If you feel you need some grounding with the concepts presented in this chapter, it may be helpful to go to Chapter Fourteen immediately after you have read this chapter and to try some of the suggestions and exercises.)

WITNESSING THE PERSONALITY

On the way toward awakening, we have to find creative and ingenious ways of seeing ourselves *doing* the roles of the personality. This detached seeing is the only way that we get to know the ins and outs of the personality. We have to become capable of seeing it act from its patterned conditioning in order to transcend it. Since we are taught to perceive that we *are* the limited personality, one would suppose that this would be pretty impossible. The difficulty is in the seeing. When we are identified with the personality, meaning, "I think I am the personality," it is very difficult to see the limited self clearly. Who is it then that would be doing the seeing, if we think we are the personality? It would be rather like an eye trying to see itself, as Alan Watts so succinctly said, somewhere back in the sixties. To wake up, we have to choose to take the position of the witness and observe from outside the personality.

At first it does take a bit of reorientation to be able to see ourselves *being* the limited personality. But the fact is that we can actually witness the personality from a viewpoint *outside* the personality structure itself. This does, in itself, prove that we are not exclusively locked into the personality. Nor are we the personality. Our true nature is as limitless consciousness. As we see and understand the limiting patterns in the personality, so are we liberated from them and able to know ourselves as eternal, loving presence.

So, shifting our perception to witness the personality
is immediately possible and extraordinarily beneficial.

A witness is already present to some extent for everyone. We have a part of ourselves that watches the personality *doing* life all the time. We have all seen ourselves at one time or another doing things like: overreacting, being irrational, oozing with charm to try to get our way, fibbing, co-dependently enabling a friend, and so forth. We have all watched ourselves indulging in gross behavior patterns like these that are self-destructive and manipulative or even sometimes in subtler patterns that are limiting in some way. When there is recognition of this fact, it is possible to develop and strengthen that witnessing aspect of ourselves. Strengthening the witness is important so that it can help in uncovering the limitations and unconscious aspects of the personality.

To begin developing and strengthening the witness, it is enough simply to ask inwardly for this to happen. In a prayer or affirmation in your journal, ask that your witness officially be instituted. This begins the process. You can repeat the prayer or affirmation as often as you like—weekly, daily or many times a day—which will help to strengthen the witness. The more frequently, the better. This not only consciously reminds you that you are not the personality, but you also invite the magic of grace to assist you in remembering. Over time, as a natural by-product of practicing the processing techniques outlined in Section Two, your witness will develop and grow. For now it is enough to begin with this simple suggestion as we explore more about what the witness is, how it works and what it does for us.

THE WAY OF NEUTRALITY

There is a way through the labyrinth of life, which is all bound up by the law of opposites. Sometimes called the middle way, or the third way or the razor's edge, it is the way of neutrality, where we surrender the idea that we should be attracted to or repulsed by anything, whether to the negative or positive side of any polarity. We choose instead to identify with the neutral place, the center point between the two sides. Here the witness has the power of observation without the reactivity of judgment. Developing the ability to view life from the neutral position assists enormously in extricating us from the turning cycles of the wheel of karma. The center is the eye of the storm, the still-point, the hub of the wheel.

The rule of thumb for the yogi is to be neither attracted nor repulsed.

This does not mean that we will never again experience pain and pleasure or any other states of mind and feeling. These pairs of opposites are the juicy experiences of life itself. Rather, something else happens. An aspect of us, the witness, detaches from the extremes, from the swings between the negative and positive polarities and from that neutral place, just observes. This does not mean that the experience of flop-flopping from one side to the other won't happen. It will, but now we will also have a witness observing this flip-flopping. And that makes all the difference. It means that part of us, the witness, is not flip-flopping. It is just observing the action.

With the witness focused on the neutral place at the center point between negative and positive poles, the dynamic of all polarities changes. Awareness placed at the neutral place between the positive and negative poles has the immediate effect of stabilizing the whole situation. We are the witness, holding the central position between the extremes. Balance happens because we are no longer identifying with the two extreme poles. It becomes a new grounding point from which to view the changeable reality of polarized extremes. Normally we ground on one side of the polarized state and are forced to view life from that one-sided place. If instead we are grounded on the stable point in the center between the two extremes and witness them, we can choose to let them pass right through the awareness field, leaving us more stable, calm, and centered. Life still happens, but the witness has a view from the center which is much more all encompassing. It allows us to be more dispassionate about the turbulent ocean of dramas, called *life*. It facilitates ascension to a higher vibratory state—beyond identification with polarized positions.

THE FULCRUM

Letting go of identification with the personality is really difficult unless there is something else with which to identify. The witness serves a purpose here. Gaining a neutral witness is

Fig. 6-1. *The neutral witness adopts the position of balance between the two sides of a polarity. It becomes the fulcrum of our awareness field. It is outside the turbulence, turmoil, and subjectivity of life.*

something that can be likened to opening another channel in the awareness field. We already have the two channels that go with being human—the negative and the positive. And we add an extra channel. For example, it is as though you are purchasing a new cable channel for your television. Previously you had only two on your television, the negative one and the positive one. You are adding a third, a neutral channel, which is the neutral witness. You don't give up the experience of the other two; you add a third (Fig. 6–1).

The neutral witness is a very important component in transformation and ascension. That neutral position is really what is also known as being centered. The neutral witness is awareness being awake at the center. It is the core. It keeps us stable, balanced and grounded. The blessing it brings is that it allows us to see the big picture on the subject of our issues.

> *The neutral witness is actually*
> *your connection to your higher self*
> *and to the absolute Self.*

When you have lived with your witness for a while, you realize that it is a way to access your higher self. As the witness gets stronger, you see that it is higher consciousness, the superconscious awareness, where pure intelligence, pure being, all knowledge, can be accessed. When the neutrality of the witness has been well developed, it functions as the *inner teacher* simply by being the state of unity consciousness, the source from which all intelligence and inspiration issues.

As the witness merges into everyday awareness, it helps to clear the mental and emotional bodies and awaken them. Having a witness wakes us up! We are actually awake when we are in it. With negative and positive positions we are immersed in the content of life's drama.

One of the initial stages of the clearing work is living more from the heart and from the soul, a much deeper level than the personality. The witness takes us there by allowing awareness to ascend out of the old reality. The witness is integral to the process of ascension. It helps awareness to leave one level and to move to another. It is no small feat to move consciousness to another paradigm. To do it, everything must be done just right. With the witness anchoring the awareness in timeless eternality, it is possible to let go of the old way of being.

Eventually we come to see that the witness
is an opening from the limited personal mind
into the universal mind.

THE BIASED WITNESS

Many people say that in the beginning their witness seems more like a judge than a witness. Ideally the witness maintains a neutral position in the overall panorama of perception, meaning that it is without any negative or positive bias. Most people's ordinary, everyday awareness is most definitely polarized and laden with bias.

This biased witness is often an internalized parent. The nature of the ego is to imbibe the parental conditioning we get in childhood so completely that eventually we do not need parents on the outside to condition us anymore. In other words, our parents and those who conditioned us are now inside of us. They are now internalized programs that run on automatic, influencing our projections and reminding us of our judgments, even though they may not physically be present in our lives. Even if we consciously try not to be like our parents, unless we have done some inner clearing work, we are still generally living *in reaction* to them and to the way they conditioned us. Our projections and judgments then would still be influenced by our parents, whether we think we are like them or not.

Transforming the judge witness, or the internalized parent, into a neutral witness takes place as we develop an ability to find the neutral position between the negative and positive extremes. The processing methods presented in Section Two are specifically designed to bring awareness to the middle way, the place of neutrality or balance between the extremes.

By observing bit by bit that we are not the traits of the personality and by deepening our ability to witness, so do we awaken. In our letting go of identification with those traits, they gradually drop away, and the personality becomes clearer. As the personality clears, outer life becomes easier, more abundant, more easeful and fulfilling, and inner life is held in truth.

DETACHMENT INCREASES YOUR CAPACITY TO LOVE

The word *neutrality* is a synonym for detachment. Neutrality sounds bland and boring to some. I use it because it indicates the spot between negative and positive when talking about magnetism. When used in a spiritual context, there is a hidden component which the word *neutrality* implies, and that is the light of the superconscious awareness that comes in when neutrality is present. Something magical happens when we engage neutrality. In that moment, our human, polarized world comes into balance, and eternity enters our lives. That brings great beauty, light and presence. A space has been created for the superconscious to enter. As long as we are grabbing onto one side of a polarity, we are keeping the superconscious out. *Detachment* also sounds bland and boring but is desirable because it supercharges our experience of life with the presence of the superconscious.

Detachment is not to be confused with suppression or denial or avoidance. Indulging in these kinds of unbalanced behaviors is not what we are talking about here. This would keep us firmly rooted in the separate system by sweeping things under the carpet and shoving them into the unconscious. This does not work and is not what detachment is about. Detachment is not about pretending that we are not experiencing thoughts and emotions passing through us. Rather it is the ability to experience these things, both positive and negative, fully, consciously, and simultaneously know that we are the Self. This ability comes as a result of the clearing work.

Likewise, sometimes people ask if detachment means they cannot experience love for something. Quite the contrary is true. The more detached we become, the more our capacity to love intensifies and the more it becomes purified and clear, as paradoxical as that may seem. In practicing detachment we learn how to love in a universal way. When we are polarized, there is prejudice in our love; it is biased. We experience love or not-love, and even hate. There is a split in our universe, and we are subject to attraction and repulsion. We can never be whole-hearted about anything because half of us is attracted, and the other half is repulsed. Not to be whole-hearted is not to know about love. We have to be whole-hearted to experience love—love in the true sense of the word.

It is a common and very obvious error of perception to think that
favoring the polarized system at the expense of the superconscious
will enrich our experience.

OUR FEAR OF DETACHMENT

Some individuals fear that by practicing detachment they will lose everything. That is a very normal notion. It is what the ego thinks will happen. Humans fear loss above all else. In truth there is no such thing as loss, not in any absolute sense. So, when we exit the system of judgment and separation, there is no experience of loss. There is only the ecstatic light of eternal, timeless presence on the other side of the little egoic membrane that we are all locked into. But we are terrified that it means endless loss to break the walls. That is the message the ego sends into the awareness when we try to break out. This is why hardly anyone tries to escape the egoic cage.

In fact, what we are remembering as we face the exit door is the primal loss that we took when we fell out of the whole—the *all that is*. Once upon a time, we were one with everything, had infinite power and love, and then something happened. The psyche is not quite sure what, but it seemingly lost it all in a split second when it incarnated into a body and became imprinted with humanness.

The negative side of the human imprint is an imprinting with loss and guilt because we interpreted what happened to us as a mistake on our part—we fell from grace and became wrongdoers, sinners. We fear taking another big loss like the original one. We fear losing the little we have left. And we run these fears mostly unconsciously. It makes us paranoid about our choices, puts a damper on risk-taking and keeps us feeling very attached to material things and to the status quo of the limited personality. Eventually, as we process, we come to realize that we are being governed by an illusory imprint, giving us false information, and we can more easily let it go. We are then able to use different motivations for our choices, and we break free.

Eden is on the other side of the egoic veil of fear. Unfortunately most people do not even know consciously that they have come to the doorway out of the separate system and have turned around and walked away from it. They reached the doorway without even realizing that they were right in front of it. Until we have a strong neutral witness, the door cannot even be seen; the whole process of running away is unconscious. This is how the world stays in place, with people avoiding major changes at all costs. Detachment is one of the keys to the doorway.

Another Way, an Uncommon Way

Very often, a seeker will wake up to the feeling that there has to be another way. This is usually accompanied by an intense desire for change. When the passion for changing our circumstances is in place and when there is an unshakable determination that this will happen, the shifts take place easily. This is the birth of the state of detachment. It is the first inkling that there is more to life than what is right in front of us and that we do not have to settle for the same old routines. An awareness dawns that we are caught in routines that are just repeating themselves endlessly in this system of high and low, negative and positive. We see that no matter how much the scenery changes, we are replaying the same old routines. The witness is the one who is showing us this. Even if we do not know we are using the witness, it is the one getting us started on the path. It is the one who holds us and keeps us stable as we let go of the old, limiting egoic stuff and as we change and take risks, fueled by a determined commitment. Change is possible then because we are supported by the neutral witness, which is a constant, invariable state in our lives. In a world of variables, it is a changeless state.

Eventually you will give up identification with personality and choose to identify
with the witness. Then you will see for yourself that the witness is the Self.

WE ARE PURE AWARENESS

We begin to see that what we have identified as ourselves, the surface personality, is really just the veneer of the play of consciousness through beingness itself. In fact, the core of our being is the essence of all beingness. We, in essence, are nothing but pure awareness, the ground of being itself. This becomes clearer as we do the processing work.

Another powerful tool to help us realize this is meditation. Meditation, in conjunction with the processing, is invaluable in helping to develop the witness and to accelerate our awakening. Often we first notice in our meditations that the thoughts we would normally identify with sort of flit by. We are not inclined to grab onto them. Then we begin to see that we can do this while in action. What we have discovered is that it is possible to be quite detached from them. We can watch them; they come, and they go. We do not have to follow them, get involved in them, embroider them, or even track them. They simply seem to arise in our awareness field of their own accord. If we abstain from hooking into them, they just pass on and go away, leaving a space until the next one comes up. This is ideal. With the onset of enlightenment, eventually the distracting thoughts go away altogether.

If we are not the thoughts, then who are we? Who is watching the thoughts? Enter into the space between the thoughts, and let it permeate you. It is in this space between the thoughts and because of what you discover there that you will realize the benefit of the egoic processing work you have done.

It is in this space between the thoughts that
you first find yourself being pure awareness—just being.

There is a continuous stream of thoughts passing through your awareness field when you meditate. But somebody or something is aware of the stream of thoughts. Who is that? What or who is it that perceives the flow, the play of thoughts going by, yet seems to be unaffected by and unattached to the thoughts? As well, who is this witness who is able to see and know the personality? With this realization that *I am not my thoughts or my personality*, comes the question, "Then who am I, or what am I?" The truth is seeing that *I am essence through which the thoughts and states of personality pass.* This state is the witness, self-aware, observing, being awareness, being the Self. The witness is the ground of being. It is pure awareness, you as essence—a very perfect, pure, undivided, unadulterated you. It is you as the totality, you as unity, you beyond the flow of consciousness, beyond the turning of the wheel.

This simple penetration to essence is the reason I recommend practicing meditation as an important and vital part of Self-discovery. You have to become quiet enough at times to actually *see* this state, to realize that it is what you are and to realize, to make *real*, the understanding that you are not the thoughts or the personality. Once you have discovered your true identity is not the personality, it is very easy to begin applying this knowledge to your life.

WE ARE NOT OUR STATES OF MIND

People often interpret the cultivation of the neutral witness as the development of a flatness in their lives, making it really uninteresting. The presence of a neutral witness does *not* mean that we will become neutral, boring sticks-in-the-mud. The technique does not work that way. In fact we will be living life with a fullness that we may never have had before.

The experience of all of the states of mind that we associate with the personality and with our interaction with the world will continue to pass through us always. In fact we will live it *more intensely, feel more involved*, but in another way less affected or buffeted by it, more able to enjoy it for not taking it so seriously. The neutral witness always knows that the experiences life offers are simply one side of a pair of opposites. We can suffer losses such as break-ups of love relationships, financial problems and career set-backs, and we can thoroughly enjoy gains such as new-found romances, financial windfalls and worldly successes. Life, as change, comes and goes. We, as pure awareness, remain eternally.

As we discover this, we begin to experience real freedom, because we see that life is a shadow play, a hologram of light. We see that the flow of consciousness and all the countless states of mind that dance through our awareness are simply the play of existence unfolding before us. We begin to know our own immortal soul by not being so bound up in the drama of our lives. This is very liberating. It is the beginning of real freedom in our consciousness and is a great accelerating of our Self-discovery.

FEELING GROUNDED — FAITH

No one can be secure when they are grounded on material things. Attachment to houses, cars, clothes, money and other kinds possessions means that we believe it is these things that are our support in the world. It means we are not detached and therefore not able to be in the witness. Material things are transitory; they come and go. If we are grounded on the transitory, which everyone is to some degree, we will be devastated when these things are taken away. What we do not see is that they were never meant to last forever. They are the things of this dream world, and their appearance and disappearance must be accepted with equanimity. If we can see past the transitory and ground on the clear light of the Self, the superconscious, we will feel and be quite secure, no matter what is happening around us. When adversity strikes, we will have inner peace. That is freedom.

Faith is a state which is talked about a great deal, especially in the Christian religion. It is something which we seem either to have or not to have. In the harsh and cynical world, faith is something seldom seen. Sometimes it is even seen as a hindrance to getting ahead in the world because it is construed as a kind of naiveté, gullibility or flakiness, not pragmatic, logical or empirical, and not based on the rules of the so-called *real* world. That is not the kind of faith we are discussing here. That is a state polarized with cynicism and skepticism, and is not actually faith. Faith in the highest sense of the word means being grounded in ultimate reality and choosing to live by spiritual principles, secure in the knowledge of the support which the spiritual principles offer. It is a state grounded in the visceral acceptance of knowing we truly are not separate from the whole.

There is nothing wrong with having material things—or with the material world per se. They are just things. The hook here is if we become dependent on them for our spiritual well-being. If we expect that possession of things will lead to fulfillment, this is unfair to ourselves and to the material world. It is quite possible to live in balance with the material world if we live by the spiritual principles.

Faith means being able to completely know that living by spiritual principles will support our lives, even in the material world. Because we are deeply rooted in truth, grounded on our eternality, we don't have to worry about the material world; it will take care of itself.

> *Faith, in its most expanded aspect, is the*
> *full and openly acknowledged awareness*
> *that there is essentially no separation between*
> *us and the eternal Self.*

This last realization is the most powerful of all. From thinking that we are dependent on money or other material securities, we will find eventually that we are completely supported, even materially, by the Self. This realization is the beginning of total freedom because we have the power to stay poised and centered no matter what kind of adversity strikes. In that state we remember where we came from and who we are and are not disturbed by the turbulence. Like a cork bobbing on a stormy sea, we are unaffected by the waves—we are unsinkable.

Eventually we will also find ourselves wanting to let go of addictions and dependencies on substances, success, security, position and power. It does not mean that success, security, position and power won't come to us; they may. But we are not seeing them as our way of fulfillment, as a substitute for liberation or for knowing who we are. These things are wrapped up in erroneous images we have about ourselves.

All of this letting go can sound very frightening. For many people, their worst fear is that if they let go of their attachment to possessions, they will end up on the street as a bag-person, pushing a shopping cart, living in a cardboard box! If this is your worst fear, it is important to remember that you are letting go of the *attachment* to the possessions, not to the actual things themselves. If you are successful at witnessing the fear, knowing it is just the erroneous warning sign on the exit door of the ego, you will get quite a different result than that worst fear. Rather, when you are detached, you become open enough to be in a flow with life. The wonder of perpetual renewal in daily life, the vast simplicity of love and the wisdom of all the ages flow into your system as the power of the Divine within quickens. You become fully established in the witness. Paradoxically you never lose anything except your limitations, and life becomes abundant—very often materially. You become part of the amazing synchronicity of the cycles of nature, yet acutely and sweetly aware within yourself of the infinite variations that the play of existence offers. Life becomes poetry, and you, the artist.

The teaching is well-known in Christianity as Jesus' sermon in Matthew 6:19-34:

Do not lay up for yourselves treasures on earth, where moth and rust destroy and where thieves break in and steal; but lay up for yourselves treasures in heaven, where neither moth nor rust destroys and where thieves do not break in and steal. For where your treasure is, there your heart will be also....Do not worry about your life, what you will eat or what you will drink; nor about your body, what you will put on. Is not life more than food and the body more than clothing? Look at the birds of the air, for they neither sow nor reap nor gather into barns; yet your heavenly Father feeds them. Are you not of more value than they? Which of you by worrying can add one cubit to his stature? So why do you worry about clothing? Consider the lilies of the field, how they grow: they neither toil nor spin; and yet I say to you that even Solomon in all his glory was not arrayed like one of these. Now if God so clothes the grass of the field, which today is, and tomorrow is thrown into the oven, will He not much more clothe you, O you of little faith? Therefore do not worry, saying, "What shall we eat?" or "What shall we drink?" or "What shall we wear?"... For your heavenly Father knows that you need all these things. But seek first the kingdom of God and His righteousness, and all these things shall be added to you. Therefore do not worry about tomorrow, for tomorrow will worry about its own things. Sufficient for the day is its own trouble.

SEEING THAT FEAR IS A GUIDE

Fear is a guide because it shows us when we have fallen out of the witness into negative ego and when we are operating from separation. Everyone comes face-to-face with fear on a fairly constant basis—it is the antithesis of faith. Fear is a separator, and faith is a connector. To have faith is to see beyond fear and doubt. Faith is the fused state resulting from the unification of fear and its opposite, courage.

Egoically, fear begins to take hold of our awareness with a doubt. Something comes along and triggers doubt. Then if, instead of dismissing the doubt, we let it in and believe it, we will fall into fear. Doubt is an apparent crack in the fluid, unbroken nature of our existence and in the perfect continuity and synchronicity of our lives, in the moment that it arises.

The shadow of doubt opens the door to fear, which immediately comes up and says, "Something is wrong. Something is about to ruin my day." Doubt, which is *not knowing*, lets us fall into fear—fear of the unknown. There is always an element of the unknown when we are in fear. Even if we have a *could*, a *maybe*, or a *what if*, or endless possibilities as a focus for our fear, the fear is there because we don't know for sure what will happen next. We are ungrounded and free-floating in nothingness when we are in fear. Fear happens because we are susceptible to it, due to the imprinting with duality and the separate self.

Living in the separate self, we hold a belief that life contains random events beyond our control, outside of us and disconnected from us, which happen by chance and without any obvious meaning or purpose. We call these events *accidents*. Doubt allows this. This belief is part of the limitation of this system.

An accident shatters our composure and puts us into the unknown. We simply do not know in the moment what is going on. If the belief in randomness is true, then anything could happen at any time. This is completely unnerving. And it is certainly the way things look on the surface, with limited vision. The imagination can run riot when faced with an unknown. It has a way of filling in the blanks and then believing what it just imagined— generating more fear. People will make up stories to explain the unknown.

It is the belief in randomness beyond our control that seems to generate doubt, which leads to fear. There is no full understanding of cause and effect in most cultures, especially in the West. Limited seeing does not allow that the cause of some seemingly outside event can be inside us—in the patterning in the unconscious. It does not allow that at some level we have set up the circumstances to cause a dance of negative-positive attraction-repulsion. And the effect is seen in the outside world. We probably have no idea with our limited per- spective what it is in us that caused the situation.

When an event happens that touches our lives in some way, especially if it is a negative way, it is certainly helpful to ask inwardly what our part is in this event. It may be some- thing that if we process it would change our outer circumstances significantly.

In fact our fluid nature is already patterned to respond to duality. It does not just hap- pen in the moment of doubt. The schism is already present, held in the unconscious where we can't see it, in the human imprint, and this makes us susceptible to doubt and to the fear that follows. We will discuss the human imprint in great detail in Chapter Eight—The Human Imprint.

It would be true to say that everyone has periods of varying length when everything is fine, when we are in the witness, in our fluid nature and experiencing fullness. Then some- thing triggers us, and we fall into the separation of duality. When this happens, we lose much of our awareness because our vibration drops. When we get triggered and react, our resources for seeing and knowing truth are mostly gone. We are susceptible to patterned reactivity when we lose the witness.

In Chapter Eight—The Human Imprint, there is a road map that describes the states we fall into when buying into doubt, so that we can recognize them when it happens, know where we are and begin processing to clear ourselves.

NOT BLAMING THE OUTSIDE

In the separate system people often blame the outer circumstances for their states of mind, because the outside is the trigger for their reactivity. They believe that this absolves them from any involvement in the situation. But reactivity is the responsibility of the reactor. If we react to a trigger with blame or fear or anger, then our patterns are the culprit. They are generating the responses we are having.

For example, let's say a man has a tyrannical boss who triggers him with irrational and unfounded criticisms of his work. There are many different ways the man might handle the situation. He could get angry and blame the boss, as though the problem is outside of him. Or he could feel victimized and betrayed and blame life. But these are egoic reactions and are a sign that he has patterns that need to be dealt with. For example, the reactions could be coming from the inner wounded child who desperately needs approval from an authority figure in order to feel self-worth and who fears disapproval. It is best to uncover this kind of pattern, to take responsibility for circumstances and to clear the pattern. If he puts the blame outside of himself and if he does not deal with the reactions and the patterns underlying them, he will simply continue to re-create similar situations in the future.

If the man was working at developing his witness, he might ask, "Why did this happen? What are the patterns in me that are creating this reaction and ultimately manifesting this whole situation?" It would open the possibility of investigation and of processing. It is not circumstances but how we respond to them that is the issue. Always ask, "What am I to see about this for my own growth?" We cannot count on changing the way the world is, but we can change the way we handle the circumstances that come our way. If we accept the responsibility and process our reactions, we will eventually live in equanimity with everything.

It is important to realize that the patterned reactions originate in the egoic subconscious. The patterns are usually triggered by fear and create contraction. We reinforce the patterns with our feelings—feelings which seem real and are there because we bought into the patterns!

We were conditioned to give the feelings and patterns full reality, to make them master of our lives. We have been deceived and deluded by our conditioning, and everyone in this system has allowed it. However, since we have so successfully been involved in the deception, we can be just as successful at dissolving it. We must try to learn to face our conditioned reactions from an expanded place of truth and not let them stop us in our actions or in our gaining of understanding.

Life experience appears to support the idea of randomness. Yet life is not random. As we own the outside and look at how we are connected to it by polarity, we can come into a working arrangement with it, bringing more integration and balance. We can move beyond being the victim of random circumstances—for example, tyrannical bosses—by doing our processing work. With the development of the witness and an expanded, more universal heart, and with the strengthening of faith through processing and integrative work, we become so secure inside that fear is then seen with new eyes. Our perception has attuned to something else—a much deeper understanding of the way things are. Fear is seen as something no more real than anything else in the separate system.

Fear is just a frequency,
like everything else in this reality.

For most of us, fear feels very real. It seems to be an indicator that life is about to serve up a lemon. The problem is that if we believe in this level of reality, that could happen. When we live in the world of competition, danger, unknowns, variables and probabilities, we have to deal with fear. At root all fears are really a fear of loss. And this is based on the belief that there is such a thing as loss. Viewed esoterically, loss is a perception that we have taken on. In this world-view when change happens, we are inclined to interpret it as a loss if it appears to deprive us of something. This is an interpretation of circumstances of which we have only a partial view. If we could see the whole circle or cycle that is passing through us, we would realize that often change is simply moving us to something else. Often with enough time to see how we have come full circle, we realize that there was no actual loss—just change.

Life certainly appears to back up our beliefs of loss and limitation. But remember that the outside is a reflection of our own projections and that our projections are based on our imprinting. Loss is an imprinting. In this world the possibility of loss seems to dog our footsteps practically every minute of the day. Most people are terrified of losing something they value. It could be anything from a few dollars to a house, to a loved one—from the most trivial to the most significant.

It is because of the human imprinting of the separate system in which we live that we are programmed with the polarity of *loss* and *gain*. The imprinting says that deep down we all feel so inadequate in our limited state that we are constantly chasing possible gains. And by chasing one side of a polarity, we are constantly reminded that its opposite could be catching up with us. Chasing gain has become a habit; it makes us constantly opportunistic. We do it automatically and do not remember the origin of the behavior. We accept it completely in ourselves, since danger and loss appear real and since trying to beat the system is second nature.

One of the things that gives rise to fear is an acceptance of the idea that there is an unknown. An unknown could contain anything—danger, harm or even death. The sense of an unknown comes from the feeling of being locked into a body—alone, separate, limited and alienated from all that is outside us in this random world—a world that is unpredictable and basically beyond our control. It is based on the belief that we are helpless and victims of circumstances. The unknown is a perception from our separate state. If we could see, we would realize that the unknown just contains more of life and that the things we fear are really disowned parts of ourselves.

With a change in perception, it is possible for us to see a less limited viewpoint, in which we know ourselves as part of a greater whole, of an ultimately intelligent transformational cycle—our evolution. As the witness develops, we will see we are learning lessons that are necessary for the soul's eventual journey back into the full realization of our inner and outer God nature. And the changes that we must go through are part of the evolution of wisdom in the soul. They are not expressions of loss and gain. As the saying goes, "Everything that goes around comes around." In the end there is balance, completion and peace.

SAMADHI—A DIFFERENT PARADIGM

Samadhi is a Sanskrit word which describes a state of unity. It is the presence of the oneness, showing from behind the polarities, and is an advanced stage of witnessing. We use the Sanskrit because there is no equivalent English word. As we develop the witness and do the processing work with the ancient principle of the unification of opposites, freeing our energy and fine-tuning the mind, emotions and body, it is the appearance of samadhi which signals the beginning of our liberation from the limited personality. It describes a state of awareness and perception that is not ordinarily accessed by most people in the normal course of life. However, it is a state that theoretically everyone is capable of reaching at some point should they try. When samadhi begins and is noticeable to the conscious mind, it is a sign that balance and harmony are beginning to birth within us. The dawning of samadhi is the intuitive knowing of the truth of our origin in the unified field. Until then it is a veiled and latent part of the mind. Yet as we begin to experience it, our awareness penetrates to the source of all states, to the unity underlying all extremes of polarization.

Samadhi awakens in us when we are fairly clear
of the limiting beliefs associated with the personality programming
and when we are able to witness most aspects of ego.

We experience samadhi as the consequence of a quiet mind and of profound states of inner and outer balance and centeredness in our energy. The centeredness experienced in the state of samadhi means having a field of awareness large enough to encompass both sides of all polarities. We are not stuck on one side of a polarity, but are neutral and in the center of them all. Samadhi is a particular kind of balance and alignment of the attention field which allows knowing higher truth from our own luminous core, the Divine within.

The experience of samadhi will come intermittently at first. It is felt as a vast stillness or expansion into an indescribable internal silence—the end of the spin. It is what the Christian church calls *the peace which passeth all understanding*. Don Juan, the Toltec sorcerer in the books by Carlos Castaneda, calls it *stopping the world*. Eventually it brings us a direct perceptual experience of the pure undifferentiated state of unity. As we gain it more frequently, we live in ever-increasing coherence with our outer world. Samadhi is the precursor to enlightenment and as it becomes evermore present within us, we will begin to experience states of enlightenment. Eventually an experience of complete inner fulfillment manifests.

CHAPTER SUMMARY

Here are some of the main points we have introduced so far:
- The witness watches the personality act from its patterned conditioning.
- To begin developing and strengthening the witness, it is enough simply to ask inwardly for this to happen. It develops as a natural by-product of doing the processing.
- The witness is a neutral observer.
- The rule of thumb for the yogi is to be neither attracted nor repulsed.
- Witnessing does not mean that we never experience pain or pleasure; it is like adding a third channel of awareness.
- The neutral witness adopts the position of balance between the two sides of a polarity. It becomes the fulcrum and is outside the turbulence, turmoil and subjectivity of life.
- The neutral witness is actually our connection to the higher self and to the absolute Self.
- The witness is an opening from the limited personal mind into the universal mind.
- The biased witness is often an internalized parent.
- Detachment increases our capacity to love.
- Detachment is not suppression or denial or avoidance.
- It is a common error of perception to think that favoring the polarized system at the expense of the superconscious will enrich our experience.

- We fear detachment because we fear the potential of loss.
- In a world of variables, the witness is a changeless state.
- When we give up identification with the personality and identify instead with the witness, then we will see that the witness is the Self.
- We are pure awareness, through which thoughts and states of personality pass.
- It is in the space between the thoughts that we first find ourselves being pure awareness—just being.
- Meditation is an important and vital aspect of Self-discovery, as it helps us to see we are not the personality.
- We live life more fully from the place of the witness; it does not mean life becomes boring.
- Faith is the full and openly acknowledged awareness that there is no separation between us and the eternal Self.
- In detachment from material things, we are letting go of *attachment* to them, not necessarily to the actual things.
- Fear is a guide.
- Fear is just a frequency, like everything else in this reality.
- Samadhi is an advanced stage of witnessing and is a state of unity.

SUGGESTIONS FOR PUTTING THEORY INTO PRACTICE

1. Make a prayer or an affirmation that your neutral witness be instituted. Repeat it as often as you feel necessary. Write in your journal about any shifts in awareness that you perceive.
2. Put up sticky notes at home and work that say things like, "Am I in my witness?"
3. Practice being neither attracted nor repulsed. Write about your experience.
4. If you have never meditated, learn how.
5. In meditation, ask inwardly, "Who is watching the thoughts?" and "Who am I?" Later, write about your experience.
6. Do you consider faith to be a sort of naiveté or gullibility? In meditation, try to feel the kind of faith that is not polarized between these states and skepticism or cynicism. Pray that true faith be strengthened in you.
7. Do you blame the outside in situations that trigger you? Make an inner commitment to take responsibility. Instead of blaming, ask, "What are the patterns in me that are creating this reaction and ultimately manifesting this whole situation?"

The light of the body is the eye: if therefore thine eye be single, thy whole body shall be full of light. (Matthew 6:22)

—Jesus

SEVEN

SEEING THE LIGHT

Although the spark of light which we are is connected to everything in the cosmos, embedded in the whole, so to speak, we think we are separate, autonomous entities, isolated in bodies, with space around us separating us from all other entities. This is simply not the case; it only appears to be so. Despite the discoveries of contemporary physics, which show us that we are not seeing things as they really are, we doggedly continue to trust appearances and only believe what we can see. We do this automatically because of our conditioning. Clearing the ego definitely creates a major shift in our perception about how things really are, which is more in line with the cosmic truth about the unity of all things.

Just as a prism refracts white light into rainbow colors, the duality of the separate system refracts the white light of unity into its myriad separate parts. All of the species, races of human beings and the amazing diversity of forms here on Earth are aspects of that refraction. Yet we see and live with all this and forget that it all originates from the one, from the pure golden-white light. On the path of Self-discovery, we gradually develop the ability to perceive life from this place of oneness. With new eyes we learn to see oneness in everything, beyond all dualities. When Jesus said, "If therefore thine eye be single, thy whole body shall be full of light," this is what he was referring to. Since it is the spinning of the dualities that drains the body of light, we become illumined when we can see and know the oneness as our reality. Our bodies literally fill up with light.

In this chapter we will examine four main topics. The first is life in the separate system as illusion and how the illusion is like a hologram. The second is the importance of being able to perceive life in a new way—from the level of energy—and the importance of holding onto our energy and light, so that we can reach higher states of consciousness. The third is a brief look at the anatomy of the light body—beyond, yet containing the physical body, and including the chakra system. The fourth is about moving beyond the consciousness of extreme polarity into the new paradigm of the heart, which is a system of greater flow.

MAYA

Once upon a time we were one with everything. We had access to all of eternity. That was before we took our first incarnation into the limited, separate system and found ourselves locked into bodily consciousness, deeply identified with the body and with only a partial view of the whole. Where did the rest of eternity go? It went into that part of us veiled from sight—the unconscious.

The partial view we have here in this world is described in the Eastern philosophies as just a really clever trick on the part of *Maya*. Maya is a Sanskrit word that describes existence as illusion. It is Maya, or illusion, that continuously deceives us into thinking we are separate and that diverts us from finding the absolute truth. The duality of this world and the personality are aspects of Maya. Sometimes depicted as a female goddess in the ancient Sanskrit literature, she is the source of the veiling technique and the creator of the illusions of existence. It is said she hid the rest of creation from us, behind the veils of unconsciousness. Maya is the reason we fall *asleep* into unconsciousness when what we really seek is to *awaken* to superconsciousness, to more of ourselves. Waking, we see that existence is illusion, is Maya, always in a flux, always in constant change.

When we become capable of observing our personality programming in the light of ultimate reality, we understand it in a completely different way than before. As we awaken, we see more and more clearly that it is an erroneous and mistaken identity—part of the phenomena and appearance of the illusory world.

What does it mean to say that the world is an illusion? It has to do with the way we see our reality. For the person living a fairly unconscious life, the world seems very real. We are taught to believe that the world is what it appears to be—solid, seemingly indestructible form, matter. *Real* for most of us means the material, the earth, matter. Our mental and emotional reality, although quite pervasive in our day-to-day existence, definitely seems more ephemeral and less substantial than the forms of the material world. Our dreams at night are quite ephemeral and not real to us at all once we wake up, though when we are asleep they seem real. More real, less real, seemingly unreal—what is being perceived here? What does *real* in this context really mean?

When we first begin Self-discovery, the material world still seems to be very real and the inner world seems to be quite unreal. Yet one of the first things we begin seeing, after practicing meditation and Self-discovery for awhile, is that life is actually quite ephemeral. How is it possible to transition from feeling the permanence and substance of solid matter and thinking it reliable, to seeing the world as ephemeral? It has to do with our original belief in the description of the world that we were given as we were growing up, which says that the world is real, solid, permanent and reliable. In Self-discovery we soon grow out of the conditioned way of believing everything we were told. As we process and practice meditation regularly, we begin to see with new eyes. What we see is that the world is not a permanent structure; it is always changing and is actually quite ephemeral. Then we discover that it is not so different from our dream world. It just operates with different rules. For example, when we are asleep, the dream world has a sense of time and space, but when we wake up, we realize it is relative. From our waking state, we see that time and space in the dream world are not fixed and permanent; we perceive that they are not real. The sense of time and space as we know it in this physical world is also a relative state to our perception. Time and space do not make this world any more real than the dream world. Finally we begin to see that none of the things we take as part of this reality are anything solid or permanent at all—they are all completely transitory and temporal. They are illusory and unreal.

This new perception of reality comes into being because, as your vibration ascends, you are able to see and flow with change, to the point that even your sense of yourself in this world is as a flow of light and awareness and not a solid or fixed self. Then finally comes the realization that the only thing that is real, meaning permanent, changeless and eternal, is the omnipresent sense of divine presence, which is always with you—all the rest is a dream, an illusion.

What does this mean to us in practical terms? Does the sudden discovery that life is an illusion mean that it is no longer of interest, has become dull, uninteresting and without meaning—that one should surrender all motivation to evolve and grow? Many times in my years of teaching, I have had people ask me this. They say, "Why, after all is said and done, should I bother having any experiences at all, since none of them are real anyway?" No, it absolutely does not mean that. Just try to not have experiences! It is impossible not to have experiences.

Having experiences is what we all came here for. Having experiences does not make life more real. Not having experiences will not make life any less real. Wouldn't it be nice if the disasters were not real and the successes were? Unfortunately there is no chance of that. What are we actually talking about here?

We are talking about existence not being real
in the way that we have been taught to see it.

When we define ourselves in relation to the real, solid world or feel that the world must be real since it is all that we have—we make it so important, we depend on it so much, and we have so much to lose. In this scenario, we live in fear of loss all the time. And all of our concerns seem to weigh very heavily on us. This is unnecessary. This world is a transitory world, and everything changes constantly. We can learn to be in acceptance of and at peace with this fact without clinging desperately to our idea that it needs to be stable, lasting and permanent. When we cling to things, we have such a difficult time with change. We become stuck, hooked to the material, unable to flow with the beauty of creation and eventually unable to accept our inevitable death. It is certainly true to say that one day it will be time to die. This is in the flow of the things of this life.

If we consciously accept the transitory nature of this world and remember that we are not the personality or the body, which are also transitory, we are free. When we awaken to the fact that we are eternal, we will know beyond a doubt that one day when this world passes away, we each will remain, not necessarily in our present form, but as essence, as the true Self.

THE HOLOGRAM: A METAPHOR FOR EXISTENCE

Holographic art is all done with laser beams. It appears to be quite real, yet it is complete illusion. To make a hologram of an object, the holographic artist begins with a small photo of the object. The photo must show all the shading, to give the impression of volume and depth and to create a three-dimensional, lifelike quality. The resulting hologram will project an exact replica of the image in the photo, not a flat and two-dimensional one, as is the piece of paper on which the photo is printed, but as though the object is in three-dimensional space, like a sculpture.

Let's imagine that the holographic image is in front of us, and together we are going to take a walk around it. It is life size, and we can walk right up to it. Since it looks quite solid and real, we walk around it and discover that it has a back and a front. It is realistic in every way, and could be mistaken for an actual object frozen into stillness. And yet if we try to touch it, we find there is nothing but colored light floating in the air. Our hands pass through the image quite easily. The hologram is nothing but light. Since it looks so realistic, it is a bit of a shock to discover there is actually nothing of substance there at all, just the air in which it floats.

The analogy of the hologram is a wonderful way to illustrate the illusion of life and the truth about the ground of being, the unified state. Life appears to be solid and real, and yet it is as insubstantial as the hologram. This world that we all regard as real and solid is a dream—fashioned from vibrations of colored light. In a hologram, all that is really there in actuality is the air—which in our analogy equates to the unified presence. With the hologram, we tend not to notice the air; it seems to be hidden. In life, we tend not to notice the unified presence, but rather we only see what we have been trained to see—the illusory forms.

LEARNING TO SEE ENERGY

On the path of Self-discovery, we will find ourselves beginning to unlearn the old, separate way of perceiving and moving into a more unified way of perceiving. One of the first changes of perception is the dawning of an ability to see energy. The truth about life is that everything is energy, and energy is also consciousness. It is possible to be more aware on the level of energy. Each of us is capable of seeing the world around us energetically, not just as solid form.

Seeing energy does not literally mean seeing the different energies with our eyes, although it can. *Being a seer* means perceiving in some subtle way the reality which is usually beyond the senses. We grasp much more about the dynamic of circumstances when we are able to witness and perceive what sort of energy is playing out in the world around us. For example, we see how our own personality patterns, as well as others', are involved in daily interactions and dramas. It takes an expansion of our awareness and a deeper understanding of what we are observing to see in this way. By witnessing and by being fully present, we perceive things taking place energetically below the surface of any situation.

Focusing on issues about energy is an intrinsic aspect of Self-discovery. As we clear entrenched patterns, a tremendous liberation of trapped energies in the mind, emotions and physical body takes place. Eventually we find that our overall life force increases enormously, and we are able to perceive much, much more about life. This assists us not only in practical ways, such as in achieving success in the world or in having healthy relationships, but also in seeing more of the subtlety of our own personality patterns and of other people's behavior patterns, which is a major asset on the path of spiritual awakening.

The Celestine Prophecy, a book by James Redfield, that millions of people have read, focuses particularly on the topic of seeing energy. The story illustrates how we can learn to perceive from the level of energy and how that ability allows us to see things in a more connected and more detailed way. This supports our growth, making it easier to let go and to change. When we see the interconnectedness of life, we feel safer discarding old personality patterns and other attachments, as well as surrendering into the experience of change and transformation. As an example take when we see the interconnectedness of life through experiencing synchronicities. An example of synchronicity might be a situation when three people in the course of a week recommend seeing a certain movie. The movie, it turns out, holds a special message for you, helping you through a dilemma you were in. Another example might be when you find yourself thinking about an old friend whom you have not thought about for years, and then suddenly the person calls you. During the conversation you realize it was very important that you reconnected, because either you were able to help the person in some powerful way, or the person helped you in some way.

Synchronicities, also intrinsically part of the plot in *The Celestine Prophecy*, are a comforting reminder that there is a more cohesive intelligence at work than just our own limited intelligence. Synchronicities show us that there is not just chaos *out there*, wreaking havoc beyond our control, and that there are no such things as coincidences. It is easier to remember that we are connected to a flow of inner and outer coherence when we have experiences of synchronicity. When we see and acknowledge them, we are beginning to perceive life from the level of energy. It is important to us as a species to see and feel our connectedness, because humanity is in its worst suffering when feeling disconnected. Feeling connected is a reflection of our ancient memory of knowing unity.

Here are some of the other ways in which we are able to perceive from the level of energy:

- ◆ by watching body language and seeing the emotional content
- ◆ by listening carefully to someone speaking and hearing the emotional content
- ◆ by discerning subtle resonances and feelings within our own bodies
- ◆ by using psychic perception, an inner knowing
- ◆ by using clairvoyance, the subtle seeing of light, energy or images on other levels
- ◆ by using clairaudience, subtle hearing on other levels

As children we had access to some or all of these subtle faculties. Most of us were discouraged from holding onto them, and we lost them. As we become clear, they tend to open up again. Learning to use them even a little brings a depth and richness into our relationship with the outside world. Unfortunately it is not within the scope of this book to do an in-depth study of these states. However, they are worthy of mention because they are assets to perception and are often one of the consequences of the clearing work.

THE LIGHT BODY ANATOMY—THE CHAKRAS

We have many bodies other than the physical; the complete, all-encompassing body is really a body of energy and consciousness. We also have a mental body, an emotional body and a vast light body as well. On the path of Self-discovery it is important and fairly inevitable that we will become acquainted with all of them. For the purposes of our discussion, we will take a cursory look at the light body, also sometimes known as the *subtle body*—often seen by psychics and called the *aura*. Even if you are currently unable to see or feel your own light body or others' light bodies yet, it is important to know what the light body is and something about how it works. By knowing about its existence, we learn to feel it more, and we become more conscious of strengthening it. The work of strengthening it supports the spiritual awakening process. As we clear the ego and awaken, we become capable of perceiving the energy movements in the light body. Knowing about it in advance will be helpful for this reason. Here we will take a brief look at the anatomy of the light body, including the chakra system. It is not within the scope of this book to do a

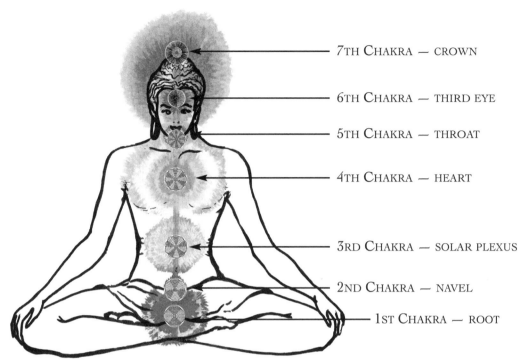

7TH CHAKRA — CROWN

6TH CHAKRA — THIRD EYE

5TH CHAKRA — THROAT

4TH CHAKRA — HEART

3RD CHAKRA — SOLAR PLEXUS

2ND CHAKRA — NAVEL

1ST CHAKRA — ROOT

Fig. 7-1. *The chakras are energy centers in the subtle body. Seen clairvoyantly, the radiating rays resemble flowers or wheels. They are the interface between the subtle body and the physical body.*

thorough investigation of the anatomy of the light body and chakra system; there are many other books on the subject. But rather, our intention is just to give an introduction to them and a general understanding of them.

Chakras are energy centers in the body and are active at all times, whether we are conscious of them or not. *Chakra* is a Sanskrit word that denotes circle and movement, or it can be translated as *wheel*. Chakras are associated with aspects of the physical, mental and emotional bodies. We have many chakras within, and even some beyond, the physical body. There are seven main chakras in the body, and they are the ones we will address here (Fig. 7-1).

There are aspects of consciousness and behavioral characteristics associated with each chakra. When we meditate on the chakra, often we can perceive the levels of consciousness that are described below. We have mentioned only the basic aspects of consciousness associated with each chakra; there are actually many more.

The first chakra is called the root chakra and is located between the anus and the genitals, at the base of the spine. The consciousness associated with the root chakra is that of security, physical survival, the fight-and-flight mechanism and life-and-death struggles.

The second chakra is located between the navel and the genitals. Sexuality, procreation, creativity, the nurturing emotions and family issues are associated with it. It is a doorway into the infinite.

The third chakra is located at the solar plexus. It is the power center and is where we work out issues of power-powerlessness, tyrant-victim, win-lose, success-failure, and dominance, manipulation and control. It is where we learn the lessons associated with polarized power, authority, name and fame.

The fourth chakra is located at the heart and is often called the heart chakra. The consciousness associated with the heart chakra is that of love, faith, devotion, duty and compassion. It is also associated with the ins and outs of love relationships—rejection and acceptance.

The fifth chakra is located at the throat and is the energy center of the voice, expression, artistry, knowledge, mastery and surrender to divine will.

The sixth chakra is located between the eyebrows and is known as the third-eye. This is the energy center of conscience, wisdom, insight, clairvoyance and psychic perception.

The seventh chakra is located at the top of the head and is known as the crown chakra because it sits on the head like a crown. It is a vortex of energy that opens upward like a funnel. The royal crown that kings and queens wear is a representation of it in physical form. The crown chakra is associated with our divine connectedness, or union with the *all that is*.

As we process and meditate, we develop a sensitivity to the chakras and can sense them energetically. Most of us have felt them at one time or another, especially in the physical body, but we are not aware of it because we are not taught to perceive energy or consciousness in this way. For example, when we experience an extreme loss, let's say losing a large sum of money to a competitor in a business dealing, the feeling could be described as *being punched in the stomach*, or maybe even feeling nauseous. These are feelings in the third-chakra area, which is associated with winning and losing and power and powerlessness. If we could actually see the third chakra in the aura in this instance, which clairvoyant people can, we would notice that the energy center looks out of balance, wobbles, and is leaking energy. One loses light, or leaks energy, in a situation of loss. In a balanced person under normal circumstances, the chakra looks like a very even, shiny, spinning vortex of energy. Often in an instance of loss like in our example, there is the desire to eat. This is because food tends to put energy or life force into the stomach area and helps to ground us. It is a natural reaction because at some level the body is telling us that we have lost light and energy and are feeling depleted in the third-chakra area. So, you can see that the physical body gives us clues as to the state of our consciousness. By becoming aware of and more conscious of the energy in the physical body and of the energy centers called chakras, we are able to know when we need to process, and we can learn to be more balanced and to hold onto our light.

Here is another example of our physical body giving us information about the energy of the subtle body, one which many people have experienced. When we receive devastating news, like the death of a loved one, or anything that could be described as *heart-breaking*, the first reaction might be to put a hand over the heart. Again, this is the body showing us that at some level we are aware that we feel like we lost something that we need. We become aware that we are leaking light and losing energy from the heart chakra; therefore the hand goes up to try to hold the light in. By becoming aware of these things, we can retrieve the neutral witness while we experience the emotions and process the situation in order to become more balanced and detached from loss and gain in the physical world.

HOLDING YOUR LIGHT

To reach higher states of consciousness, we have to have a lot of light and energy. Our consciousness is like a pendulum. It oscillates with our imbalanced thoughts and emotions. The still point in the center is the place of the neutral witness (Fig. 7-2).

When we are out of balance and spin or oscillate mentally and emotionally, we lose our light and energy; the life force is pushed out. It is like a windshield wiper that pushes the water off the windshield. And every time we swing wildly, we lose more. We are left drained, and often our physical health suffers. By strengthening the subtle body through processing and meditation, bringing us into balance, we learn to hold onto the light and not to dissipate it unnecessarily.

The loss of light and energy happens because there are *holes* in the subtle body created by the process of the conditioning we experienced in childhood. Where there are imbalances in the personality, there are holes in the subtle body. Light is always coming in, as our true essence is a flow of divine light and of connectedness to source. But sometimes we lose it faster

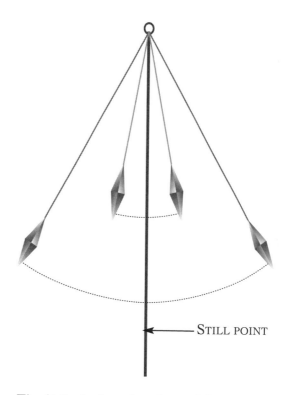

STILL POINT

Fig. 7-2. *As the string of a pendulum gets shorter, the pendulum quickens. It oscillates less and less extremely and moves closer to the still point. As we process and identify more with the neutral witness, we shorten the string of the pendulum.*

than it comes in when we are running below par. Every time we are successful at witnessing and balancing our unbalanced personality patterns—for example our wild mood swings—we are filling in the holes.

When we lose a lot of light, we drop into negative states and get depressed and unhappy. We become depressed because of insufficient light. When we are full of light, we are happy, poised and confident. We are inspired, creative and turned-on by everything. We have energy, and this gets us through the day without dragging.

Strong, luminous light bodies are usually the prerogative of the young and strong. For them it is not so vital to have a lot of balance in the personality and such a strong witness. But as we age and as our patterns become more entrenched, we continue puncturing the light body further and further with our unbalanced behaviors, negative beliefs, and self-destructive attitudes. We have to be more careful as we get older because we lose light more easily. By developing the witness and using the processing techniques in Section Two, we balance the personality, strengthen the subtle body, and hold light more easily in the whole system of bodies. It is essential that we stop the oscillation and reach the still point if we want to hold our light, to improve the quality of life and to reach higher states of consciousness.

THE LIGHT BODY ANATOMY—THE SHUSHUMNA

Let's take a look at more of the anatomy of the light body (Fig. 7-3).

The light body has a core or central axis. In Sanskrit it is known as the *shushumna*, and it corresponds roughly to the physical spine. The shushumna is the luminous core of enlightenment within each one of us. Most people in the separate system are unaware that it exists and rarely feel it. All the veils of the conditioned personality—fears, imbalances, negative and limiting belief systems, and so forth—have been wrapped tightly around it and have hidden it from our conscious view. In fact they resemble a coating of thick, black leather, like a sleeve, around the shushumna. They constrict and cut off the natural flow of light and energy that would normally move up and emanate from the shushumna through our physical body. As we ascend in vibration, peeling away the veils of ego, letting go of the beliefs in separation and limitation, we become conscious of the light literally ascending and emanating from the shushumna, connecting us all the way up, from root chakra to crown chakra. This is why when we meditate, it is important to keep the spine straight and erect to assist the flow of light in ascending the shushumna.

In the East the light or energy that moves through and animates the body is called *kundalini*. Kundalini is our vital life force. It comes from the Sanskrit word, *kundal*, which means *coil*. Seen clairvoyantly, kundalini is coiled at the base of the spine, like a snake, and when awakened, moves serpent-like up through the body.

When a single, thread-like flow of light, or kundalini, ascends all the way up the shushumna from root to crown, uninterrupted by egoic limitation, the state of samadhi begins. Samadhi, as described in the previous chapter, is an advanced stage of witnessing and is the precursor to enlightenment. As we clear constricting, limiting egoic patterns and as we progress on the path of Self-discovery, the thread widens and our samadhi state evolves and grows. Samadhi is an actual experience of the light of the shushumna. Light is unity and contains information. When we enter samadhi, we download the information in the light/ unity consciousness and later it is decoded through the mental body, where we become conscious of multidimensional understandings. For example, we may gain insights

Fig. 7-3. *The shushumna or core (body's axis)*

into a current process which would help to unravel a destructive behavior pattern, like overeating or smoking. Many of the world's great scientists, artists and leaders have access to higher realms of light—whether consciously or unconsciously—and therefore are able to receive information and brilliant new ideas in this way. Light is sometimes experienced—usually in meditation—as a blissful, ecstatic, ever-expanding presence; it is the unconditional love of the Divine.

The light of the shushumna is experienced as unified or non-dual awareness. Traditionally, developing awareness of the shushumna is done mainly with meditation practice. With meditation, doorways gradually open in one's interior space and the consciousness is flooded with the state of non-dual awareness that is our natural state. This experience is often a very spectacular form of realization of the oneness.

However, using the processing techniques in Section Two, we are able slowly and gently to thin out the veils, allowing the non-dual awareness to seep through and to realign the ordinary everyday awareness, bringing us very easily and gently into a wonderfully integrated state of awakeness.

THE LIGHT BODY ANATOMY — THE IDA AND PINGALA

The *ida* and *pingala* are the Sanskrit names for the flows of energy that form the bi-polar electromagnetic field of the body. They take the form of a double helix and wind themselves around the shushumna (Fig. 7-4). Consciousness, or awareness, moves along these flows, perceiving negative and positive, good and evil, and the other dualities of life in the separate system. Our attractions and repulsions in the electromagnetic field spin the energy through the ida and pingala. The ida is the passive, or yin, descending flow and is associated with the feminine energy. The pingala is the active, or yang, ascending flow and is associated with the masculine energy. As we balance our consciousness through the unification of opposites, our awareness is able to perceive from the shushumna as well as from the ida and pingala. This is the adding of the third channel of awareness, described as the witness in the previous chapter, to the channels of negative and positive. The witness is actually outside the electromagnetic field of the polarized zone. As we balance yin and yang, feminine and masculine, we find our-

selves less and less in the either-or mind associated with the limited, dual system and more and more in the state of centeredness and detachment associated with the witness.

It is interesting to refer briefly here to Genesis 3:22-24 in the story of Adam and Eve. After Adam and Eve had eaten the forbidden fruit, learned of good and evil and taken the fall, "Then the Lord God said, 'Behold, the man has become like one of Us, to know good and evil. And now, lest he put out his hand and take also of the tree of life, and eat, and live forever'…the LORD God sent him out of the garden of Eden to till the ground from which he was taken.

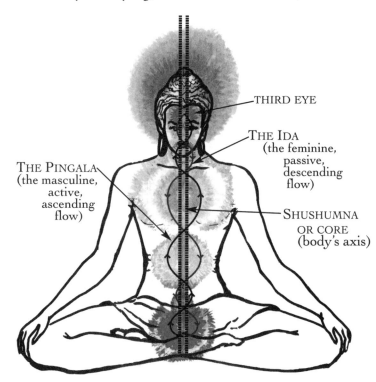

Fig. 7-4. *The ida and pingala, waves of force which flow in a double helix around the shushumna. Please note that this simple two-dimensoinal diagram does not accurately depict the three-dimensional quality of the double helix.*

So He drove out the man; and He placed ...a flaming sword which turned every way, to guard the way to the tree of life." I believe the story is referring to the anatomy of the light body. The tree of life is the shushumna, and when we eat of its fruit, we live forever, i.e., we know our true nature as eternality. But from our fallen, separate state there is a flaming sword guarding the way to it, and therefore it is not easily accessed. When one views the shushumna clairvoyantly, it looks like a flaming sword.

You will notice in the diagram that the ida and pingala begin just below the third eye. This is where the either-or mind begins. Below the third eye is where we perceive the duality, which encompasses the sixth through first chakras. The witness is often centered at the third eye. Above the third eye is the crown chakra, which, in addition to the shushumna, is where we perceive our connection with source. And to refer again to Jesus' statement in Matthew 6:22, "If therefore thine eye be single, thy whole body shall be full of light,"— we see that when our flow of awareness ascends to the third eye, i.e. the single eye, then we begin to be illumined to our true nature as unity.

THE PARADIGM OF THE HEART—THE SYSTEM OF FLOW

With this processing work we are moving through one of the densest veils in human consciousness, from the third chakra to the fourth chakra. This is an aspect of *ascension*—moving from the old paradigm of polarized power and powerlessness into the new paradigm, which is heart-centered and of a more unified nature. The density of the consciousness which keeps the two paradigms separate is reflected in the physical body as the diaphragm, which is a very thick, muscular and restrictive partition, like a ceiling above the third chakra. There is a knot in consciousness there, which is squeezing the shushumna shut very tightly, and which we are loosening and untying as we do the processing work. In the East it is known as *the knot of Vishnu*. When it opened for me, my guides called it *Heaven's Gate*.

Let's look at the difference between the two systems. The third-chakra system is the world of polarity—win-lose, tyrant-victim, authority-subservience, power-powerlessness. That realm is about the battles that we fight every day, the losses we take, the victories we have. It is a system of alternating expansion and contraction. This is life in the world of extreme duality.

With the egoic clearing work we are bringing all of that to a conscious awareness, balancing it out by seeing all the missing pieces. In doing this, the heart gradually opens more and more. We move up to the next level, where we have faith, trust, vision, balance, compassion, and we learn to stay open more easily.

The new paradigm is another system. It is a system of the awakened heart, of continuous flow and emanation of energy, in which the energy moves differently, like a wellspring bubbling up from the earth. It does not expand and contract, is not subject to extreme attraction and repulsion and is not empty some of the time and full some of the time. We know loss and gain in the old system. The new system is not contained by the same kind of heavy polarization. It is less limited, allowing a state of almost continuous fullness. As soon as there is an outflow of energy, it is replaced by a new inflow of energy. So, there is never an empty state. It does not oscillate so extremely between negative and positive. The system of the awakened heart is not an either-or, win-lose system; it is a win-win system.

When we begin the path of Self-discovery, we are living between the two worlds. Although we talk about the two paradigms as distinctly separate from each other, in truth an individual moves gradually between the two over a period of time, often living in both simultaneously. It is not possible to leap all at once into the new paradigm. This would blow all our circuits; it is too much voltage for our old selves to handle. It takes time for the body to integrate the differences and for the circuitry of the body to hold the new vibratory rates. Like an old house needing new wiring, the body must be able to hold the new experiences. Often after we do a session of processing, we feel like we are being re-wired, and literally this is not far from the truth of it. With the wiring of the old paradigm, we hold the potential within us to experience the light of the shushumna for only a few seconds. That would translate into a peak spiritual experience. To hold the experience for longer, we must be re-wired time and time again and gradually become accustomed to it. By using the processing techniques, there is a weaving of the schisms, or fault lines, in our subtle bodies, which results in a re-wiring of our circuitry, making us more whole and able to experience our wholeness.

To bridge the old and the new paradigms, we take on the intermediate persona of the spiritual warrior. Living from the persona of the spiritual warrior, we choose to live in complete integrity with our own inner truth and with the world around us. We are willing to see the world as a mirror of our own projections and not blame the outside for our own limitations. We address our unconscious egoic issues and our destructive belief systems with the intention of dissolving the old personality and moving our awareness into the heart. By adopting the persona of the spiritual warrior, we have a vehicle to help us gradually move into longer and longer experiences of the light of the shushumna.

CHAPTER SUMMARY

Here are some of the main points we have introduced so far:

- ◆ Existence is not *real* in the way we have been taught to see it.
- ◆ The material world is transitory and ephemeral, and life is like a hologram.
- ◆ Seeing life from the level of energy, we perceive more about our own and others' egoic patterning, and more of the interconnectedness of life, including synchronicities.

- The light body anatomy includes: chakras, the *shushumna* and the *ida* and *pingala*.
- *Kundalini* is the vital life force that moves through and animates the body.
- To reach higher states of consciousness, having light and energy is important.
- We hold light when the ego is clear and balanced.
- We lose light when the ego is not clear and is out of balance.
- As we clear the consciousness of the third chakra—polarized power issues—we move through the *knot of Vishnu*, or *Heaven's Gate*, and into the paradigm of the heart, the system of flow.

Suggestions for Putting Theory into Practice

Looking At the World Around You

Looking and seeing are two different things. We look at things, yet we do not really see them clearly. This is because of our imprint of separation, which has made sure that we have limited faculties. We tend to do limited seeing and limited hearing. When we listen to something, we are able to take in only a small fraction of what we are hearing without losing focus. It is the same with seeing, when we look at something we take in a very limited amount of data. To increase seeing, try to draw an object. Most individuals feel that they do not have any artistic ability, but really it is just that the seeing is not fully enough developed to depict an object clearly. Everyone has an artist within. The problem is in the seeing. We look at the world constantly, but we are continuously selecting only a fraction of the data available. When one draws something, there is a deeper investigation of the nature of the object. By doing this exercise, you will realize how selective your seeing is.

- Select and draw an object you really like, something simple to start with, such as a shell, a leaf, a vase, a flower, a teacup, etc.
- Draw something appealing but more complex, such as: a vase containing a flower, a statue, your sleeping pet, a tree, etc.
- Go out into the world, to a place which inspires you, preferably a place which you find beautiful, relaxing and peaceful. Stay there long enough to find a place of peace and calm inside yourself. All the time that you are there, take the time to really look at your surroundings. What kind of terrain is it? Can you see the horizon? Is there vegetation? If there are buildings, what kind of buildings are they? What are the predominant colors in the scene? How does the light look, and how does it affect you? How are you affected by the light and color of the scene? Describe in detail in your journal all the things about it that you notice.

I give you the end of the golden string,
Only wind it into a ball,
It will lead you in at Heaven's Gate
Built in Jerusalem's wall.

— William Blake

EIGHT

The Human
Imprint

There are countless ways of viewing and describing the organization of human consciousness. Because it is an integral whole, it really does not matter which way we view it. Since any way we choose would be an artificial construct of the analytical mind, we can come up with innumerable ways to dissect and describe it, and if they work to create understanding, they serve their purpose. There is no absolute right or wrong way, and because of this, many models are currently available.

In this chapter we have chosen to use a model that introduces you to the structure of the ego in a way that will be the most useful for your processing work. The particular one presented here is called the Human Imprint. It is an upward-and-downward-spiral model. During inner journeys in deep meditation, I have seen that egoic energy held in separation actually takes the shape of an upward and a downward spiral. This correlates to the upward and downward spiraling flows of energy in the subtle body, which are the ida and pingala.

When we take incarnation in the separate system, consciousness is literally imprinted with energetic flows that form these spirals. Viewing our consciousness from the perspective of this upward-downward spiral model is helpful because it is a particularly graphic way of seeing the ego's underlying structure, or *blueprint*, as opposed to its surface content. Being able to see beyond the superficial layers and into the underlying structure is a road map, a golden thread to liberation from separation. As we explore and understand the blueprint, we gain a much greater insight into what aspects of the personality really need to be changed. We see more clearly where the major limitations and unconscious aspects of the personality patterns are, and this leads us to balancing and releasing them.

The upward-and-downward-spiral model is a useful tool to discern when you are acting from your ego. It helps to develop the vigilance you need and to remind you when to get into your neutral witness and process. It is a map for understanding how awareness spins, cycling into negative and positive, and what its upper and lower limits are.

The spin of consciousness within the electromagnetic field—and the resulting upward and downward spiraling of our energy—profoundly affects how we see life. The blueprint for our mental, emotional and physical states is an intrinsic part of these spirals in that a whole spectrum of vibratory states of mind and emotion is imprinted in the upward and downward spiraling energy. In the course of our transformation work, we must examine all the states of awareness on this human blueprint and see how they affect our personal patterning and behavior. In this chapter we will explore all these concepts in greater detail. Let's begin by taking a look at the difference between content and structure.

CONTENT AND STRUCTURE

Content is the *story* aspect of one's life. It is the current drama which is unfolding for us today. It is the surface appearance of things, the superficial scenery, the window dressing of a particular act of the play, the *who said what to whom*. The content is not what we are interested in. We are much more interested in the structure, which underlies the content.

> *Structure is the underlying skeleton,*
> *which holds in place the patterns of behavior.*

We are easily deceived into thinking when the scenery changes that we are having different experiences and that real change is happening. It is only as we begin to look at the underlying structure of each drama that we begin to realize we are constantly replaying the same old dramas.

EXPANDING AND CONTRACTING

The best way to demonstrate the human imprint is from the point of view of the *up and down movement of your attention* through the electromagnetic field and of its spinning and *spiraling* nature. Because of the nature of the electromagnetic field, which pushes and pulls attention, awareness moves constantly in what seem to be directional flows. When we are in a good mood, we seem to spiral up, and when we are in a bad mood, we seem to spiral down. This apparent up and down spiraling movement really comes about because our consciousness is expanding and contracting. Our colloquial language reflects this. If we are having a good day, we say we are feeling *up*. If we feel badly, we say we are feeling *down* or that something is a real *downer*.

Probably everyone at one time or another has felt the spin of the upward or downward spiral but has not consciously realized it. Often when we experience some kind of major loss in life, we tend to feel dizzy—a sign of a spin. This is one physical symptom that is a reflection of the spin downward in consciousness. Sometimes when we experience a loss or a disconnect, we say we feel as though *the plug has been pulled* or that we feel *drained*. Our language reflects the movement of awareness, similar to the way water spirals down a drain when the plug has been pulled. Or we may feel someone else's consciousness as *spinning*. For example, if you have ever been peacefully quiet and alone when a very excited person enters the room and explodes enthusiastically with news, you may have felt like he or she was in a *whirlwind* or as though a *hurricane* passed through the room. Or if the person was very angry, you may have felt like you were hit by a *tornado*.

Spiraling down slows our vibration, and everything—mental, emotional and physical—contracts. This is the negative side of the ego and does not feel good to us. Spiraling up is a speeding of vibration where everything expands, and this is the positive side of the ego. We tend to feel more attached to the positive, upward side of the energy flow. It feels better to us because we generally prefer to feel expanded rather than contracted. Because God or heaven is associated with a faster vibration and with expansiveness, we have developed the idea that being in the positive side is the way home. As described earlier, this is a problem because of the law of opposites—we cannot stay on the positive side long enough to raise the vibration enough to find the Self, before something triggers us back into the negative side. We are constantly bound by the fluctuations of the upward and downward spirals moment to moment, in our daily interactions with life. If something triggers us with fear, we go down, and if something triggers us with a positive reaction, we go up. The permanent raising of the vibration, which is known as ascension and which leads us to the Self, is done by transforming the boundaries of the ego through clearing the patterns and by holding to the middle way—the way of the neutral witness.

The parameters of our egoic patterns set limits to our expansion and contraction. We can only expand a certain amount before we find ourselves contracting again. So too, we can only contract to a certain extent before the situation will turn into its opposite, and we begin to expand again. This controlling by the ego moves our attention in a kind of infinite loop.

These upper and lower limits are the boundaries of the ego, beyond which we cannot venture without the kind of shifts which result from the clearing work. The clearing work permanently changes the patterning, and therefore the boundaries of the ego begin to dissolve and expand. The only change the ego can institute for itself is a swing between negative and positive, in other words, to the other side of any polarity. This creates the illusion of change but is not a real changing of the position of the boundaries, just another change of scenery.

THE HUMAN IMPRINT—A DESCRIPTION OF OUR ORIGINAL SEPARATION

Everyone in a human form is imprinted with a certain organization of consciousness, which is the blueprint for being a human. We all have the same basic *stamp* at the most fundamental level—the stamp or mold of the human form. This basic engineering, common to all humans—can be likened to the way in which there is a basic engineering common to all makes of cars—the internal combustion engine. Yet there are variations from one model of car to another. A Rolls Royce is not like a Volkswagen, yet they both have internal combustion engines that run on the same principle. So, too, there are variations in design from person to person, although our basic structure or blueprint is the same. Amazingly, though we are all unique individuals at the surface, we are all the same at root. I will explain how this is possible in the next few pages. The common denominator of our shared blueprint is the stamp of *duality*, the schism between negative and positive, caused by the electromagnetic field.

As we discussed earlier, the effect exerted on consciousness by the electromagnetic field gives rise to the pushing and pulling forces of attraction and repulsion, causing spinning cycles, which oscillate between negative and positive. Within the framework formed by these energy flows, a spectrum of vibratory frequencies is introduced. These are a wide spectrum of mental and emotional states—states of tremendous variety, which are available to all humans. We are each imprinted with these mental and emotional states, and we each have the potential to express them.

THE PRIMAL SEPARATION

In the beginning there was *That*, the eternal, infinite, omnipresent, unity consciousness. And then something happened to disturb *That*—a vibration began, something which we might interpret as movement or action. The vibrations seemed to gain momentum until unity consciousness seemed to shatter and fragment into millions of different parts. Somewhere in this shattering, individual pieces of consciousness (us) seemed to descend or *fall*, so to speak, into separation from the whole. And so, at the origin of each individual self, a *piece* of consciousness becomes veiled from the whole. Then it reorganizes itself into this structure of the downward and upward spirals. This fall was seemingly a spiraling of consciousness downward. This imprinted pure consciousness with a series of negative states. The sequence of the imprinting of the negative states is shown in the list that begins on the facing page. The downward spiral is common to all humans.

The next imprinting to take place was with the positive, upward spiral. It consists of all the opposite states to those states on the downward spiral. This too is common to all humans. We will discuss the upward spiral later on in this chapter.

Patterns, which later develop in the individual personality, are formed from the states held in the negative downward spiral and the positive upward spiral. Humans, within their egos, are always spiraling either down or up. The spiraling down replays each time we have a negative experience, whether of a minor or major nature. We repeat the fall sometimes several times a day when our buttons are pushed by small or large issues. The conditioned, individual patterning about loss, overlaid on the imprint, triggers us into believing that we are experiencing some sort of loss, and we fall again.

The imprinting of the downward spiral happened in a split second. This mere moment at our origin contains all of the negative states we now know and experience in this life. In that split second we passed through a profound shattering of our wholeness and felt the most traumatic sense of loss and of ripping away. We experienced and imprinted a series of states of mind, one after another. This takes the form of the downward flowing spiral, which progresses steadily into slower and slower vibrations the further we descend. In my perception this is the "fall" described in the story of Genesis. We did, in effect, within the illusion of the separate system, become separated from God consciousness and from our sense of inner connectedness to our non-dual state held in the shushumna. We became beings destined to live in separation, cycling between the negative and positive magnetic downward and upward flows of the ida and pingala.

The list of words below provides a general outline of the downward spiral and represents a skeleton structure of the negative ego. Take a moment to really study these words; they are the themes which haunt our dark days here in this world. Especially notice the order in which the states progress. The sequence reflects the feelings we go through after experiencing a loss or disconnect:

The Downward Spiral
SHOCK
SHATTERING
DOUBT
CONFUSION
SUSPICION
FEAR
REJECTION
BETRAYAL (let-down)
ABANDONMENT
LOSS
DISAPPOINTMENT
PAIN

BLAME
ANGER
RAGE
FEAR
SELF-BLAME
GUILT
SHAME
SELF-RECRIMINATION
INADEQUACY
HATE OR SELF-HATE
REGRET
DESPAIR
WORTHLESSNESS
HOPELESSNESS
MEANINGLESSNESS
DESOLATION
DESTITUTION
ANNIHILATION
DEATH WISH
KILLER INSTINCT

It is important to note as you look at the words that they can be seen two ways; either they can be turned inward on oneself, or they can be projected onto others. For example we can hate ourselves, or we can project hate onto others. We can turn the death wish into a desire to commit suicide, or we can project it onto the outside in the desire to kill someone else.

ARE WE EACH UNIQUE, OR ARE WE ALL THE SAME?

The fact that we all hold the same design, that we are all imprinted with the same downward and upward spirals, seems to imply that we are all the same. How then does this account for our perceived uniqueness? Just as with the earlier analogy to the automobile and its internal combustion engine, the appearance of uniqueness has to do with the particular design we have chosen for our patterns. The unique design is overlaid onto the imprint and gets its individual nature by putting a greater emphasis or magnetic charge on some states and by down-playing others. For example, one person might have a pattern whose main focus is guilt. When that person experiences loss or disconnect, he or she would tend to spiral down into some form of guilt, perhaps passing quickly and fairly unconsciously through the first half of the states on the downward spiral. The person would remain feeling guilty for a while before moving further down the spiral or spiraling back up again. Another person might have rejection, betrayal and abandonment playing big roles in his or her makeup, while guilt does not have much charge on it at all.

As individuals we are capable of experiencing many subtle nuances of the states described in the upward and downward spirals, in endless permutations of light and dark. The designs can become more and more complex until they resemble amazing labyrinths in consciousness.

How does this express in our lives? It means that until we start to wake up, we act out behaviors that are habitual, daily routines. And the grooves wear deeper and deeper, instituting more structure all the time. The personality becomes an entrenched design—a pattern, a labyrinth with established pathways and openings. Desires, fears and experiences shape the labyrinth in particular ways. Some people's designs are apparently more functional than others', although everyone's pattern is exactly what they need to learn their lessons. Bad and good experiences each will teach certain lessons in conformity with the soul's purpose for its evolution.

To give you an example of how this might look in a practical sense, let's look at a woman who desires a relationship. Let's say her conditioning is such that her pattern's emphasis is on rejection, betrayal and worthlessness. She may or may not be totally conscious of her desire or her patterning. The more unconscious she is of these things and the more habitually she runs the pattern, the deeper the grooves she would dig for herself in her particular design. In her relationships, she will experience situations in which her partners trigger her feelings of rejection and betrayal, and then she will spiral down into feeling worthless. Over time, if her unconsciousness continues, her pattern would become more entrenched and would accordingly limit her range of choices in a relationship, drawing toward herself the kind of partner that would trigger these feelings more and more. If she has a fairly balanced consciousness and is not easily triggered by a partner to experience these feelings, her design may appear to be highly functional, and the relationship would appear to work in a beneficial and happy way.

If she has an unbalanced consciousness, then the design may seem very dysfunctional, and her relationships would appear fraught with turbulence and unhappiness. She may have many experiences of relationships that end because she feels rejected and betrayed by her partner, and then she may spend a period of time after each relationship feeling worthless. Generally with very deep grooves in the pattern, i.e., lots of unconscious patterning, our designs are extreme and convoluted and we tend to have experiences which are more polarized and unbalanced. The more we make the patterns conscious and work at balancing and clearing them, the more centered, balanced and happy our lives seem to be. Whether the relationship feels like a good or bad experience—usually some combination of both—the woman would have the exact experience she needs to have in order to learn the lessons her soul has chosen.

Experiencing the rejection, betrayal and worthlessness, having the happy or sad relationship, is not necessarily either good or bad. It is simply life experience and soul evolution. On the path to awakening, we are choosing to make our experiences, lessons, desires and other states of mind as conscious as possible and to witness them. As we become more conscious, life becomes very smooth and peaceful, and we tend to experience higher and higher potentials of happiness, success, creativity and physical energy.

REACTIVE PATTERNS TRIGGER THE DOWNWARD SPIRAL

The downward spiral runs automatically when triggered by any of life's negative experiences. For example, if an experience on any given day triggers a reactive pattern, we may drop rapidly through all the states from *shock* to *betrayal*, pause momentarily to feel and register the betrayal, then free-fall all the way down to *meaninglessness* and *despair*. In this example, we have fallen so fast that we do not see ourselves pass through all the other states in between.

The unification of opposites techniques are used to process and heal situations where we may have *fallen*. In order to do this we must recapitulate the reaction we had in the situation we were in at the time and *slow everything down*. With the slowing down, all of what we felt in that moment can be examined and processed. In processing the difficult situation we are in, it is most helpful to retrieve and describe as many of the imprinted states as possible. The processes work best when we are able to include every feeling, thought and action—including all the information about the thing that triggered the fall in the first place.

Patterns relating to falling down the spiral form the basis of the negative ego, with its fixated and rigid nature. Each of the states on the downward spiral forms the underlying structure of each negative experience. We need to look below the content, though, to see this. The states on the downward spiral are the themes which play an important part in holding the patterns in place. The patterns associated with the downward spiral will begin to shift only as we identify more with the unified, neutral observer, who is able to witness these patterns, as we remain detached from the patterns and as we identify less with the downward spiral.

There is a tremendous contracting of awareness and energy as one falls into the downward spiral. The overall experience is of feeling loss or of many losses, and we get imprinted with this. In fact, the original spiraling down, the original human imprint, feels like the cause of our biggest loss, the ultimate loss, the loss of our godhead. At times, as one works with the imprint, it feels like the *primal scream*, a split second of unbelievable agony in which everything we value disappears (Fig. 8-1).

The downward spiral is the origin of victim consciousness, which seems to be rampant and especially visible in the world at the moment. The word *victim* is not on the list for the downward spiral because the whole list is the persona of victimhood. As we each contain the downward spiral, we each have the potential within us to feel like a victim. As with all personality programs, the victim personality is bound in a push-pull with its unconscious opposite side. In other words when we feel like victims, we tend to draw toward ourselves people and situations which become the mirror for us—reflect to us the opposite, unconscious side. There are three archetypal personas which play the opposite of the victim and are important enough to mention here, so that we can know enough to witness them if we encounter them.

photo: J. Lathion, © Nasjonalgalleriet

Fig. 8-1. The Scream, *by Norwegian artist Edvard Munch*

One is the *tyrant*. The tyrant is the bad authority figure that interacts with the victim by controlling, dominating and manipulating the victim. The victim, in return demonizes the tyrant. Another is the *savior*. The savior is the good authority figure, which the victim glorifies and idealizes. The victim perpetually wants to be rescued by the savior. The third is the *rebel*. The rebel plays out aggression toward the authority figure, wanting to become the one in power and control. The victim is the opposite of the rebel in the sense that the victim submits to and is powerless in the face of the authority figure. It is not within the scope of this book to fully explore these four archetypal personality patterns, but at least by knowing about them, we can be more aware of them and witness them. We all contain all four archetypal personas in our personality patterning, and so we all have the potential to experience living out those personality types.

Therefore, we also all have the potential to draw toward us as mirrors those archetypal personality types, who will act out our unconscious opposite side for us. If you take some time to reflect on situations in your life that feel unbalanced, no matter what the *surface content* looks like, you will generally find that underneath, in the *structure* of the situation, these four archetypes are playing out some unbalanced dynamic.

The downward spiral and all the accompanying personas are things to process, clear, and eventually be free of altogether in order to live in a permanently instituted state of unity. By clearing them, we are no longer attached to any of the states involved in this imprint or bound by the parameters it sets for us. And, yes, this is possible. When we reach that place, we become fully conscious of our enlightenment. Gradually working on these states begins to create an opening in the awareness, which leads to this awakening. So even a little bit of clearing goes a long way!

THE FALL IS A LOSS OF CONSCIOUSNESS

The original fall left us with such a loss of light and awareness that when we enter the negative side of the ego, we feel powerless and worthless. This is one of the reasons that most people avoid the negative at all costs. The average person will develop all sorts of compensatory mechanisms to avoid having to feel those states.

For someone on a spiritual path who is still trapped—even somewhat—in the imprint and who takes a fall, it is a loss of energy and spiritual power in the light body such that it would affect the person's ability to enter and stay in samadhi. For instance someone may be having a blissful experience of samadhi one day, and then a letter arrives from the Internal Revenue Service about taxes. If the situation is something unexpected and *shocking*, the person may react by falling down the spiral. How far the person falls is governed by how bad the situation is and how clear of the downward spiral the person is. He or she may stop at *betrayal* for instance, or at *fear* or *anger*, or go all the way down to *despair* and *hopelessness*.

When we are clear of all attachments and patterns relating to shock and the other states in the spiral, we cannot be thrown off-center by anything, even the Internal Revenue Service. The fact is that until we are clear, anything triggering any of our worst fears cuts us off from the whole and sends us down the spiral.

Most people, when they find themselves in the negative side of the personality, whether conscious of taking a fall or not, would describe themselves as being in a depression. They would probably not waste too much time trying to sort out what the associated feelings are or where they come from. They would most likely just say that the feelings are coming up because of some incident that happened or that they are coming up out of nowhere. But either way, the feelings are more acknowledged out of nuisance than anything else, and the pervasive feeling is that something must be done outwardly to fix the situation.

Nowadays many people just take Prozac or some similar drug to take the depression away. Drugs such as Prozac mask the symptoms, and someone may be satisfied with that for many years. Anything is better than feeling the feelings—than being depressed. When we are depressed, we are not really socially acceptable. For the most part society expects us to feel *up* all the time. When we are not *up*, we are ashamed to face others and tend to hide until the depression is gone. Given that we are all subject to the law of opposites, it is inevitable that we will feel depressed at least some of the time. It is normal and to be expected.

When there is no commitment to make the unconscious conscious, the potential for growth is lost in such a situation as a depression. Whereas if we make the commitment to do the clearing work, all of our experiences, states of mind and emotions, even the negative ones, are valuable and are honored as opportunities for growth.

THE STORY OF ARIADNE'S THREAD

Do you remember the Greek legend about the hero, Theseus, who went to Crete from Athens as a slave, to take part in the dangerous bull-dancing rituals? He hadn't been there long when he decided to escape. Bull dancers were allowed to leave only if they were willing to go down into the labyrinth below the palace and slay the Minotaur, a monstrous half-man and half-bull. No one had succeeded until Theseus decided to try.

Fig. 8-2. *Theseus and the Minotaur battle in the labyrinth.*

This was dangerous obviously, not only because of the Minotaur, but because it was inevitable that one would get lost in the labyrinth. However, one of the King's daughters, Princess Ariadne, had fallen in love with the handsome hero, Theseus, and she agreed to help him. The metaphor is of the merging of masculine and feminine to create the wholeness needed to become ready for the descent into the downward spiral.

At the entrance to the labyrinth, she gave him a spool of golden thread, which he unrolled as he walked through the labyrinth, until he found the Minotaur. Theseus slew the Minotaur after a fearsome battle, and because of the thread Ariadne had given him, he was able to find his way out of the labyrinth to freedom (Fig. 8-2).

For us Ariadne's thread is a metaphor for the witness. It helps us to enter and to find our way out of the labyrinth of the downward spiral. When we fall into the negative states of the downward spiral but are solidly established in the witness, this makes all the difference. For example, to be stuck in meaninglessness without a witness would be to believe the feelings, to make them real, and this is often unbearable. The witness gives the understanding that the meaninglessness is just another egoic state and not real at all.

THE WITNESS IS THE THREAD OF UNDERSTANDING

It is the support and understanding held by the witness that makes it possible to move further down the spiral than many souls would consciously dare to go. In the interests of waking up completely, the seeker must look at the death wish and the issues around dying with dispassionate eyes. This can only take place with the support of the witness.

When there is a witness present, we know why we are in the downward spiral—it is to clear and become enlightened. We know, too, that the ego is illusion, and we don't make the feelings real. We know that they are not who we are—so we know they can be cleared. There is no comparison in this instance to someone falling into this state unprepared and without a witness, becoming stuck in a state such as meaninglessness. That could be unbearable. With a witness, there is no temptation to *act out* from the confusion and from the sense of overwhelm.

As the seeker experiences those heavy states from the place of the witness and with the knowledge that they are not real, as well as with the intention to clear them, the emotional charge begins to dissipate and dissolve. When the downward spiral has been explored and cleared, there is a deep knowingness that there are no further labyrinths and minotaurs to be endured. We have seen it all and have found that all the minotaurs were just aspects of the egoic mind.

THE MAP FOR EXITING THE SYSTEM

The downward spiral is the road map for the journey home. Its value is that it allows you to get your bearings along the way. When you find yourself stuck in your egoic patterning, when you have lost your witness and are off balance, you can refer to this list of states on the downward spiral to see what stage of the negative ego you are cycling through. You can remind yourself to witness your states of mind, to process them and to release them, which leads to balance, clarity and liberation. You can track your descent from the place of the witness, knowing that none of it is really who you are.

Using the map usually becomes most necessary when you are quite far along in the work—in fact it is most useful for the homestretch. The homestretch happens when you have done most of the preparatory work. In other words you have balanced and married the inner masculine and feminine to some extent. You have developed a strong witness, and you have developed a warrior spirit.

RE-EXPERIENCING THE IMPRINT

Whenever we perceive an experience of loss, we re-experience our original imprint of falling down the downward spiral. In childhood, this is how we are conditioned—traumas of loss, whether big or small, send us down the downward spiral and begin to institute the patterning of separation, which sets the personality in place. As we age, the grooves of the personality deepen until they have become quite structured. Why then, you might ask, does allowing oneself to go down the spiral now, as a seeker, have a different result? The answer has to do with your intention and commitments.

The commitment to institute the patterns of separation is firmly in place at birth. We made the commitment to have an experience of life lived in separation, in the system of duality. It is the experience we came here for, and we need to live out that destiny. It is not until the commitment has been changed to one of *releasing* the patterns of separation that it becomes possible to descend the spiral and to watch the feelings unravel and dissolve before our eyes. Becoming a seeker reverses the commitments in favor of finding unity, and our lives begin to move in that direction.

This is because, as with the labyrinth, the way into the system is also the way out. We must relive our traumas from an emotional level, re-experiencing the pain, fear and anger associated with them, but with awake, witnessing eyes, in order to have them dissolve. They become a doorway out of the system—just as they were once a doorway into the system.

In meditation we can recapitulate the experience of our original fall down the downward spiral simply by asking inwardly for it to happen. It may not happen immediately, but spirit will eventually give us the experience in meditation when we are ready. This is quite helpful when we have the intention of descending in order to clear the imprinting. It gives us a valuable insight into what happened. The experience is different for everyone, and it does not even necessarily have to be a traumatic experience. Some people re-experience the fall as being sucked down the downward spiral. Others report an experience of being pushed down or of being catapulted down, and some even report floating down quite consciously. By examining the particular variation of your own experience in meditation, you gain a fundamental understanding of the basic constructs of your personality. For example, if you felt pushed down, you might tend to develop the personality patterning of a passive victim. Re-experiencing the original imprinting can be very helpful in seeing the deeper constructs and tendencies in the personality patterning.

THE RETURN JOURNEY IS A REVERSING OF THE SEQUENCE OF SEPARATION

The road map of the return journey shows us that we approach our integrative work by reversing the order in which the separations originally happened. As a reminder, when we originally "fell," the order in which the separations occurred is first a subject-object split between totality and the soul, and next a split between the soul and the individual self, which includes the simultaneous schisms of masculine-feminine (or yang-yin), negative-positive and conscious-unconscious. So in a broad sense, the unifying and balancing of masculine-feminine, positive-negative, and conscious-unconscious frequencies in the personality will be one of the first phases of the work and will begin the process of taking us back into soul consciousness.

Reconciling and balancing these schisms is well worth the time it takes—since it smoothes the way and brings us much closer to home! For example, when you first start the integrative work, the aspect of feminine and masculine issues will form an overarching theme. Even if it seems that you are not working on relationship issues, the gender frequencies involve the polarities of yin and yang, which for example are aspects such as: passive-active, subservience-dominance, weak-strong, and receptive-active, just to name a few. These are the sorts of frequencies that are involved in the feminine-masculine split.

When this phase is complete and the masculine and feminine have found the marriage of spirit, the next phase is about addressing the subject-object split between soul and godhead—which means the dissolution of the coating, or veils of illusory identity, and finally the realization of the unified state.

CLEARING THE IMPRINT

The first noticeable change in clearing the imprint is that you are able to maintain a witness who observes what is happening, who stays present with the situation and who is able to witness the emotional body spin down the spiral.

Even though the emotional body may feel all the emotions
of the downward spiral pass through it
and even though the physical body may contract in reaction,
if the witness stays present, a clearing has taken place.

Maintaining a witness in the heat of the moment means that the pattern will be seen as a pattern and not be made real. Even though the emotional body automatically runs through its feelings and even though bodily sensations, such as waves of heat or contraction, still are in effect, a clearing happens. With the act of conscious witnessing, the mental-emotional charge in the body caused by the pattern will eventually begin to dissipate and disappear. The presence of the witness ensures that the pattern weakens.

Usually in the beginning you will find that your witness will come in after the fact of the incident. This is because we are not naturally taught to witness, but rather we are taught to make things *real*. So this is the best that one can hope for at first as the witness develops. Even if the witness comes back several days after the incident, that is better than not having one at all. As soon as you get a witness to the situation, it is time to process it. Even a delayed process is better than no process at all. It does not matter how many days have passed; a process is always good for changing the situation in the future. A future situation will always come up under a different guise, until you have cleared the pattern. So in the beginning, it hardly matters *when* you do the process, as long as you do it.

Until you have begun to work with the processing techniques in Section Two, which will help develop and strengthen the witness, you can practice witnessing your emotional reactions as they arise from time to time simply by remembering to ask yourself inwardly, "Am I in my witness?" Or as suggested in Chapter Six, simply make a mental affirmation or prayer to the effect that you would like to have a more present witness. You can do this as often as you feel moved to. The more frequent, the more conscious you will become.

THE SPLIT SECOND TO WITNESS

The separate *I* makes you believe that the feelings you experience are *who you are* and therefore that they are important and matter—and have to be validated and listened to. In this instance no detachment or neutrality is present. Our choosing to be deceived happens because we are *identified* with the two spirals of the ego, thinking that they are who we are, that we are the sum total of all those states on the downward and the upward spiral.

Thinking we are the personality, we give them our power—the power we would use to dissolve veils and to re-enter into the essence. We are unable to stop falling until we give up our identification with the spirals. As humans we are unable to give up identifying with the separate self until we begin identifying with the neutral witness.

The state of neutrality puts us in touch with essence, and the identity is shifted away from the egoic spirals to the essence, to the shushumna, our true state. As we identify more with the witness, we have a moment, a split second of grace, when we can choose whether or not we want to get sucked into the spirals and the issues involved. We can choose to let go in that moment. We begin to understand that when we make something matter, we get *matter*! We become *material*—we become denser. As we are more and more able to witness that split second and to choose letting go, we become lighter and experience our marriage in spirit.

THE DARK NIGHT OF THE SOUL

A person seeking spiritual awakening does not miss opportunities to explore consciousness. As the commitment to awaken deepens, the extremes of consciousness present themselves for further exploration. The highs and the lows, the ups and the downs must be examined, experienced and released. Most people choose not to have these experiences, especially the lows. But as we enter advanced spirituality, we choose quite consciously to clear the downward spiral and the upward spiral. Of course, we cannot work on one without working on the other. When we process the negative side, we automatically surrender the positive side as well.

This means that at a certain point on the path of Self-discovery, one may make the conscious commitment to explore the states on the downward spiral with the intention to know and experience them fully. It is like the metaphor of Theseus and Ariadne, where the hero chooses to enter the labyrinth and to slay the Minotaur. In the Judeo-Christian context, it could be considered a deliberate descent into an inner Hell with the intent to clear it out of one's system. Before the ego can be let go of, it must be known and understood in all its extremes. This phase of the clearing work is also sometimes known as *the dark night of the soul* or *the veil of tears*.

The worst fear that comes up for most people when they hear these words is that the phase of dark night of the soul or the veil of tears will never end. Of course this is simply not true. It is just a fear built into the design of the ego, which is about not moving beyond its own boundaries. The fear is the warning sign on the gate that says *do not go past this point at all costs!* Fear is just the veil, which is designed to hold the boundaries of the ego in place so that the pattern does not change or expand. And of course this is much of what the clearing work is about—moving beyond the boundaries of fear into the knowledge of the Self, into an experience of our wholeness, of our true nature.

So of course the idea that the negative states are an endless realm is not true. Although it is designed to make us believe otherwise and although it may seem infinite, the ego does have parameters. The exploration of the downward spiral is not about going out into the infinite where perhaps the worst fear is that we could get lost. It is simply about taking one step at a time, maintaining the witness position and clearing the downward spiral little by little.

The ego's furthest parameters are beyond the reach of most people's conscious mind. Uninitiated souls simply do not choose to go there. People without strong commitments to wake up and to explore the truth of existence cannot handle the deepest, darkest depths of negativity—as they often cannot handle the extremes of the positive side either. When a seeker chooses full enlightenment, the soul will choose to explore those depths and the related heights, knowing that it is a small price to pay for liberation from the ego and for enlightenment.

The dark night of the soul is often done in stages, over a period of months or years, so that the seeker gradually becomes more and more accustomed to being in those states, despite the intensity. Each time we consciously choose to examine the downward spiral is like a mini dark night. Being prepared is everything and takes time. The journey into the depths will not happen until the individual is ready and seeks it. Preparation includes bringing balance through the masculine and feminine to some extent and developing a strong witness and a warrior spirit. Without this training, there is no dark night of the soul—just a depression, which most people may not be able to handle without Prozac. The distinction here is that the dark night is a productive experience; it releases us from the bondage of the ego and leads to liberation.

Often people who are on the path of raising their consciousness or seeking spiritual liberation find themselves in situations in which they have descended the downward spiral without a witness. Most people have not been told about and prepared for the experience. On the surface these kinds of situations could look like failed relationships, money problems or loss of a job. And these experiences may result in periods of feeling despair, depression, destitution, meaninglessness, hopelessness and worthlessness. Not understanding that these states of mind are just ego, and that experiencing them with a witness is a powerful opportunity to clear them and wake up, usually means that the person will feel confused, victimized and betrayed by life or God for having to feel so bad. As spiritual seekers it is important to remember that at some level we have committed to go down there and clear these egoic states. We need to remember that the dark night of the soul is just a temporary situation, that we are navigating and clearing the labyrinth and that *this too shall pass*. With a witness, we become free. And, using the processing techniques presented in Section Two to balance and clear the downward spiral, we can move through the dark night fairly quickly.

THE UPWARD SPIRAL

At our origin, after we imprinted the downward spiral, we took on an imprinting of all the opposite states as the positive upward spiral. This imprinting all happened in a split second. We tend to talk about it happening in the past because we live in and believe in time. In fact, although it seems we first incarnated eons ago, it would also be correct to say that we are continuously imprinting this upward and downward spiral in each moment, based on the choices we make. We do exist outside of time. Time is just an illusion of our separate system—of the maya.

When you first look at the list of words that comprise the upward spiral, you may think that these are the ideal states. They appear to be the states everyone aspires to. Why would we want to change these states? This is a good question, asked by awareness attracted to the states on the upward spiral. For most people the list below is the *attraction side* of the attraction-repulsion polarity. So this is a reminder that in the ego all states are polarized. It is not possible to always live only in the positive side without the spin of consciousness bringing us around again to the negative at some point.

It is a common mistake to think that the states of mind listed on the downward spiral are ego and that the states listed on the upward spiral are not ego. They most certainly are. All these states are part of our dualistic, egoic nature, in that they are bound by the law of opposites, which states that everything in time will turn into its opposite. All the states listed are dynamically bound together; we cannot have one without the other. As hard as it may seem, in our processes we must surrender both sides, the negative and the positive, to ascend into non-polarized, unified consciousness. Each word on this list of states is the corresponding opposite to each word on the downward spiral list.

The Downward Spiral	The Upward Spiral
SHOCK	STILLNESS
SHATTERING	COHESIVENESS
DOUBT	CERTAINTY
CONFUSION	CLARITY
SUSPICION	SECURITY
FEAR	COURAGE
REJECTION	ACCEPTANCE
BETRAYAL (let-down)	TRUST
ABANDONMENT	CHERISHING
LOSS	GAIN
DISAPPOINTMENT	SATISFACTION
PAIN	PLEASURE
BLAME	PRAISE
ANGER	PEACE
RAGE	CALM
FEAR	COURAGE
SELF-BLAME	SELF-PRAISE
GUILT	INNOCENCE
SHAME	PRIDE
SELF-RECRIMINATION	SELF-RIGHTEOUSNESS
INADEQUACY	COMPETENCE
HATE OR SELF-HATE	POSSESSIVE LOVE
REGRET	GRATIFICATION
DESPAIR	EXULTATION
WORTHLESSNESS	SELF-WORTH
HOPELESSNESS	HOPEFUL
MEANINGLESSNESS	MEANINGFUL
DESOLATION	FULLNESS
DESTITUTION	ABUNDANCE
ANNIHILATION	EXISTENCE
DEATH WISH	WILL TO LIVE
KILLER INSTINCT	INSTINCT OF SELF-PRESERVATION

The pull from the heaviness of the negative side to the lightness of the positive side is irresistible at first. For the most part we are programmed to constantly strive to hold the states of the upward spiral. We try to spend as little time as possible in the negative and as much time as possible in the positive. This is the trap inherent in the system.

Remember, we cannot be attached to one side and not have to deal with the other, because they are irrevocably bound together at this level. We need to be able to see the value in both sides and to make them both conscious. Someone who has made the commitment to spirit to ascend in vibration cannot maintain the old way of staying in the positive by sweeping the negative under the rug.

The old way is about being caught in duality and about not awakening fully and permanently to the knowledge of higher vibratory consciousness. It is an old solution to life which works only because of the commitment to the nature of separation itself. We must move on from that modality now if we are to become aware of our true destiny as one with our immortal divine nature.

CLEARING INFANT ISSUES

As we progress deeply into the furthest recesses of the egoic extremes, we come up against the earliest issues imprinted in this current life. These issues are most likely *samsaric* (past-life tendencies) and are echoing through into this lifetime. Because the journey home is a reversal of the outward-bound journey, they come up late in the processing as we near the end of the letting-go process. We retrace our footprints, and this takes us back to childhood, when many of the patterns were set in place.

From there we progress to the pre-verbal stages of infancy. These stages are difficult to process because there was no verbal registration of the experiences, and therefore there is no easily accessed memory. In fact, at first glance it looks as though it is quite impossible to clear this early infant conditioning, due to the loss of memory. Yet somehow it all works out. There is plenty of help from the unconscious at this stage.

INFANCY AND YOUR AWAKENING

Toward the end of the process of letting go of the ego's old form, we deal with the most intense and densest issues related to the bottom of the downward spiral. These are the things which happened in earliest infancy and in utero.

It may surprise you to know that for almost everyone born into a human body at this stage of humanity's evolution, infancy is a life-and-death struggle. Most of us certainly do not remember it this way, if indeed we remember it at all. But should you decide to explore those regions of your unconscious, you will discover this for yourself. Even if your parents are loving and wanted to have you with them, the level of unconsciousness which exists in most people today is such that your parents probably did not have sufficient know-how to protect you from this life-and-death initiation. In fact most parents are contributing to it, however inadvertently, in their ignorance of what babyhood is really all about.

Fortunately, there are signs of a new way of approaching this most important phase of a baby's initiation into the world. More people are becoming aware of the importance of holding the babies and nurturing them for longer periods until they are older. Many mothers are breast-feeding longer and feeding their babies not by a schedule but when the babies are hungry. Some parents are not having their baby boys circumcised, which is an incredible trauma to an infant. Home births and underwater births are not so uncommon anymore and tend to be more nurturing for infants than being brought into the bright lights of a hospital where they are taken away from their mothers for periods of time. But most newborn beings in this world are still not cared for in the proper way. Unfortunately this only became clear to me when I did the work of clearing my own infancy, not when I was a new mother still in my twenties. I look back on my own insensitivity at that time and wish it could have been different, knowing that even insensitivity seems like violence to an infant. What must real violence do? I can only wonder at the extreme levels of density and separation into which the negative ego can be contracted.

Birth and infancy are a repeat performance of the original primal separation. The birth experience, with its descent of the birth canal, is a re-initiation of the original downward spiral. Only this time it has the added weight of the individual's samsara.

We repeat the experience of the primal separation by arriving naked and helpless in an unknown world, with nothing but a deep sense of having lost everything. The journey down the birth canal is dangerous, and we must face death in order to have this dubious life—dubious because it is life in a dualistic world. It means we must live with the loss of the memory of where we came from and of who we are, and we find ourselves divided into polarity. In this way we have lost all our original power and our original resources. We lie helpless, vulnerable and exposed, completely dependent on those who may or may not love us, completely unable to take care of ourselves. At least that is how it feels to the infant. If those feelings are reinforced by traumas in the early infancy experience, such as circumcision, unsatisfied hunger, not being held or breast-fed long enough, which to an infant can all seem like life-threatening situations, they become a victim consciousness in the child and eventually in the adult.

Infants do also have the capacity to get their needs met; they are not as powerless as they appear. They have the power to yell. If their crying is met with a suitable and satisfying response, they will develop in a fairly balanced way. If their needs are not sufficiently met, they develop compensatory behaviors. They have the power to be little tyrants—raging for attention with a noise that is terrifying in its strength. They think they are fighting for their survival, and this may or may not actually be true. If the child has a destiny to be with unsupportive parents, then tyrant or no tyrant, its spirit will eventually be broken, and victim consciousness will become a major part of the child's programming.

It is not within the scope of this book to delve too deeply into the patterns of childhood, but suffice it to say that these birth, infancy and childhood experiences manifest as many different egoic patterns and permutations, depending on the soul's commitments for the life. I am trying to convey here the implications of the raw confrontation that infants have with the bottom of the downward spiral. The most intense feelings that arise as we do the infant clearing work are the fear and pain of being alone, disconnected, abandoned and helpless, and of having no resources.

These are terrifying when they are imprinted, and in the clearing work they can lead us into the most advanced level of the clearing process—the fear of dying and the desire to die. Seeing, processing and surrendering the fear of and the desire for death, as well as the fear of and the desire for life is the last stage of the awakening process, before the dawning of a significant level of clear light comes in. You will most likely need to go through clearing the sequence of the downward spiral quite a few times before complete, continuous awakening is present. The technique called *squares* presented in Chapter Eleven offers a simple and profound way to help explore and clear desires and fears such as these.

Our Parents Are Not To Blame

Since the infant has been stamped with the human blueprint already as part of its original separation experience from the godhead, it is not really the parents who *do* the programming. The parents are there simply to institute the design that the soul of the child has chosen for its life.

So you may ask, "How can the parents do anything different than what they find themselves doing? And how can anyone in this world ever change?" The answer is that the parents can't do anything differently than what the child has planned for its destiny. However, change is still possible.

Change for the child and for the parents can come in by degrees through the conscious choice to transform. Parents can lessen the density of a child's samsaric imprinting by being willing to take the journey to a more balanced ego themselves. Then in the process of growing up, the children are able to transform, too, by a kind of osmosis with their parents. Gradually the children will be affected by the parents' letting-go process.

As the children grow and come to accept the responsibility of their own transformation, their own children will become clearer. In other words the parents and the children must all take the journey of transformation, so that over time everyone will be less dense.

We chose, at a soul level, the patterns our parents are commissioned to institute for us into the soft clay of our new bodies. We cannot blame them. If we are still at the stage of blaming, then we are not owning the outside as our own unconscious.

If you find yourself blaming your parents for your issues, it is important to get in your witness and get out of your victim. It is the victim that feels innocently abused by outside circumstances. In our scheme of things, there is no such thing as an innocent victim. We have all made choices that were within the laws of cause and effect, and when we suffer, it is because of choices we make that cause the suffering.

It is so extraordinarily empowering to take on the realization *that you did it to yourself*—because if you did it to yourself, you can undo it as well. It is very easy and feels really good in the moment to blame something on the outside. Yet the consequences of such blame are so far-reaching and so disempowering that they are as dangerous to your wellbeing as substance addiction. It is important to learn to take responsibility and process your own consciousness in order to empower and liberate yourself.

If something were truly outside you, you would have very little power to change it. Your only hope then of changing the outside would be to resort to manipulation, domination or control of some sort. Do not be tempted; it is not worth it. These are dangerous solutions to choose, with terrible effects on your spiritual wellbeing. Separations would be set up, with effects that would lock you into the old form of ego until you stopped doing them. Take back your power and own your issues now. Make a commitment to create change by processing rather than by trying to control or create superficial change in your life. Processing creates shifts on the outside, as well as inside you. You have a very good chance of freeing yourself forever from the patterns limiting you and of birthing your liberation from duality.

FACING THE PROJECTIONS

As you begin to do the clearing work, it becomes necessary to face the past times when you did project blame toward the outside. As your witness becomes stronger, you will be able to feel the painful and fearful feelings of the innocent victim, even those of the infant, but with a witness present, so that you are dissolving them and not strengthening them by making them real. Eventually you will be ready to look at and to clear the actual human imprint itself, the first *cause* of the *effects* of your life, and to re-enter the unified state of the heart.

Since the human imprint is such a deep experience of loss, clearing it is mostly a matter of looking at the feelings of rejection, betrayal and abandonment, which we feel toward God in the negative unconscious. As these very painful states clear, we are able to experience the releasing of the knot of Vishnu, the opening of Heaven's Gate—which separates the third chakra from the fourth—and to feel energy flow upward, unobstructed, into the heart.

These states clear because we are able to choose to love and forgive instead of believing that God *did something to us*. Even if the story of our fall from the godhead is inaccurate, we have been told that story since time immemorial, and it has ingrained itself into the unconscious, where it awaits some sort of reprogramming.

OPENING THE HEART

As we move out of the human imprint and the old egoic reality, which is one of extreme separation, we move into the consciousness of the heart. The heart holds a greater sense of connection to the whole. Initially the heart allows tolerance and acceptance of others. In time this grows into reconciliation, forgiveness, mercy, compassion and eventually into unconditional love for ourselves and our fellow humans. It is in this journey toward love and the growth of the heart that we will find happiness.

It is in the heart that we are able to see more of the truth of how things are. And it is in the heart that we grow into selflessness, humility and into a more expanded knowing of who we are in our capacity to love. Undertaking the path into heart is a journey. It must be taken if our awakening is to be complete, balanced and well-rounded.

As we become permanently established in living from the heart and fully open to the unconscious, we are established in Self-knowing. People who believe that they have opened the heart permanently but who have not cleared out the egoic shadow in the unconscious are still subject to the heart's closing when they enter the downward spiral. When something negative happens to them in life, they drop back into the separation again and find themselves in pain, loss, confusion and self-doubt.

The heart will not open to its infinite nature and will not stay open until most of the negative ego has been released. Unless we are clear, the heart cannot bear adversity without closing.

In the consciousness of the separate system, the heart is like a valve;
it opens and closes with positive and negative stimuli from the outside world.

For example, when someone gets angry with us, usually our feelings get hurt, and the heart contracts and closes. When someone says they love us, the heart expands and opens. In permanently instituted heart consciousness there is no closing of the heart under negative circumstances, and we live in higher states such as compassion, unconditional love, generosity, forgiveness and humility. These are primarily heart states and are associated with the open heart. As mentioned previously, there is a more comprehensive list of the higher states that we begin to live in as we clear, listed on page 174 in Chapter Ten—Triangles.

STAYING IN ONENESS

Clearing the human imprint and coming to the neutral place is much more powerful than we can know at first glance. Being able to fully witness the human imprint brings us to the core of our existence in this world. This is the place in us where we find the doorway into knowing the Self.

This is the awakened state, beginning as a small, still presence, becoming more developed, more pervasive with time and with recognition of its presence. It will always feel like a timeless moment, where life's spin is on hold and a knowing of truth is found. As it strengthens and as we are able to identify with it, we come to realize that it will always be present with us, even when the transitory nature of the ego flip-flops, back and forth. We eventually come into knowing that it is who we really are. Staying in the neutral place, we are *in* it; we *are* it—watching as it gradually quickens and becomes our luminous inner presence—an eternal light illumining awareness with truth.

CHAPTER SUMMARY

Here are some of the main points we have introduced so far:

- The upward-and-downward spiral model of viewing consciousness is a helpful tool in order to see the ego's underlying structure.
- Content is the superficial appearance of life. Structure is the underlying skeleton, which holds in place patterns of behavior.
- Consciousness moves up and down and expands and contracts. The upper and lower limits are the boundaries of the ego, beyond which we cannot venture without doing the clearing work.
- All humans have a basic blueprint at a fundamental level. Our common denominator is this stamp of duality.
- When consciousness "fell" from the whole, the separate pieces (us) reorganized into the structure of the downward and upward spirals.
- The downward spiral is the negative ego. The sequence of states represents the feelings we go through after experiencing loss or disconnect.
- Like the many types of internal combustion engines in cars, we, too, are all unique yet have the same underlying design.
- Reactive patterns trigger the downward spiral.
- The fall is a loss of consciousness.
- Ariadne's golden thread is a metaphor for the witness, which helps us to find our way out of the labyrinth of the downward spiral.
- The list of words on the downward spiral is a map to exit the system.
- Whenever we perceive an experience of loss, we re-experience our original imprint of falling down the downward spiral. In childhood, this is how we are conditioned into the patterning of separation.
- When we choose to consciously re-experience the downward spiral with a witness, we release and dissolve egoic patterns, and it becomes the doorway out of the separate system.

- The return journey is a reversing of the sequence of separation.
- Even though the emotional body may feel all the emotions of the downward spiral pass through it, and the physical body may contract in reaction, if the witness stays present, a clearing has taken place.
- There is a split second to witness, when we can choose not to get sucked into the downward spiral.
- The dark night of the soul is an exploration in consciousness to clear the downward spiral and is often done in stages over months or years.
- The upward spiral is usually what we are attracted to and is the opposite of the downward spiral.
- Clearing infant issues is one of the final stages of egoic clearing.
- For most people infancy is a life-and-death struggle.
- Our parents are not to blame.
- It is necessary to face our projections of blame onto the outside.
- As we move out of the human imprint, we move into the consciousness of the heart.
- Clearing the human imprint helps us stay in oneness—in the awakened state.

SUGGESTIONS FOR PUTTING THEORY INTO PRACTICE

1. Begin to discern between the content and the structure of your daily experiences. Pick one experience and write in your journal about its content versus structure.
2. Meditate on the list of words on the downward spiral. Can you feel how you cycle through these states whenever you experience loss or disconnect?
3. Write the list of words on the downward spiral on the inside cover of your journal so you can refer to them whenever you are experiencing the negative ego. This will serve as a reminder to witness the feelings and to know they are just ego. Use the list as a map to exit the system.
4. How do you play out the roles of victim, tyrant, savior, rebel? How do others in your daily interactions play out these roles with you? In your journal, write about what you see.
5. In meditation ask to be given an experience of your human imprint—your original fall down the downward spiral. It may not happen right away, but when it does, write about the experience in your journal.
6. Do you blame your parents for your issues? If so, write about what you blame them for and why. Ask for grace to help you release the feelings. Forgive your parents.

SECTION TWO

THE MARRIAGE OF SPIRIT TECHNIQUES

Know Thyself

—The Delphic Oracle

*I dwell within; I am without. I am before and behind. I am in
the south and I am in the north. I am above and I am below.
The wave, the foam, the eddy and the bubble are all essentially
water. Similarly, the body and ego are really nothing but pure
consciousness. Everything is essentially consciousness, purity
and joy.*

—Shankara

Introduction to Section Two

The *unification of opposites* techniques are mental tools to help us unravel the knots of the mind. They offer a very fast way to balance our lives and wake up and were given for this particularly accelerated time we are living in. They are age-old principles, truths from the ancient mystery schools and traditions, and have been revamped and streamlined for the modern era.

The following seven chapters progress from the basic method, polarities, to a more evolved level of processing, which includes: the triangles and squares techniques, some advanced applications of the techniques, as well as developing and strengthening the neutral observer, or witness. The methods may seem like simple little diagrams, but they are actually incredibly precise renditions of deep metaphysical laws.

Since you probably have a pretty good idea by now as to why you would want to clear the ego, the purpose of this section is to offer the methods of how to clear the ego. The first three chapters of Section Two contain the three primary exercises associated with The Marriage of Spirit teachings—polarities, triangles and squares. Each one works at a slightly different level of awareness, relative to mind, emotions and body.

Working with the first exercise, polarities, brings about fundamental shifts in consciousness that are most closely aligned with mental processes, or with one of our subtle bodies called the *mental body*. It is the simplest of the techniques, and each chapter progressively builds on its principles, moving into more advanced techniques.

Working with the second exercise, triangles, effects significant changes and clearing in the emotions, or what we call the *emotional body*. This level of consciousness is often more difficult to address because the triggers that cause emotions in each one of us are so buried in our subconscious.

Working with the third exercise, squares, helps to manifest the deepest and most last-ing changes in consciousness—so much, in fact, that we can heal and raise the vibration of the physical body.

The combination of these three exercises results in a holistic approach of clearing and healing—effecting change in the mental, emotional and physical bodies. It is not impor-tant, at this point, that you completely understand the distinctions between the exercises. In more advanced stages of practice, when you have been working with the exercises for a while, you will be able to intuit which exercise is best for specific instances in your life. You will also be able to move back and forth between techniques as necessary to achieve the best results for your particular situation. We have presented the exercises in this order because of the way they build on each other.

The remaining four chapters in Section Two contain suggestions for getting the most out of the exercises, as well as offering some more advanced techniques. They also talk about combining and/or modifying exercises to achieve specific goals.

Being Mindful of Your Purpose

Before exploring what clearing ego actually is, let's also take a look at some of the things it is not. First, the clearing work is not about *fixing* or *rearranging* the egoic structure. Most psychological work and many other forms of personal growth work are associated with restructuring the personality so that it is more functional and healthy. Having a healthy, functional egoic structure is very important in order to move into Self-discovery more deeply. But *clearing* is a defining characteristic of the Marriage of Spirit work. The Marriage of Spirit work transforms and clears the ego so that eventually nothing remains but the Self, so that the clear light can shine through, unobstructed. The best analogy is the one Ram Dass has used, likening the ego to a prison. We don't want to rearrange the furniture inside the prison; we want to open it up so that it is not a prison anymore.

Second, this work is not about *doing*. Many people get confused about this aspect of the egoic clearing work. They wonder, "If enlightenment is about not *doing* anything, then why do I have to *do* this work?" It is not a *doing*; it is an *un-doing*. We are undoing the per-sonality, which leads to letting go and to moving into the neutral witness.

Third, the work we are presenting here is not about *getting rid of* the ego. Sometimes people misinterpret the egoic clearing work for this. The confusion is based on a miscon-ception that because we are trying to clear the ego, we are implying that the ego is bad or that there is something wrong with having an ego. Most people in this world are in the ego and will stay that way. This is a world where one learns with an ego. An ego is just a struc-ture. It is a way of organizing consciousness so that it can take form. It would be very diffi-cult for consciousness to be here in the world without an ego or without a structure on which to base itself. The ego is the teacup, and the consciousness is the tea, held and contained by the cup. The consciousness has to have a structure to hold it in form so that it can be present in the world. It is not an issue of good or bad at all. A misinterpretation like that would come from the little child—the little inner child who is concerned about being bad, or not being bad, or wanting to feel good, and defending that it is good rather than bad. This work that we are doing is beyond good and bad. It is about moving into unity consciousness and improving our lives. We are seeking a completely new kind of egoic structure—something that is not blocked or clouded with a lot of extraneous, unnecessary detail, old memories of bad experiences from childhood, or all sorts of ideas that are obsolete, have no power, or that affect our lives in a negative way. These are things that we are better off without. We can live much more easily without them. The new form is wise, all encompassing, and grounded in truth.

So, if the processing seems as though it is an attack on the ego, that would be in your interpretation. It would be about feeling attacked yourself, and of course, you are not the ego anyway. The ego is just the structural organization that allows consciousness to exist in this world. You are clearing the structure so that its lines are simple, clean, aesthetic and balanced. You will still have a form for consciousness when you finish this work. It will be more balanced because you will know who you truly are—you will no longer be identified with the personality.

BLUEPRINTS IN CONSCIOUSNESS

The system of human existence, what we like to call *the separate system*, or the *system of duality*, is a structure held in place by each person's unconscious acceptance of its rules. It is a structure that is, for the most part, hidden in our subconscious. As soon as we become aware of its existence, the rigid hold that this structure has on our lives begins to diminish.

Pain and anger don't seem so real when we see that they have love or joy as an opposite. When we realize that the system is just many frequencies that pass through us, we can take it all much less seriously, and we become much less immersed in it. The content of life, the window dressing, is what fools us all the time. We get deceived by the ever-changing scenery. We don't see that the underlying structure is just a game—the game of life, of course.

As we begin to explore how the game of life works, we become liberated from it. Being liberated does not mean that we go away and never play anymore. We play more easefully and feel freer. We are not as bombarded or as hurt by the content. It no longer seems so real. We have more fun with it when we know it is not real.

So, in this book we examine the structure of human consciousness as a way of analyzing the system in which we live. To give an analogy—if you want to learn about a large building, how would you proceed? You may take the elevator up to the tenth floor, perhaps, and look down so that you get a different view on it. You may peek into one of the rooms, and you get an idea of what is in it—gilt-edged mirrors, paintings and fine furniture. But basically what you are looking at is the surface, the content, the furnishings of the building. If you want to get to know it a lot more explicitly, the obvious solution would be to go down to City Hall and to pull out the blueprints, the plans created by the architect in the process of designing the building. If you want to make the acquaintance of it in fine detail, you need to see how it has been structured and put together. You need to locate the plumbing and electrical installations, the switch boxes, the elevator shafts and everything that is hidden when you are inside the building, getting a whole different viewpoint on the building. That is what we are doing. We are taking a new look at human consciousness by pulling out the blueprint to see how it all works. We will have a much clearer idea when we have seen it right to its core. We are not simply taken in by the gilt-edged mirrors, the fine furnishings, and the trappings of life, the superficial joys of the building.

By doing this, we begin to see that the Self permeates the whole building. The Self is throughout the building—in every atom of it, even in the air in the rooms. There is nothing it is not. However, until we have examined the blueprints and the underlying structure, we are generally not conscious of this. It is only after going to City Hall and *waking up* to the underlying structure that we are no longer fooled by the surface appearance. In doing so, we become conscious—we become the witness to the whole thing. Becoming the witness is the birth of awakening to our true nature as the Self.

And that is life. Most people see only the surface. But if you want to wake up, you need to see the blueprint—because when you do, you see yourself. You examine the world through your own personality. The edges of your personality are actually the edges of the world—your world—your description of the world.

So it is time for you to examine and look carefully at who you are or who you think you are in your human form. Because as you get better at it, as you progress, you will awaken to a new you—the real you—and you will surrender your old form. That does not mean you will disappear in a puff of smoke and vanish without a trace. No, there will still be a body there. If you stand in front of a mirror, you will still see a body. Other people will see a body; you will look just the same. But you are not; you are different. Inside, you see the world differently. You have a different description of who you are, because you have seen the blueprints. This gives you a tremendous advantage in dealing with your life because you have mastery of the egoic self, rather than its having mastery over you. Rather than being swept along by the roller coaster of life and being fooled by the trappings of the world, you are living from soul consciousness. You are seeing the world with clear eyes and living in truth.

DEVELOPING THE RIGHT MINDSET— YOUR NEUTRAL WITNESS

In order to *see* our patterns of thought and behavior, we need to dis-identify with the personality—with the emotions, thoughts, and physical pains/joys that make up daily life. To this end, we can view our world from a more detached perspective, a perspective somewhat similar to the fulcrum point on a teeter–totter. As emotional triggers send the egoic self spiraling up or down a range of emotions based on ingrained patterns of response, there is a part of us, that connection to the Self, that remains a detached observer of everything that is going on. From this neutral witness's perspective, as we are increasingly able to access it, we will be able to understand why things happen the way they do in life, which is the first step toward making positive change.

How do we initially access and cultivate a relationship with the neutral witness? Paradoxically, it would seem, a natural by-product of working through the exercises in Section Two is the development of what we call the neutral witness. It is a scenario of *which comes first, the exercise or the witness?* In this case, you need to get into the exercises in order to practice being aware from a detached perspective. As your neutral witness develops, the exercises will take less time and yield more powerful results.

At this point, it is simply enough that you understand the concept of the neutral witness and desire to access it for your own personal growth. Say a prayer about it and ask for help. You can also use some of the suggestions in Chapter 14—Developing the Witness to encourage progress. There are some simple signs that will help you judge whether you are truly in a neutral witness state at various times in your life. On a mental level, you may acknowledge from time to time your connectedness to people and things around you. You may also experience mental understandings of truth, which could result in a newfound tolerance and love of others, or in wisdom. On an emotional level, you may experience an episode of sadness and crying, but you also maintain a sense of being okay. You descend the negative spiral, but are conscious and detached about the descent. You may also experience states such as compassion, generosity and humility, which are also indicators of the witness state. On a physical level, even in the face of stressful situations, you may feel an inner calmness and sense of overall peace, a lower heart rate and slow, deep breathing.

So, we have two sides of a pair of opposites. Right in the middle is the point of balance, the fulcrum. That is where the neutral witness is situated. (See the illustration on the following page.) Neutrality has great power. If you can maintain a position of neutrality, you can detach from negative experiences even as they happen to you.

Remember that in the beginning it is very difficult to detach. We run on automatic and get caught up in life's dramas because we cannot help ourselves. We may even see ourselves choosing to get caught up, but we cannot stop it. We just find ourselves in the same old behavior patterns of ego, which is like a loop in a computer program. That is why it is

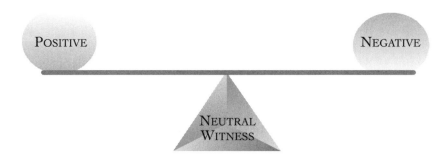

The neutral witness

important to stick with the exercises, continuing to devote time and energy toward doing inner work—which will eventually enable us to assume the role of the neutral witness, at will, under any circumstance.

HOW TO USE SECTION TWO

Take your time with each chapter; they are not meant to be rushed through. Each technique will help you move a lot of stuck energy, and so it is important for you to honor yourself and your body as you learn to process. It is best to pace yourself throughout this section according to your own discernment. You will get the most out of it if you spend at least a week or so on each chapter, as each technique will take some time to master and as the exercises at the end of each chapter are designed to take a few days to complete. You can turn this section into a seven-week course. Or if you prefer a more formless approach, just move through it at your own speed. Especially, it is most important to spend plenty of time digesting and practicing the technique in Chapter Nine—Polarities, as this is the foundation for the rest of the techniques.

The ultimate goal is to make the processing techniques your own. There is no right and wrong to any of this. There are some suggestions for putting theory into practice at the end of each chapter just to help you get started. Please don't let this format restrict you. The tools are offered in the spirit of service, so that anyone can freely take them, adapt them, build on them, enhance them and use them however is best. Get creative with the techniques. Make up your own style. Share them with others.

The techniques are presented in their current order because each chapter's method builds on the previous chapter's method. But when you have finished learning all of the methods, you can use them in any order you wish. Apply them to your life as you see fit, according to your own intuition and discernment.

You can use any personal blank notebook to do any of the methods. If you are serious about change, it is an excellent idea to keep a good notebook. As you continue to do the clearing work, you will be exploring your patterns of thinking and behavior more deeply. Because life cycles around, you will want to review what you did previously. You will see how we all return to cycle through the same thing again and again. The chances are that the second time you do the process, you will go a lot deeper. Keeping a good journal also helps to ground your experiences in the physical world. You bring it from the realm of ideas and formlessness into form and make it more tangible.

The Marriage of Spirit methods are not intended to be the only tool you use. It is best to supplement your processing work with other forms of spiritual practice, such as: meditation, hatha yoga, emotional release therapy, or others.

There is a story/testimonial at the end of each chapter. Each was written by a person who had profound transformational experiences with the Marriage of Spirit processing techniques. I hope their examples will deepen your understanding of the potential for processing and inspire you to continue with your processing work. It is important to remember that these examples make good stories because they are about spectacular issues. Remember that often it takes longer to get these kinds of results. The degree of change you see in your own outer world depends on how ripe for transformation you are and how dedicated you are to your own spiritual growth.

Here are some suggestions to make your processing pleasant and successful:
- Pick a suitable time with no interruptions, allowing enough time to complete at least one full exercise. Especially in the beginning it is important to give it your full concentration. Initially, you may find yourself spending a few days reading through a chapter and working on your first exercise concurrently, and this is to be expected.
- Choose quiet surroundings.
- Turn off your phone's ringer.
- Get a new notebook and dedicate it exclusively to processing.
- Get two different colored pens or a highlighter.
- A thesaurus and a dictionary of synonyms and antonyms are also helpful.
- Remember to date each processing session.

If the techniques are helpful, you may find that using them becomes a way of life. There are many people for whom this is true. Hopefully you will find that by using them, they help you master the art of life in the world of duality. Life becomes much more easeful, joyful and uplifting, as you dance with grace.

The ego is like a stick that seems to divide the water in two. It makes you feel that you are one and I am another. When the ego disappears (in samadhi) one realizes Brahman as one's own inner consciousness.

—Sri Ramakrishna

NINE

POLARITIES

The polarity processing method is a perfect tool to use to free yourself. You can use it to process the polarities involved in experiences that you would like to clear, experiences that are non-productive and self-destructive—that you would choose not to have happen again.

When an unpleasant experience has already happened, there is nothing you can do about it. You cannot undo it. But you can take a look at it and clear it. Or you can take steps toward clearing it so that a similar experience does not happen again. So when a bad experience is over and you feel terrible, you realize it did not help you at all, and you say to yourself, "Well, I'm not going to do *that* again." At that point, you need to process it.

Usually, it is not possible just to use your will and say, "I will not do that again." Sometimes you can. What we are talking about here has nothing to do with will. This is about clearing away the programming that makes you do those non-productive things, so that you have *less desire or fear* next time.

You cannot always clear a bad experience completely with one process. If it is a deeply ingrained behavior, you will have to do it again and again—the *same* process. Every time it comes up, you do the same process, but each time you do it, you shave another layer off the grooves you have cut in the past. And the desire to go on that old track gets less and less. Finally you will erase the pattern completely. Processing peels off these layers just like layers of an onion. So do not be discouraged if you do a process, have a clearing, and then three weeks later it seems like you are in it again. It is the next layer down.

THE POLARITY PROCESSING TECHNIQUE

We begin by finding the pairs of opposites that are involved in the situation. The very beginning level of this is presented here. Later, we will get into more advanced levels. This level is very simple really.

You will need to get a journal. Just a spiral-bound notebook is fine. Keep it exclusively for your processes. Always date the top of the page so that you can keep track of the processes over several months. This will be helpful later.

STEP ONE—PICK AN EXPERIENCE

Processing can be used for many types of experiences. It may be a very old experience from childhood or a more recent one. This process works to untie knots in the mind no matter when the incident occurred; it is even useful with clearing samsara (past life tendencies). For example, the incident could be a memory of being scolded and humiliated by your second grade teacher, or it could be an argument that you had this morning with your spouse or roommate. The processing also works for more severe traumas, things such as sexual abuse or the death of a loved one. You can even use the method to clear experiences that don't involve another person. Perhaps it is a situation that happened when you were alone, like having an accident and hurting yourself; or one that is internal for you, like a vague sense of depression or worthlessness for no apparent reason; or one involving something inanimate, like never feeling you have enough money or food. These can all be worked with using the polarity processing method.

Let's say it was a very negative experience that just happened, and it has left you in shreds. You have calmed down a bit, and you are coherent enough to be able to address it. So, you sit down with your notebook.

STEP TWO—WRITE ABOUT THE EXPERIENCE

You have to tell the story to yourself and write it down. You can do *stream-of-consciousness* writing, if that works for you. Just say everything. You don't have to write it in a careful way. Don't edit it, either inside your head or on the paper. Don't even bother to punctuate it if you don't want to. Just write it down as though you were a child spilling out the story to a parent or friend. It is especially important to write about your feelings, thoughts and states of mind that occurred around the incident. Keep asking yourself, "How did/does this make me feel?" Use lots of adjectives and be very descriptive. If another person is involved in the story, it is also important to describe your perception of that person, too. Make sure to empty your cup completely. The more you capture all of the thoughts, emotions and states of mind involved, the bigger the breakthrough you will have. Be very extravagant with your use of the paper; get it all down.

If you feel you tend to struggle with writing, you might try talking into a tape recorder and then transcribing the story onto paper. Sometimes that works really well for people without a lot of writing experience; it is easier to be in the emotions of the incident if you don't have to focus on the writing.

An Example Story

Here is an example of a story written by someone we will call Paul. Of the thousands of processing stories we have worked with over the years, we have purposefully chosen this example because it is a very simple example and because it is a situation that most people will have no trouble identifying with. It also is a good example of how you can process an apparently mundane occurrence, gain tremendous insight from it and experience a deep healing. It is important to remember, however, that you can also process issues of a much more traumatic nature using the methods presented here—issues such as bankruptcy, divorce or being fired. By working with Paul's story in each chapter throughout Section Two of this book, hopefully you will see how processing something simple can evolve into something profound.

I was driving on the freeway, and I was in a hurry to get home for an appointment. I always allow myself a little extra time, but the freeway is usually not very crowded. This particular day there were not too many cars. At one point there was a cement truck in front of me, going pretty slow, and there were two cars between me and the cement truck. At about the same time, because of some construction work, we began to approach a flashing-arrow sign way up ahead, indicating we were supposed to move into the left lane, since the two-lane freeway was about to merge into one lane. So of course, one of the cars in front of me pulled out into the left lane to pass the cement truck, in order not to get stuck behind it. The other car did not pull out. It stayed behind the cement truck. So, I started to pull out into the left lane to pass. But just at the last second, the car between me and the truck decided to pass the truck, too, and so she pulled out right in front of me, causing me to slam on my brakes. I started swearing and said to myself, "Watch where you're going! You're going to kill us both!"

Then, the strange thing is that as she passed the truck, she slowed down to the same speed as the truck. So, I was hemmed in. And, she decided not to pass the truck. Instead, she let the truck in ahead of her! The truck was going about 45mph in a 65mph zone. So, then the truck was ahead of both of us in the single lane. I was really angry because I was feeling like I was going to be late, like this driver in front of me was totally crazy, dimwitted and idiotic and going to cause an accident. I got very impatient. I sometimes tend to be impatient in my life, and the freeway is where it shows up the most. I got hot under the collar because I knew we were going to be crawling along for about ten minutes before the freeway opened up again into two lanes, and I was going to be late.

Finally, the freeway opened up into two lanes, and the cement truck moved over into the right lane. But! Then the slow driver decided to stay in front of me in the left lane, still keeping pace with the truck on the right. So I couldn't pass, and we were all doing about 50mph in a 75mph zone. I thought, "What is going on?! Maybe she is sick or something." So, I honked. No response. I started to tailgate, getting up really close to her bumper. She just ignored me. She was breaking the law by not yielding. Then a few more cars were starting to pile up behind my car. I was thinking, "You are a complete insensitive jerk. What if I or someone else had an emergency? What if I or someone else needed to go to the hospital?" I felt like a total victim. With the car in front of me tyrannically controlling the situation, I felt like I wanted to kill her and was in rage. It escalated from minor irritation to feeling like if I had a gun, I would have shot her tires out!

I was taking it all very personally. Never mind the cars behind me—I can't get through. It wasn't an older person. She seemed quite young, and young people usually speed, not crawl. She was toying with me. There was no other explanation. Finally, she pulled over, taking her sweet time. Only when she decided to let me by did I get a look at her. She looked about 19, and she was snickering at me. So, then I got really enraged. I almost gave her the finger. But I thought, "No, no, restrain yourself. It's not worth it."

So, my exit came up, and I got off the freeway. I was trying to calm down. There was somewhat of a witness there, but in the heat of the moment, I really had absolutely no witness. I felt very helpless and powerless because there was nothing I could do. Indignation. Impatient. Anger. Fury. Killer instinct. Everything came up within ten minutes. It was so weird, too. People just don't often behave like she did.

I wasn't late, but I was so angry that somebody would purposefully manipulate and slow me down like that. What a pain in the butt. She was controlling the whole situation. I had a lot of heat in my body as a result, a prickly sensation. I felt really contracted, and it took me about half an hour to unwind. I was still seething when I got home. I couldn't release the feelings. I wanted to release them at her, let her really know what I thought, but of course she wasn't available. Finally I was able to calm down and neutralize, but it took a long time before I could let go and forgive her. My reaction was so over the top. Instead of being calm, I just blew up. Usually I handle things like that a lot better.

STEP THREE—PICK OUT THE THEME WORDS AND PHRASES

With a colored marker or highlighter go back through the story, and pick out all the theme words and phrases. Theme words and phrases reflect states of mind that have a charge for you. This includes feelings and emotions as well. You want to find words and phrases like: CONTROL, ANGER, HELPLESS, VICTIMIZED, CAUSE AN ACCIDENT. These are all themes.

*Theme words and phrases reflect the structure
of the experience rather than the content.*

As we discussed earlier, the content of the experience is the surface story of what happened, who said what, and when, and what the worldly details looked like. This initial step belongs in the writing of the story. The content of the story is actually irrelevant except that it leads us to the next step, which is to find the structure of the story. We are looking at the underlying *structure* of the experience, the blueprint or template. To find that, we have to go deeper. The content is world stuff, stories, drama. It is a distraction. We cannot work with it for change because it is too superficial.

*We must focus on looking for theme words and phrases that
represent the states of mind, not the content.*

With this process we are trying to see our characteristic patterns of reaction. We are not looking for the information content of the story. For example, this story's content is about drivers, freeways, construction work and a truck. We are looking for the emotional and mental states and the way the personality pattern usually reacts. We are looking for the *juicy* words and phrases, the ones that have a *charge* for the personality, the ones it reacts to. Often, adjectives and adverbs are juicy.

Theme words and phrases such as: HURRY, IMPATIENT, ENRAGED, INSENSITIVE JERK, BREAKING THE LAW, TOYING WITH ME, POWERLESS, and BLEW UP are the constructs, the frequencies, that are structuring the story. Those are the forces that are shaping the circumstances. The structure is made of the actual frequencies of the experience, the states of mind that were present. In some other story, the themes might be something like: SURPRISED, SHOCKED, CONFUSED, UNCERTAIN, DOUBTFUL, PAIN, BETRAYED, FEAR, GUILT, APPROVAL. We underline these kinds of words or highlight them with a marker.

It is also important to know that there is no right and wrong to this method. You need to feel and discern for yourself what your own theme words and phrases are, what has a charge on it for you, what your own underlying structure is. You can even make up your own words! Sometimes these are the most powerful ones to work with, because they are unique to your patterning and your life.

When you write the story, you do not necessarily have to write down only the states of mind which *you* are experiencing. If you are having a disagreement or conflict with someone and you saw that *they* were bursting at the seams because they were so angry, you put down ANGER. It does not make any difference whether it is your state of mind or theirs. What you want to do is extract the structure of the whole experience, yours and theirs. So write what you see them doing and what you feel yourself doing. *Both.* You are processing their stuff and yours. The reason you do that is because *their states are as much a part of the experience as yours.* Whatever you see before your eyes is your own unconscious stuff. You are having somebody else act out your projections for you. So, you process *both experiences* with the understanding that *everything is part of the pattern that you are addressing.* That is the basic premise for doing this work.

That is how you really effect integration, when you *own everything*, what you see outside of you and what you feel inside. In the beginning it is enough to make an inner commitment and intention to own everything. As you develop your skills with the processing method, your witness becomes stronger and more of the unconscious becomes conscious, which will allow you to really see that you are everything. So, in the beginning you simply need to say the words and make the intention that you *own the outside* as you. With practice, you will experience it, and you will gain a visceral understanding of the principle. If you have resistance to that notion and you are just not ready to own the outside as part of the pattern, here are some suggestions. You can re-read the early chapters of this book which discuss and detail universal laws such as this one. You can meditate and ask inwardly for help. You can ask to be shown what the block is and how to remove it. Perhaps you can make a leap of faith, try out the processing tools, and just see if they will work for you.

EXAMPLE OF STORY WITH HIGHLIGHTED THEME WORDS AND PHRASES

Here is what Paul's story looked like after he underlined his own particular theme words and phrases. All of these words had a charge on them for Paul:

> *I was driving on the freeway, and I was in a <u>hurry</u> to get home for an appointment. I always allow myself a little <u>extra time,</u> but the freeway is usually <u>not very crowded</u>. This particular day there were not many cars. At one point there was a cement truck in front of me, going pretty <u>slow</u>, and there were also two cars between me and the cement truck. At about the same time, because of some construction work, we began to approach a flashing-arrow sign way up ahead, indicating we were supposed to move into the left lane, since the two-lane freeway was about to merge into one lane. So of course, one of the cars in front of me pulled out into the left lane to pass the cement truck, in order not to <u>get stuck</u> behind it. The other car did not pull out. It stayed <u>behind</u> the cement truck. So, I started to pull out into the left lane to pass. But just at the last second, the car between me and the truck decided to pass the truck, too, and so she pulled out right in front of me, causing me to <u>slam on my brakes</u>. I started <u>swearing</u> and said to myself, "<u>Watch where you're going</u>! You're going to <u>kill</u> us both!"*
>
> *Then, the really <u>strange</u> thing is that as she passed the truck, she <u>slowed down</u> to the*

same speed as the truck. So, I was <u>hemmed in</u>. And, she decided not to pass the truck. Instead, she let the truck in <u>ahead</u> of her! The truck was going about 45mph in a 65mph zone. So, then the truck was ahead of both of us in the single lane. I was really <u>angry</u> because I was feeling like I was going to be <u>late</u>, like this driver in front of me was totally <u>crazy, dimwitted</u> and <u>idiotic</u> and going to <u>cause an accident</u>. I got very <u>impatient.</u> I sometimes tend to be impatient in my life, and the freeway is where it shows up the most. I got <u>hot under the collar</u> because I knew we were going to be <u>crawling along</u> for about ten minutes before the freeway opened up again into two lanes, and I was going to be <u>late</u>.

Finally, the freeway opened up into two lanes, and the cement truck moved over into the right lane. But! Then the <u>slow</u> driver decided to stay <u>in front</u> of me in the left lane, still <u>keeping pace</u> with the truck on the right. So I couldn't pass, and we were all doing about 50mph in a 75mph zone. I thought, "What is going on?! Maybe she is <u>sick</u> or something." So, I honked. <u>No response</u>. I started to <u>tailgate</u>, getting up really close to her bumper. She just <u>ignored</u> me. She was <u>breaking the law</u> by <u>not yielding</u>. Then a few more cars were starting to pile up behind my car. I was thinking, "You are a complete <u>insensitive jerk</u>. What if I or someone else had an <u>emergency</u>? What if I or someone else needed to go to the hospital?" I felt like a total <u>victim</u>. With the car in front of me <u>tyrannically</u> <u>controlling</u> the situation, I felt like I wanted to <u>kill her</u> and was in <u>rage</u>. It escalated from <u>minor irritation</u> to feeling like if I had a gun, I would have <u>shot her tires out</u>!

I was taking it all very <u>personally</u>. Never mind the cars behind me—<u>I</u> can't get through. It wasn't an <u>older</u> person. She seemed quite <u>young</u>, and young people usually <u>speed</u>, not crawl. She was <u>toying with me</u>. There was no other explanation. Finally, she pulled over, <u>taking her sweet time</u>. Only when she decided to let me by did I get a look at her. She looked about 19, and she was <u>snickering at me</u>. So, then I got really <u>enraged</u>. I almost <u>gave her the finger</u>. But I thought, "No, no, <u>restrain</u> yourself. <u>It's not worth it.</u>"

So, my exit came up, and I got off the freeway. I was trying to <u>calm down</u>. There was somewhat of a <u>witness</u> there, but in the <u>heat of the moment</u>, I really had absolutely no witness. I felt very <u>helpless</u> and <u>powerless</u> because there was <u>nothing I could do</u>. <u>Indignation</u>. <u>Impatient</u>. <u>Anger</u>. <u>Fury</u>. <u>Killer instinct</u>. Everything came up within ten minutes. It was so <u>weird</u>, too. People just don't often behave like she did.

I wasn't late, but I was so <u>angry</u> that somebody would <u>purposefully</u> <u>manipulate</u> and <u>slow me down</u> like that. What a <u>pain in the butt</u>. She was <u>controlling</u> the whole situation. I had a lot of <u>heat</u> in my body as a result, a <u>prickly</u> sensation. I felt really <u>contracted</u>, and it took me about a half an hour to <u>unwind</u>. I was still <u>seething</u> when I got <u>home</u>. I <u>couldn't release</u> the feelings. I wanted to release them at her, let her <u>really know what I thought</u>, but of course she wasn't <u>available</u>. Finally I was able to <u>calm down</u> and <u>neutralize</u>, but it took a <u>long time</u> before I could <u>let go</u> and <u>forgive</u> her. My <u>reaction</u> was so <u>over the top</u>. Instead of being <u>calm</u>, I just <u>blew up</u>. Usually I handle things like that a lot <u>better</u>.

STEP FOUR—MAKE A LIST OF THE THEME WORDS AND PHRASES

Remember, it is important to pick out your own theme words, based on your own intuition and on what has a charge for you. You may not have chosen the same ones as Paul did. You must do whatever you feel works the best for you.

During the course of the experience, Paul cycled through a number of states of mind and saw the other person in the story doing the same. These states of mind should all be underlined in the written version of the story. Then, on another clean sheet of paper, rewrite all of those underlined words from the story, making a column with them down the left side of the new page. This way, you are isolating all the states of mind in the story— yours and the other person's. Usually they are all negative, but if there are positive states, put those down as well. You must generate a list that is as long as possible. To get it as long as possible, you have to go into all the subtle nuances. Remember to be really extravagant with paper. Do not try to economize at all. Write everything possible. The more words you get, the bigger the breakthrough. Usually when you write these lists, they end up being a few pages long. You can get quite long lists out of a story. The longer the better.

Once you have understood how the processing works, it is no longer necessary to write down the story. You can go straight into making the list of words.

EXAMPLE LIST OF THEME WORDS AND PHRASES

Here is the list of theme words and phrases that Paul extracted from his story. Look at how short that story was and how many words he got out of it.

hurry
extra time
not very crowded
slow
get stuck
behind
slam on my brakes
swearing
Watch where you're going!
kill
strange
slowed down
hemmed in
ahead
angry

late
crazy
dimwitted
idiotic
cause an accident
impatient
hot under the collar
crawling along
late
slow
in front
keeping pace
sick
No response
tailgate
ignored
breaking the law
not yielding
insensitive jerk
emergency
victim
tyrannically
controlling
kill her
rage
minor irritation
shot her tires out
personally
I
older
young
speed
toying with me
taking her sweet time
snickering at me
enraged
gave her the finger
restrain

It's not worth it
calm down
witness
heat of the moment
helpless
powerless
nothing I could do
Indignation
Impatient
Anger
Fury
Killer instinct
weird
angry
purposefully
manipulate
slow me down
pain in the butt
controlling
heat
prickly
contracted
unwind
seething
home
couldn't release
really know what I thought
available
calm down
neutralize
long time
let go
forgive
reaction
over the top
calm
blew up
better

MORE WORDS AND PHRASES

Sometimes, as you pick out the words, they remind you of other words that could be added to your list. There may be words related to the incident that you did not mention in your original narration. Add them to your list, even if they were not in the original story and if you thought of them later. The more comprehensive your list, the more likely that you will get good results with this technique. It is important to find all of the subtle nuances of feeling. Go really, really deep in your quest to understand the situation that you are processing. Remember to ask yourself, "How did/does this make me *feel?*" Nothing is too inconsequential to be included in your list.

For example, if you have the word *anger* on your page, probe to see what the anger is made of. Anger is actually a composite word describing a great range of different frequencies, and you may find aspects like *hate, violence, rage, explosiveness, dominance, vengefulness, spite.* Use a thesaurus if you have to, to try to pick out all of the subtle nuances of energy contained in the situation. Each word represents a vibratory frequency, which fills in the picture much more clearly. The more filled-in the picture is, the bigger the breakthrough you are going to have, and the more tangible the shift will be.

Here are Paul's afterthoughts and the extra words he added to the list:

> *I realized that when she pulled out in front of me, I went into total <u>shock</u>. It was so <u>sudden</u> and <u>unexpected</u> and <u>scary</u>. My body was full of adrenaline and <u>fear</u>. Also, after I got home, got past my <u>rage</u> and <u>calmed down</u>, I realized how <u>ashamed</u> I was of how I reacted. I felt somewhat <u>humiliated</u> that such a <u>silly</u> incident got the <u>best of me</u>. I was also very <u>confused</u> about why it made me so angry, such a silly little prank the girl pulled. I <u>don't understand</u> what happened.*

shock
sudden
unexpected
scary
fear
rage
calmed down
ashamed
humiliated
silly
best of me
confused
don't understand

STEP FIVE—FIND THE OPPOSITES

Then find the opposites of the words in your list of theme words. Make a column of the antonyms (opposites) on the right side of the page. Sometimes you just cannot think of some of the opposites. That is because you have them locked in the unconscious. For those times, use a dictionary of synonyms and antonyms, which you can get at almost any book store. This is not an ordinary dictionary but one that specifically has opposites in it. You can also use a thesaurus. These come in extremely handy in this work. In fact they are almost essential because they help reveal your unconscious by giving you words you would not have thought of on your own, which is the whole point of the work.

You will notice there is sometimes more than one word possible as the opposite. A word might have different opposites depending on what the meaning was in a specific case. For example, sometimes LOVE can have the opposite HATE, and other times it can have the opposite FEAR. So depending on what *your* story was about, the opposites might not always be the same. You can write both pairs of opposites or choose the one that works best for you.

If you see a word come up more than once in the story, it may have a different meaning in different parts of the story, in which case you might have a different opposite. Or if it repeats a lot, maybe it is a really strong theme in the story, something you will want to make a note of to examine and process further.

Doing this work really increases your vocabulary as well as your ability to describe your states of mind and feelings. You are reminded constantly of what is happening in your unconscious. It is an amazing and powerful way of looking into the unconscious. When you do see the unconscious opposite, it *startles* you in a subtle way. Somehow, you immediately wake up to a bigger perspective.

When you find the hidden unconscious piece—sometimes one simple word—that has held a whole pattern of behavior in place for you, it is a revelation that allows you to expand and see much more of yourself. You get an *aha* not only when you reveal the hidden side of the personality, but there is the added component of a deeper connection with your soul. You find yourself opening to the vast storehouse of your own power that lay dormant until the unconscious was made conscious. Wisdom, heart-centeredness, compassion and the neutral witness begin to become established in your conscious awareness. Insights to a deeper perspective on life awaken in you.

EXAMPLE OF THEME WORDS AND PHRASES WITH THEIR OPPOSITES

Here is what Paul's paper looked like after he found all the opposites:

hurry	slow down
extra time	short of time

not very crowded	crowded
slow	fast
get stuck	get free
behind	in front
slam on my brakes	gun it
swearing	blessing
Watch where you're going!	Watch where I'm going!
kill	save
strange	ordinary/normal
slowed down	speeded up
hemmed in	freed up
ahead	behind
angry	happy
late	early
crazy	sane
dimwitted	bright
idiotic	smart
cause an accident	drive safely
impatient	patient
hot under the collar	cool
crawling along	zipping along
late	on time
slow	fast
in front	in back
keeping pace	lagging
sick	healthy
No response	response
tailgate	allow room
ignored	acknowledged
breaking the law	obeying the law
not yielding	yielding
insensitive jerk	sensitive being
emergency	ordinary
victim	tyrant
tyrannically	victimized
controlling	out of control
kill her	support her
rage	peace

minor irritation	major pain
shot her tires out	forgive her
personally	impersonally
I	She
older	younger
young	old
speed	crawl
toying with me	respecting me
taking her sweet time	considerate of my time
snickering at me	honoring me
enraged	calm
gave her the finger	blew her a kiss
restrain	impulsively dive in
It's not worth it	It is worth it
calm down	stirred up
witness	reactive
heat of the moment	in retrospect
helpless	capable
powerless	powerful
nothing I could do	in control
Indignation	imperturbability
Impatient	patient
Anger	joy
Fury	calm
Killer instinct	preserving
weird	normal
angry	peaceful
purposefully	accidental
manipulate	not in control
slow me down	let me pass
pain in the butt	relief
controlling	out of control
heat	cold
prickly	smooth
contracted	expanded
unwind	wound-up
seething	at peace
home	dangerous freeway jungle

couldn't release	let go
really know what I thought	stifling reaction
available	not available
calm down	get excited
neutralize	get anxious
long time	short while
let go	hold on
forgive	revenge
reaction	non-reaction
over the top	subtle
calm	aggravated
blew up	self-contained
better	worse
shock	sedate
sudden	gradual
unexpected	expected
scary	pleasing
fear	fearlessness
rage	serenity
calmed down	exploded
ashamed	proud
humiliated	haughty
silly	serious
best of me	worst of me
confused	clear
don't understand	understand

Did you notice how a word like *angry* that is repeated several times can have a different opposite each time? Paul used *happy*, *joy*, *peaceful* and *serenity* as opposites. Remember that it is okay to include words in your list repeatedly. It usually indicates that this a major theme of your current process that you may want to examine more in detail. For Paul, *angry* and *control* are some of the words repeated often.

Remember that we contain both sides of the list within ourselves.

STEP SIX — OFFER IT UP WITH A PRAYER

When you have your list, find all of the opposites and feel that you have emptied your cup, then offer it up to spirit. You do this with a prayer. You ask higher consciousness to take these unbalanced states of mind, which you have in your being at that moment, and to bring them into balance, so that clarity and a new level of seeing come to you. Then just remember to say, "Thank you," and trust completely that it will be done. Here is the kind of prayer you will want to make:

PRAYER

Oh Eternity, please take all of these states of mind which
are unbalanced in this pattern and balance and clear them. Do this so
that I may see more clearly and find my way home more easily.
I give thanks knowing it will be done.

You are welcome to write your own version of the prayer. Initially it is best to actually say the prayer, either out loud or inwardly, because it is in the spirit of what you are seeking. It is important to be precise and reverent in the beginning until the spirit of the prayer is inside you and runs automatically. After a while, you just need to hold the feeling level of the prayer for a moment—the surrender and the gratitude—instead of actually verbalizing all of it. The shift does happen. The prayer works.

It works because whenever you find both the
conscious and unconscious aspects of any situation, asking spirit to
take it and balance it for you, you will experience a freeing
from your egoic programming.

Here is how Paul chose to offer his prayer: "Divine Mother, Father, God, I offer up these polarities, these imbalances. I ask you to please take them from me. Please bring me into the place of the neutral witness, into detachment. I especially offer up the polarity of *control* and *out of control* and pray for release from this imbalance. I offer it all up and pray for grace. I trust that the changes will be made for me. I give thanks and offer gratitude. Amen."

STEP SEVEN—WAIT FOR GRACE

Wait a few minutes. Go wash some dishes, or make yourself a cup of tea. When grace comes in, you may feel a shift in your physical body or in your subtle body. Or maybe you will have some emotions pass through. Or perhaps you will suddenly start getting insights. Or that night you might have a significant dream. Or the next day you might have some special experience. Sometimes it will come in the form of a friend or mentor sharing information with you that you find meaningful. Any of these experiences is more usual than not because the layer that you have put down on paper has been lifted, and you are seeing into the next layer. Spirit will peel off a veil for you, and suddenly you can see a deeper level of the structure.

If you do not feel the shift happen, it does not matter. You may not feel it the first couple of times you do the lists. A shift will definitely happen, but you may not recognize it. It is a funny thing about consciousness shifting. One cannot always see it. Because we are identified with the state we are in at any given moment, we simply flow with the shift, not recognizing the subtlety of what has happened. With practice and a strong witness, it becomes clearer to us that awareness is shifting.

Remember that the reason the process must be repeated over and over again is because the personality is like the layers of an onion. Peel away a little bit, and there is more underneath it. You will think to yourself, "I know I've done this one before! I *know* I've already processed this!" But you've got to keep re-doing it until it settles down for you.

It is important to remember that after you have defined the issue fully
and have offered it up, what you want is for <u>you</u>
to not do anything at all. Give the issue over to spirit.

Relax, let go and allow the integration of the two sides. It will happen. It is miraculous that you do not have to continue to analyze everything and to try desperately to make yourself change. You just let go of both sides of the list. This is a very fast way to facilitate change. Most people find it much faster than some other form of therapy.

So you offer it up and let it happen. As you do this over and over again, you will find that fewer things in your life are upsetting. You will find that almost as soon as incidents happen, you can see what the opposite sides are. In fact, when you get really good at this, you don't have to write the narration. You can just jump directly to the list of words. For example, one day you may be driving along in your car, get cut off by another car in traffic, and you can just sit there thinking, "I feel ANGRY... Oh, the opposite is CALM." The writing is redundant once you really know how to do the technique. Then, you offer it up and the volatile feelings release. Eventually, you will only use the writing of narratives and lists when you have a complex situation which you cannot decipher at all.

REVIEW

THE STEPS OF THE POLARITY PROCESSING TECHNIQUE

1. Pick an experience
2. Write a description of the experience
3. Pick out the theme words and phrases
4. Make a list of the theme words and phrases
5. Find the opposites
6. Offer it up with a prayer
7. Wait for grace

PRAYER

Oh Eternity, please take all of these states of mind which are unbalanced in this pattern and balance and clear them. Do this so that I may see more clearly and find my way home more easily. I give thanks knowing it will be done.

SUGGESTIONS FOR PUTTING THEORY INTO PRACTICE

1. Get a journal that you will use exclusively for processing.
2. Pick one story from your current life to process. Don't worry too much about picking the right story to process; getting started is the most important thing.
3. Pick another story from your childhood to process.
4. Try to feel in your mind, emotions and body when a shift occurs for you. Did it happen during the initial list-making? During the offering? While finding one particular opposite? Try to be conscious of what is happening to you during the exercise, even though shifts can be very subtle.
5. If you did not feel any sort of increased clarity or sense of change in yourself as a result of completing the exercise, ask yourself these questions:
   - Did you use enough descriptive words in your narrative? (You may want to try using a thesaurus.)
   - Did you remember to dig deeply inside yourself, always asking, "How did it make me feel?" (You may try using a tape recorder so you can speak your story and be more emotional, rather than writing it.)
   - Did you completely empty your cup into your notebook, or is there more to your story?

- Did you take the time to find all the right opposites for you? (You can use a synonym-antonym dictionary to help.)
- Did you offer it up sincerely and meaningfully?
- Did you really let it go and let grace take over, or is your *do-er* trying to figure it out and to make the shift happen for you? (Remember after you make your prayer offering to *trust* and *surrender control* to higher consciousness. This may be the biggest stumbling block for most people. But don't worry; learning to surrender the *do-er* develops naturally over time.)
- Did you pray and ask for more help to be shown where you are stuck and unconscious? (Be open to receiving answers from *anywhere* and *anyone*.)
- Did you maybe not notice the shift? (Remember that this is okay and very natural in the beginning.)

6. Before moving on to the next chapter, take about a week or so to really practice and digest the polarities technique presented in this chapter.

TESTIMONIAL ◆ SURRENDER

I was living in Los Angeles, and nothing seemed to be working out. What I realized much later was that spirit was telling me it was time to leave Los Angeles and was pushing me out the door. I got a job in Seattle, knowing no one there and only one person in the entire state. The job turned out to be my worst nightmare; my boss and I hated each other. After two months she fired me. So there I was with no job and no money.

I sat down, moved into the neutral observer and asked what this was all about. There was no panic, and I heard back that it was all going to be okay. I wrote some long lists of polarities and did some squares to dissipate some of the energy about failure/success, poverty/wealth, rejection/acceptance, alone/with friends, nightmare job/dream job, and so forth.

I was down to my last few dollars and felt like giving up, but instead I trusted that grace was working things out for me on some other level. About two weeks later, just about the time my rent was due, I received an unexpected referral check in the mail which carried me through the month. The processing was working, and so I continued, making long lists, doing squares and offering them up as I felt moved to. Three weeks later I found a fantastic job. I found out later that my new boss and her boss both had a very strong spiritual orientation. I definitely could see the correlation between the shifts taking place in my outside world and the processing I was doing. I was manifesting the changes in my outer life that I so badly wanted by balancing and clearing my inner life.

That was almost six years ago, and I'm still in the same job, which is the best one I've ever had. A few months after that, after continued processing, I met a wonderful woman, and we've been together over five years. When difficult situations show up, what I've learned to do is move into the neutral observer, look at it as if I were watching someone else, ask what's really going on, and it usually clears up. Doing the lists of polarities and trusting in grace to make the shifts for me is amazingly magical. It really works.

The Great Way is not difficult
for those who have no preferences.
When love and hate are both absent
everything becomes clear and undisguised.
Make the smallest distinction, however,
and heaven and earth are set infinitely apart.

—Sengtsan, Third Zen Patriarch

TEN

TRIANGLES

Before reading this chapter, it is best to make sure you have had plenty of time to digest and practice the polarity processing technique presented in Chapter Nine—Polarities, as the triangles technique builds on the information presented there. The triangles technique helps to effect significant changes and clearing in the emotions. We reconcile the unbalanced polarities and move into an integrated emotional state. In doing triangles, we proactively assist grace with the ascension of awareness to the unified state.

STEP ONE—CHOOSE A POLARITY

To do a triangle, first choose a polarity that has a charge on it for you, some aspect of your patterning that you feel you want to work on a little further. An example might be a certain polarity that kept recurring in your story that you wrote during the previous exercise. When you have a polarity to work with, write the polarity on the bottom two points of a triangle, along the baseline.

STEP TWO—FIND THE ASCENDED BALANCE

Then try to find a word that feels to you as though it reconciles the polarity, a word that brings the polarity into balance and harmony. Write this word at the top of the triangle. When you find the right word, you move more into your heart. We call it the *ascended balance*.

It is not always easy to see the ascended state. The reason is because in finding what fits at the top, we actually have to reorganize our inner perceptions and become conscious of heart-centered emotions and states of mind. The challenge with triangles is that we are using the conscious mind to intuit the ascended balance state, whereas with the opposites technique, we simply ask grace to reconcile the polarity, and to institute the ascended balance state. Some people who really use opposites a lot still have trouble in the beginning with the triangles. This is because in finding the ascended state, there has to be a conscious awakening of the heart, of the integrated emotions. After we have done a bit of work with the opposites, grace unifies the polarities and puts us in the higher state, allowing us to find the ascended balance more easily.

THE ASCENDED BALANCE STATES

The ascended balance states are cleared emotional states. They are heart-centered states that are rather uncommon in this world. Here is a list of many of them. *Feel* how they reflect a rare level of balance, stability and maturity.

You may find it helpful to write this list on the inside cover of your journal. It becomes a handy reference when doing triangles and will act as a map on your journey to the ascended state.

ACCEPTANCE	HARMLESSNESS
ATTUNEMENT	HARMONY
BALANCE	HUMILITY
BLISS (ANANDA)	IMPECCABILITY
CLARITY	JOY
COMPASSION	LOYALTY
DETACHMENT	NEUTRALITY
DEVOTION	PATIENCE
DHARMA	PURITY
DISCERNMENT	QUIESCENCE
EQUALITY	SAMADHI
EQUANIMITY	SELFLESSNESS
ETERNALITY	SURRENDER
FAITH	TOLERANCE
FLOW	TRUST
FORGIVENESS	TRUTH
GENEROSITY	UNCONDITIONAL LOVE
GRACE	UNITY
GRATITUDE	WISDOM

STEP THREE—OFFER IT UP AND WAIT FOR GRACE

When you have found an ascended balance word, form an intention to have an experience of that state, and/or pray for an experience of it. In this way you are inviting your polarity to integrate into the ascended balance, and you are asking for your consciousness to be raised. You can assist with and participate in this process by quietly meditating as you make your offering and by: 1) visualizing your consciousness as a flow of luminous energy ascending through your body, and 2) sensing the movement through the body and the chakras. This ascension of consciousness in the body and chakras is discussed in greater detail later in the chapter. With practicing the processing techniques, you become more sensitive to and aware of this movement of energy, and you will develop your ability to experience it happening in your body.

As with the polarities and the squares, offer up your process and wait for grace. In the prayer, you can ask for the ascended balance state to be instituted as a new state of consciousness for you in place of the old, polarized consciousness. For example in an offering prayer, you might ask, "In place of the old imbalance of LOVE and HATE, I ask for the new state of COMPASSION to be instituted. I ask to be brought more into my heart."

If you can't find the ascended balance word, it still works to offer up just the polarity. In fact, if you can be in a state of innocence and not-knowingness when you make your offering, you are in a state of humility. You can say, "Please bring me to the place of whatever the ascended balance is, and I don't know what that is. Please show me." You ask for that new place to be instituted, and the understanding comes through feeling and experiencing it.

By asking to be moved into the heart and to live from the heart rather than being stuck in polarity, we ascend and balance—we live in the still point.

SOME EXAMPLES

Looking at examples may be the best way to understand how triangles work. There are many provided in this chapter. To come up with the ascended balance word, try to feel your way into it. It is a very intuitive and feeling-oriented exercise. Especially in the beginning while learning the technique, an excellent way to find the ascended balance for a triangle is to refer to the list of commonly used ascended balance words on the facing page.

EXAMPLE ONE—POWER AND POWERLESSNESS

Let's take POWER and POWERLESSNESS as an example polarity and do the triangle technique with it. It is such a big polarity for everybody. If *power* is on one bottom point, and *powerlessness* is on the other, what would be at the top? Can you guess? How about

HUMILITY? You have to practice and have a bit of experience to find that. Power and powerlessness battle each other. When humility comes, that is the end of the battle. Humility is a state of acceptance of oneself and others. It is a state which encompasses both sides.

Another example of an ascended balance word for this polarity is SURRENDER. The word *surrender* comes from the French *to deliver up* (*sur*=up/upon and *rendre*=to render). Surrender means that we are giving up the separate will, the will of the small, limited self, to God. We are acknowledging to higher consciousness that we are finished with the power games of the separate system, and we wish to give over to a more integrated and balanced form of power. We surrender the illusion of both power and powerlessness. In a state of humility or surrender we find true power, not the limited, polarized kind of power, which is always in an imbalance with powerlessness. Figure 10-1 shows how your journal page would look in this example.

Power-powerlessness is a very basic and deep level of the egoic structure. This could make it a challenging example to find the ascended balance for because aspects of the patterning may be buried deep in the unconscious. There are many sub-categories of power and powerlessness. Let's take a look at one of them and see if it is an easier example.

If we were to take the polarity of SELF-ESTEEM and WORTHLESSNESS (another way of saying power and powerlessness), then perhaps we can get a better sense that HUMILITY would be at the top of the triangle (Fig. 10-2).

Humility is the non-judgment of oneself and others. In humility we do not indulge in feeling worthless, or indulge in feeling

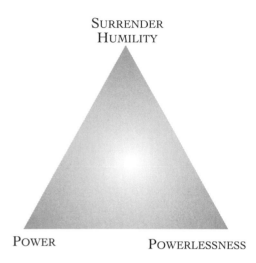

Fig. 10-1.

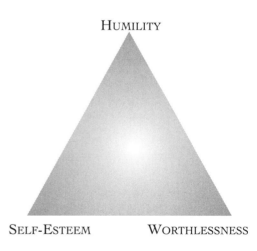

Fig. 10-2.

especially self-important. Humility is not meekness, implying sort of weakness in being humble. It goes beyond being humble. We find true inner power in the state of humility because it is an alignment with higher consciousness.

As shown in the diagram on page 107, the two sides of a pair of opposites create a pendulum effect. Consciousness swings between the two sides. It is the swinging between the two sides that causes suffering in life. By letting that feeling of insecurity…and security…and insecurity…and security…pass right through us, we are in a state of humility. It is a state of non-rebelliousness, non-willfulness, a state of acceptance, a state of quiescence in the mind and emotions. It comes from detachment and from seeing that everything is perfect just as it is.

Ordinarily we might think, "I like to feel self-esteem. Why shouldn't I? What's wrong with that?" It is not wrong. That is not the problem. It can be a polarized state, and if we yearn to feel self-esteem in an unbalanced way, we have to deal with its opposite, worthlessness, at least some of the time. Humility is a more balanced state. It is subtle, because it sees a larger picture than good and bad, right and wrong, important and unimportant. We can still feel self-esteem from the state of humility; it is just that we are not so attached to it and desperate for it anymore. From the place of humility, we can watch self-esteem come and go, and we can watch worthlessness come and go; but we are witnessing the swinging pendulum and are not so caught up in the back and forth of it.

EXAMPLE TWO — LOSS AND GAIN

Since looking at examples is the best way to understand how triangles work, we have included three more here.

If we were to have LOSS and GAIN as the two bottom corners of the triangle, what would the top be? How about NEUTRALITY? It is a very similar state to humility. Neutrality in this instance implies that we have a level of detachment around whether or not we suffer a loss or have the pleasure of gaining something. We are aware of the bigger picture—that whatever we could lose or gain in this transitory world is not permanent. The pleasure or pain of the circumstance would pass through us; we would remain unaffected and not attach to either side (Fig. 10-3).

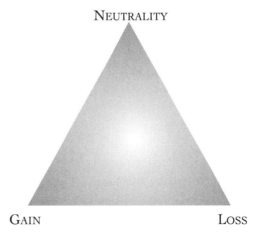

Fig. 10-3.

EXAMPLE THREE — CONTROL AND LOSS OF CONTROL

Here is an example taken from the processing session with Paul, who did the polarity technique about the freeway incident in the last chapter. Paul's biggest charge was on the polarity CONTROL and LOSS OF CONTROL. He used a few words at the top of his triangle: DETACHMENT, SURRENDER and NEUTRALITY. Paul saw his attachment to being in control of the situation, and therefore he got angry when he was not in control. He found that these ascended balance words helped him to move into his heart around the issue, to recover a level of his witness, and to view the drama from a higher perspective (Fig. 10–4).

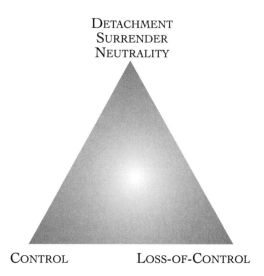

Fig. 10-4.

EXAMPLE FOUR — VICTIM AND TYRANT

Here is an example using a common polarity, VICTIM-TYRANT. The ascended balance could be many different words, depending on the actual situation of the individual—for example: SELFLESSNESS or FORGIVE-NESS. But it is helpful if you can pick out the *one* that works the best for you in that situation. Often you will find many words that fit at the top. That is fine. Try to feel all of them inside yourself and find the one that seems to resonate for you the most.

Selflessness fits because it is a state of giving up the small self, which is embroiled in the drama of being a suffering victim or an oppressive tyrant, and it sees a bigger picture. Forgiveness also works. Forgiveness is a heart state that means we have a level of tolerance

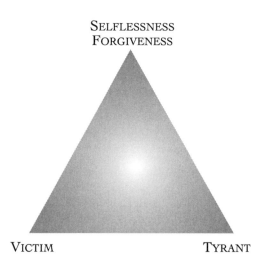

Fig. 10-5.

and understanding for both the victim and the tyrant and that we are not attracted or repulsed by either side. We need to be able to encompass both sides of the polarity without judgment in order to forgive them for being just who they are (Fig. 10-5).

NOTE: If you are having trouble with the triangle technique, you may want to jump ahead and read the next chapter on squares first, and then come back to this chapter. Sometimes, if you work out a square first, then the triangle's ascended state becomes clearer to you.

CREATE A PATHWAY TO THE HEART

In doing the polarity processing technique, you do not have to be conscious of the emotional experience of it. It just happens. If you cannot feel the ascended state, that does not matter. The polarity processing is an intellectual exercise, and the shift takes place through grace by offering up the polarity.

But with doing triangles, by finding the top yourself, you are helping to actively change the emotional body's alignment. By actually hunting around within, intuiting, you become conscious of grace shifting the pathways in your emotional body when you find the ascended balance, or *heart* word. Sometimes it can take a few days and a lot of prayer to find yourself in the middle way, for example in the state of forgiveness, or of compassion, but it is worth it because the changes are permanent.

By participating in this way, you are helping to create that ascension channel inside of you, that pathway into your heart. When you find the ascended balance, you actually are becoming conscious of the resolution of the opposites. You are consciously participating in the ascension process.

Talking about this seems very esoteric. It is really something that has to be experienced. But with time and with practicing the processing techniques, sensitivity in the body and psychic awareness develop, which do allow you to feel the movement of consciousness in your physical body, subtle body and chakras. Triangles are mainly an emotional, intuitive process, and so as you become more sensitive and are able to feel this movement, you will have more tangible and visceral experiences with the triangle technique. If you have not yet read Chapter Seven—Seeing the Light, and if you are unfamiliar with the concepts of the subtle body, the chakras and the ascension of consciousness through the body, then you may want to go back to read Chapter Seven now in order to grasp the concepts presented below.

ATTUNE TO THE MOVEMENT OF CONSCIOUSNESS THROUGH THE BODY

Upon completing the processing work, a releasing will take place. It is helpful to be able to feel the release moving through the chakras and the physical body, although it is not absolutely essential. Not feeling the release does not mean that it is not happening. Usually it simply means that one is not yet sensitive enough to feel the subtle shifting take place. However, go ahead and try to become aware of the movement. The first step is to take a moment to sit quietly and empty yourself while remaining mindful and aware of your bodily sensations. This will institute the neutral witness and will invite your focus to be on the body, simply watching to see what happens. You maximize your release by taking this quiet, neutral moment to empty your attention field and by simply witnessing whatever happens. Again if there is no perception of anything happening, don't be concerned. The movement is generally not felt when you first begin to use this process.

Let's look at the direction that the movement of consciousness usually takes as the releasing happens and as your process resolves itself. This is not always how it will move, but the following description should give a general idea of what to look for.

Most polarities, though not all, operate at a lower level, associated with the third, second and first chakras. The ascended states of balance are associated with the upper chakras, the fourth, fifth, sixth and seventh, beginning at the heart and moving up to the head. To start with, the movement of consciousness will most likely be felt in the third chakra or solar plexus area. This is one area where polarized consciousness centers itself. Initially, prior to experiencing the release and as you are processing, you may feel the polarity as an uncomfortable pushing-pulling sensation in the gut, as nausea, or as a dense, heavy feeling in the pit of your stomach. Doing triangles creates an ascension of emotional energy. So you may feel a movement in the direction of the heart, through the throat, to the third eye. You may feel this movement in your physical body or as subtle sensations in the aura. As the energy moves through the heart center, you may feel states of mind such as love, compassion and forgiveness. As the energy moves through the throat, you may feel the desire to get creative, to give voice to or to express the feelings. As the energy moves into the third eye, you may experience a new sense of wisdom about the situation. The third eye is a place of intuitive understanding of unity, which means that your experience of the polarity from the third eye will allow a viewpoint encompassing both extremes of the polarity. When the consciousness moves up into the heart, throat or third eye, you may feel a new sense of peace, calmness, expandedness and equanimity in your mind and emotions. You may feel that the previous tension or discomfort has been resolved somehow.

To illustrate this movement of consciousness, we will use the example of the polarity IGNORANCE and KNOWLEDGE (Fig. 10-6). Ignorance has the connotation of being bad, since it is a state of lack and powerlessness. Knowledge has a good connotation because it implies having information of some kind; information is power. People generally have prejudice toward those who are ignorant, and a lot of pride about their own knowledge. Intelligence is prized in most cultures, but especially in the West. Most Westerners regard third-world countries and communities of indigenous peoples as hotbeds of ignorance, and therefore inferior. In some Western countries as a way to cope with the national identity of being smart, some people pay outrageous sums of money to put their small children into programs that promise the best college placement. Most people on this planet are conditioned to believe that being smart is superior and being uninformed is inferior.

If you find yourself in a situation where you feel out of balance or judgmental regarding the polarity of IGNORANCE and KNOWLEDGE, you can process it using the polarity processing method described in the previous chapter or with triangles or squares. As you process, you may find a release start to happen for you. As your consciousness moves from the lower chakras toward the higher chakras, here is what you might experience: Resolving this polarity in the heart, where we first begin to experience unity,

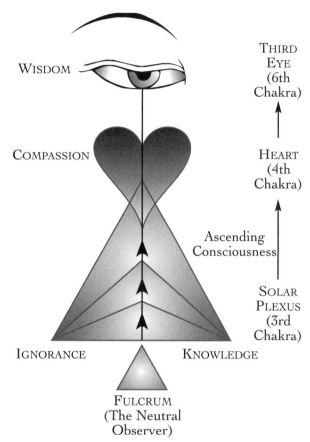

Fig. 10-6.

would awaken certain heart-centered states, based on your individual programming associated with ignorance and knowledge. For example you might come into a place of self-acceptance if you had been feeling somehow resentful of your own ignorance or self-important about your knowledge. Or perhaps if it is someone else's ignorance that you are in judgment of, you might first find the heart state of tolerance.

As you process and settle into a place of comfort with these two states, your emotional clearing could then move your awareness to a place of forgiveness. Forgiveness encompasses the whole heart, including the thymus chakra area, which is between the heart and throat. In other words the heart space expands. Compassion could happen next as the energy expands and ascends into the throat and the third eye. It is understanding coming from the third eye that resolves the situation into compassion. Compassion is a heart-expanding state of complete non-judgment. It implies an attitude of non-judgmentally loving yourself (or someone else), whether or not you (or they) have knowledge or are powerful or powerless. With the awakening of compassion, the heart energy encompasses the third eye. Wisdom or truth is associated with the third eye. Wisdom is the conscious awareness of higher truth, a place of seeing how things really are or the deeper meaning of life.

In our example the energy flow has created a pathway from the third chakra. It has awakened the heart and connected into the intuitive wisdom of the third eye. The awareness has flowed above the sense of separation in the third chakra, has moved into the heart and has been anchored in the unity of the heart. The heart has expanded to where its energy radiates up into the wisdom/truth center of the third eye. And finally the expanded heart radiates down back into the third chakra, dissolving the separation between the original polarity, initiating a new state of unity, which can now be held in the third chakra as well as the heart, thymus and third eye.

When you do the triangle technique, imagine the triangle superimposed over your third and higher chakras, where the baseline is over the third chakra and the apex is over the fourth, fifth or sixth chakra. (Refer to Fig. 10–6.) The polarity, the push-pull, either-or, teeter-totter-like scenario, operates in the consciousness of the third chakra, at the baseline of the triangle. The ascended balance operates in the consciousness of the higher chakras, at the apex of the triangle.

As you find yourself coming more and more into balance by doing the opposites and triangles techniques, your ability to feel consciousness ascending in your body and through the chakras improves. You find yourself living in states of mind associated with the ascended balance words. You begin to move from the polarized, dualistic consciousness of the lower chakras into heart-centered consciousness and into unity consciousness.

SEMANTICS

There is a difficulty in talking about much of this because of the limitations of our language in this dual system. Because we are in the dual system, words used to describe the state of unity consciousness are inadequate. We can try to approximate what the oneness is like with our limited, dualistic language, but it falls short. The Buddhists use the analogy of a finger pointing at the moon. The finger represents language and the moon represents unity consciousness or enlightenment. We can approximate where the moon is by using the pointing finger, although it is inadequate to actually touch it. We can never touch the moon with our finger, but it can point the way. Ultimately, the unity associated with Self-realization can only be experienced.

Words are symbols from the polarized world. The Bible says, "In the beginning was the word…," suggesting how this plane of existence was created—through the vibration of the words. So when you are moving to other planes, the experiences can't always be expressed in words. Very often this is where religions fail—in that people misinterpret the finger for the moon. Religions start as the finger pointing the way to the moon. Instead people think it is the finger that is important, and they start worshipping the finger.

In finding the ascended balance words at the top of the triangle, we may encounter challenges with our language. For example, we may say the word *light* and interpret it as unpolarized. We say light is unpolarized unity consciousness. But then what about its having an opposite in *dark*? Doesn't that mean it is polarized, or in the duality? We can use some words, like light, to mean two different things. Although our limited language originates from duality, there are some words, like light, that represent qualities of the higher chakras. Light can be used in the dualistic sense, with dark as its opposite, or in the unified sense, which would perhaps have the meaning *God* or *spirit*. The word *love* can be used this way, too. There are many levels of love. Unconditional love is the ascended state, and love-hate is the polarized pair of opposites.

Even using the phrase *ascended state* makes something else seem lower, which is another polarity. This does not seem neutral. In the sense of the system of *Vedanta*, the ancient teachings of non-duality, there is no high or low. Only unity is real. The high and the low are illusion. The reason we talk of high and low in this work is because we are looking at the body and the subtle body as our schematic. In the human system there are levels which appear in the relative world to be higher and lower. The whole premise of this work is to address the relative world as it is and then to transform it into unity.

REVIEW
THE STEPS OF THE TRIANGLE TECHNIQUE

1. Choose a polarity
2. Write it on the baseline points of a triangle
3. Find the ascended balance, and write it at the apex of the triangle
4. Offer it up and ask for the ascended state to be instituted in place of the polarity
5. Wait for grace

SUGGESTIONS FOR PUTTING THEORY INTO PRACTICE

1. Write the list of ascended states on the inside cover of your processing notebook for a handy reference.
2. Use the triangle technique with at least twenty of the polarities from your list of opposites in the previous chapter's exercises. Take your time with each pair, feeling the ascended balance word that is most exact.
3. Choose one polarity that is particularly charged for you. Close your eyes in meditation and feel the polarity in your body. Where do you feel it? Write about your insights.
4. Do the same with the ascended balance word. Where do you feel it? Write about your insights.
5. For one week, make a daily prayer for the ascended balance state of your choice to be instituted in your life (e.g., ask to know gratitude or unconditional love). Write about your experience.

TESTIMONIAL • HEADSTRONG

I've always had difficulty with processing. I found that I was identifying with my egoic patterns and so could not get objective enough to clear them. Whenever a negative pattern was brought to my attention, I felt I was being criticized and attacked, which then brought up my defenses so I wouldn't have to feel shame and humiliation or feel like a wrongdoer. I wanted to avoid these feelings at all cost. This, of course, served to keep my egoic boundaries firmly in place.

One of the patterns I would run was that the minute something upset me, I would fly into my head and run the drama of the story, over and over again. Analyzing, reacting, judging, fretting and obsessing to try to *figure it out*, to find a solution. I wanted to change either myself or something or someone outside of me to make things better. I would thus lose my witness and make the drama *real*. I found that somehow doing the triangles was incredibly helpful, as they brought me more into my heart and into humility with this process of rigidity, helping me to regain my witness and clear my emotional body.

One night after what felt like an intense discussion with some friends, I went to bed and, to my chagrin, started spinning the story in my head. This time, however, I caught myself and paused—I did a few triangles and could see what I was doing. I heard an inner voice say, "Let it go. The content does not matter. It was just an energy exchange, and it is done. The energy shifted for you. Let it go. Surrender." *In that moment I was able to release it.*

The next instant I felt energy move through my body—it had an effervescent quality to it that felt very blissful. I recognized that particular quality from the occasional states of absorption I would experience in meditation—a samadhi state. This lasted the night and into the next day.

That night I had the following three dreams. First I saw myself lying in bed surrounded by angels, and their presence was very protective and comforting, while my grandmother was trying to stop me from levitating off the bed. Next, I found myself in an open field with someone who appeared to be a teacher. I heard him say "Just let go," which I did and instantly flew high up into the sky as if I were a bird. The experience was exhilarating. Lastly I saw my body expand and grow until I became a giant, walking around town with most of the buildings reaching only my knees. These dreams involved the expansion that took place in my awareness. This whole experience took me completely by surprise. I had always assumed that this state of consciousness could be achieved only through deep meditation.

Through direct experience I saw that as soon as I was able to let go of my limited self, pure essence shone through. What enabled me to finally let go? I do know that the triangles helped. In finding the words *surrender* and *grace*, I was able to become conscious of the process involving my do-er. I could see that after relentless effort on my part to *do it*, I finally realized that it had to be more of an undoing—a letting go—and so I surrendered enough to allow grace to enter.

Pain and happiness are simply conditions of the ego.
Forget the ego.

—Lao Tsu

ELEVEN

SQUARES

Some years ago I had chronic fatigue syndrome. After trying many different therapies, which all helped to some extent, I had the distinct feeling that the problems I was having with the body were a process. I saw that the imbalances were mental-emotional overlays to the body, belief systems of a very subtle nature. I knew that I could look deeply into the body and process myself out of them. My rationale was that everything is consciousness, including the body. Processing will shift consciousness; therefore processing will shift the body. I would just have to find the right pieces. That was the hard part, finding the right pieces. I made a list of hundreds of polarities associated with the material plane—things like: HEALTH and SICKNESS, OLD and YOUNG, STRONG and WEAK, GRAVITY and LEVITY.

I sat on my bed and resolved not to move until I was successful in shifting my condition. It was during this time that I intuited the squares technique. I filled two or three notebooks in my determination to be healed. It took three weeks, but I found most of the issues. Eventually, after experiencing numerous subtle shifts, the most spectacular came with a square on LIFE and DEATH. This involved looking deeply into the issues of why I DESIRED TO LIVE, why I FEARED LIVING, why I DESIRED TO DIE, and why I FEARED DYING. As I completed the square and did the offering, I felt the meridians, or channels of subtle energy, in the body *pop* open and the energy begin to flow in the body again. The disability was over, and the cure seemed miraculous. I was sold on the squares technique, as you may imagine. Now I would like to share this technique with you.

Understanding the Squares Technique

This technique is a little more complicated than the lists of opposites. It is associated mainly with the physical body and the physical world, although it serves to clear the subtle bodies as well—including mental and emotional. The number four and the square are symbols for the physical plane. The consciousness is quite *boxed-in* at this level, and that creates density. The square is a very a-dynamic form. We even have a colloquial expression in our language, calling someone a *square*, meaning that they are rather conservative, stuck and boring. The dynamic wave energy of life has been contained in a box and cannot unravel itself easily.

As you read ahead about how a square works, you will see that each corner is an aspect of consciousness that is out of balance. Each corner represents some part of the ego that pushes or pulls you off center. In the normal course of our lives, we tend to live out the corners rather unconsciously. They are our desires and fears. When we live by habit or by rote and don't examine the nature of our own egos, it can take years, or even lifetimes, to live out our desires and fears represented in one square. This translates as feeling boxed-in and stuck in life, and normally we don't even know why we feel this way. Usually, most people blame the outside circumstances of their lives, rather than look within to see what needs to change in order to effect outer change.

When we have little or no knowledge of the principle of changing the inner to change the outer, we have to live out in the physical world the experience of the effect of our desires and fears. In other words, before we tumble to the fact that what limits us is the inner, egoic conditioning—our desires and fears—they will cause us to have to live out physically whatever their effects are. Until we realize this fact, we generally don't experience significant change in our lives. We may try to change the outer appearance, the window dressing, for example by changing jobs or relationships or locations, but we don't experience a real change in our lives until we begin to examine what really limits us—our egoic conditioning, which comes down to our desires and fears. This is why we often find that we have to keep repeating the same lessons and the same kinds of experiences over and over with just a change in scenery, and we feel caught in some kind of bizarre loop. The movie *Groundhog's Day* with Bill Murray offers an excellent metaphoric illustration of this metaphysical principle; it is also very funny. It is about a man who wakes up every day and re-experiences the same day—Groundhog's Day. He finally finds his way out through balancing and clearing his inner consciousness and by moving into the heart.

As you read ahead about the squares technique, you will see that it offers a much faster method of experiencing change in your life than having to live out in the physical world the experience of your desires and fears. Doing a square allows you to complete the experience mentally, rather than physically. All you have to do is write about the desires and fears in your journal. This allows you to shorten the path greatly. In fact, this is also true for the polarities and triangles techniques. Because these are all mental techniques, they offer a very fast way to transform consciousness, rather than having to live out our lessons physically.

When I was given this structure, spirit said to me that DESIRE and FEAR form a pair of opposites. Energetically, DESIRE is the pulling toward something and FEAR is pushing it away, or pulling back from it. Desire and fear represent one of the ways in which we use ATTRACTION and REPULSION. As we have seen, attraction and repulsion are the powerful magnetic forces that shape the physical world. To use the squares technique, we insert the relevant polarity into this powerful format of desire and fear.

THE SQUARES TECHNIQUE

The oscillations in consciousness, back and forth (the ups and downs in life), are kept in motion by our attractions to things and our repulsions to things, our desires for things and our fears of them. The square processing technique is a diagram for the flow of awareness and energy on a mental and emotional level. These awarenesses form projections and create the events we live with in the physical world. They shape our physical world and the body. So we can examine any one polarity in a way that also takes into consideration that pushing/pulling sensation and effect change right through the mental-emotional levels down into the physical. This is the square.

STEP ONE — PICK A POLARITY

To do the square technique, first you pick a polarity that you want to examine in greater depth. Maybe it is one that you uncovered when you wrote a story for polarity processing, a polarity that for you seems to have a lot of charge on it. For example, our old friend of the freeway, Paul, decided to do a square on CONTROL and OUT OF CONTROL.

STEP TWO — DRAW AND LABEL A SQUARE

Then you draw a square in your journal. You label the two corners on the left side of the square the DESIRE TO _____. The two corners on the right side of the square are labeled the FEAR OF _____. Then you fill in the blanks with the polarities. One polarity goes into both top corners, and the other polarity goes into the two bottom corners.

Using Paul's example, in the upper left-hand corner of this square, we write the words, DESIRE TO BE IN CONTROL, and in the upper right-hand corner we write the words, FEAR OF BEING IN CONTROL. The desire and fear of the opposite, we write in the lower two corners. In the lower left we write DESIRE TO BE OUT OF CONTROL, and in the lower right we write FEAR OF BEING OUT OF CONTROL (Fig. 11-1).

So for *any* polarity, we just attach the words, DESIRE TO... , FEAR OF..., DESIRE TO..., and FEAR OF.... Whatever the polarity is, we use the same word for both top corners, and the opposite polarity for both bottom corners. We put the label, DESIRE TO... on both the left-hand corners, and the label FEAR OF... on both right-hand corners. We always use this structure (Fig. 11-2).

Now is a good time to practice the first step of the technique. Try labeling a square in your journal on the polarity LOVE and HATE, for example. Also try labeling a square on WIN and LOSE.

DESIRE TO BE IN CONTROL	FEAR OF BEING IN CONTROL
DESIRE TO BE OUT OF CONTROL	FEAR OF BEING OUT OF CONTROL

Fig. 11–1.

STEP THREE — MAKE ALL CORNERS CONSCIOUS

Once we have labeled the square, then the real fun begins. We explore it. We look at it and try to recognize which corners we are familiar with. If there are one or two corners that we have never seen before, then we try to feel them.

We all contain all four corners of the square.
Some of them may be locked into the unconscious,
but they are all in there somewhere. It is very common to
want to go into denial regarding some of the corners.

DESIRE TO...	FEAR OF...
DESIRE TO...	FEAR OF...

Fig. 11–2.

Usually when we do squares, especially when we are working with a pair of opposites that *we really react to*, we will find that there is at least one corner (sometimes two) that we have not seen before. This is our hidden side, the part that is in our unconscious. Everything in each corner exists within us because we are all everything. It is denial to say, "I don't do that!" If we indulge in denial and avoidance in this way, we are choosing to make something unconscious.

We have to try to remember
an instance when we felt it.

SAMPLE SQUARES

Step three takes place on a mental-emotional level. Step four will involve writing about this in your journal. For now just think or feel it through, and don't worry about the writing part. Before we get into journal work, take some time to think about these sample squares.

DEPENDENT AND INDEPENDENT

That is a polarity that pushes on people a lot. The corners are: the desire to be dependent, the fear of being dependent, the desire to be independent, and the fear of being independent.

The *fear of being dependent* is very common. The image of growing old, becoming feeble and being a burden on one's family usually sends most people into fear.

But how about the *desire to be dependent*? Perhaps this corner is less easily visible and might require a little more internal examination. But if you look deeply enough, you can see that it is easy to long for someone else to take care of you, to nurture you and to provide for you. It can feel wonderful to be dependent on someone loving and strong in this way. This is the desire to be dependent.

The *desire to be independent* is pretty easy to see. Especially during the teenage years, we crave our independence. Is there a corner that you have never seen before? The *fear of being independent* perhaps? That is probably the least commonly felt corner. But if you feel your way into it, you can probably recall a time when you feared your own independence. For example, what about when it was time to leave your parents' house and strike out on your own? Or what about leaving a long-term relationship? Usually there is some degree of fear involved in these instances.

INFERIOR AND SUPERIOR

The *desire to be inferior*. Most people try their very best *never* to feel this corner! You might ask yourself incredulously, "Could some part of me really desire to feel inferior?! How can this possibly be?" But it is true. The desire to feel inferior is a part in the unconscious played by the victim. As the victim, we might find we get attention and sympathy, or we get to blame the outside and feel self-righteous, which feels good and juicy. If you look hard enough, you will probably be able to remember at least one time when you felt this. When you can own this corner, you are on the way to awakeness.

The other corners are: the *fear of being inferior*, the *desire to be superior* (we all know feeling), and the *fear of being superior*.

APPROVAL AND DISAPPROVAL

Everybody grapples with this one. *The desire to be approved of* and *the fear of being approved of*—you start suppressing the natural expression of your innate self because of these two. Most of us know about the desire to be approved of. However, a lot of people develop a self-destructive pattern so that they will not have to deal with success and with being approved of. They cannot handle it, and that feeds into the desire to be disapproved of—the rebel. The fear of being approved of is the lesser known part. It will sabotage your efforts, especially if you are working with the public in some way and just cannot handle the praise or the acclaim—or the criticism, actually. They both have the power to throw you off balance. Praise is something that everyone craves, yet when you get it, it often knocks you sideways.

Then, it leads to the *desire to be disapproved of*. For example, maybe that is the reason why movie stars sometimes do outrageous things! For the shock value. You create the outside to reject and push you away. There is juice in that.

Then, of course, you go to the *fear of being disapproved of* because some part of you doesn't like feeling rejected. It creates a loop in consciousness. The energy keeps moving, and the corners lead into each other, cycling around and around continuously.

LACK AND ABUNDANCE

We know the *desire for abundance*—everyone knows that one!

The *fear of abundance* can be a biggie for spiritual seekers since many of us have taken a vow of poverty in one lifetime or another. There is a fear that money corrupts. When doing this square, people often think, "Well, you know, if I had money, I would be a bad person." So they will not let themselves have it. It is too big a responsibility, they feel. They fear they might have to shine their shoes, put a smile on their faces, and go out there to face the world or to take care of other people.

Abundance does not have to mean money, really. So you can examine abundance to see if you have chosen abundant loving, money, generosity, creativity and relationships. The *fear of abundance* and the *desire for lack* are much less acknowledged than the other corners. These corners are usually associated with the belief that asceticism is spiritual and good. Can you find another reason?

The *fear of lack* runs very deeply in most of us. Some people's worst fear is about being poor and homeless—being a bag person pushing a shopping cart on the streets.

STEP FOUR—APPLY DATA TO THE SQUARE

So, the next step is to divide your journal page into four equal sections by drawing a large cross in the middle of the page. Label the top of each quadrant with one corner of the square. Then, in each quadrant you write down every possible way in which you know that desire or fear.

Many times, you will have too much for one corner to fit it all on a fourth of a page. In this case, you may want to use four pages, one for each corner of the square. If you run out of room using just one page, don't try to economize with paper. Be extravagant and fill up as many sheets as you need to.

Write words, short phrases, or a narrative of how you have lived out that corner. This includes emotions, thoughts, states of mind, memories, dreams and anything else that comes up for you. For each corner ask yourself, "How do I *feel* about this corner? How does/did that look for me at one time? And *why* do I desire or fear this thing? What is my motivation to desire or fear this thing?"

SAMPLE SQUARE AND JOURNAL ENTRY

A prominent theme in many processing stories is of being a VICTIM who is abused by a TYRANT. In a workshop we conducted, a group filled in the corners of the VICTIM/TYRANT square with the following responses. Before you read their responses, take a few minutes and try this square in your own journal. Then, look at the lists below. Some of their answers will probably be real eye-openers for you.

Here is how you can divide your page (Fig. 11-3). For our example, we have made lists. The lists are long enough for each corner that we have used several pages.

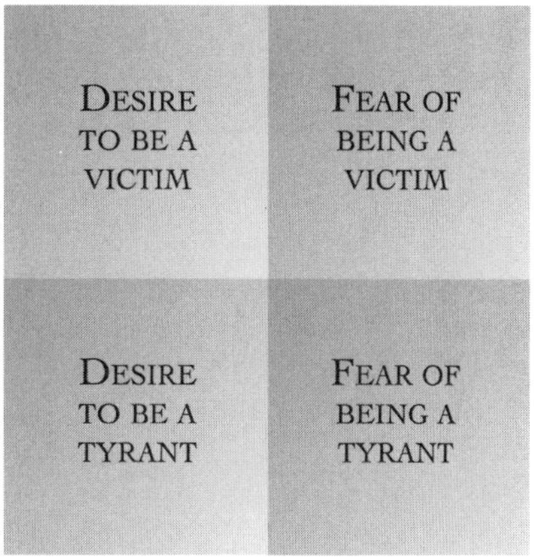

DESIRE TO BE A VICTIM	FEAR OF BEING A VICTIM
DESIRE TO BE A TYRANT	FEAR OF BEING A TYRANT

Fig. 11–3.

In the corner labeled the DESIRE TO BE A VICTIM:
feeling the need to be punished
feeling guilty
to get attention
don't have to work
self-righteousness
at least I am harmless as a victim
security of the familiar
to get sympathy

don't have to be conscious
to be a martyr
to avoid conflict
I have feelings of unworthiness
self-indulgence
balancing out bad karma
get pampering
self-pity
belonging to the victim tribe
commiserating
comparing and sharing wounding with others
to get nurturing and love
to blame others
to manipulate others
playing games
innocence
I want people to have compassion for me
don't have to be responsible
have an excuse
can't help it
justified anger
indignation
bad mouthing others
as a child when I got sick, I'd get special treatment

**In the corner labeled the
FEAR OF BEING A VICTIM:**
it's embarrassing and humiliating
I'll never get out of my rut
infantilized
powerless
fear of death
lose self-respect
lose respect of others
fear of no love
fear of no intimacy
fear of feeling worthless
being in danger

passive
pain
being vulnerable
being pitied
being terrorized
exploited
shamed
fear of dying unconscious, unawake
betrayed
lack of control
hopelessness
meaninglessness
purposelessness
weakness
inferior
degrading
depressing
impotent
losing
despair
dependent
needy
pathetic
suicide
as a child I feared my father spanking me

**In the corner labeled the
DESIRE TO BE A TYRANT:**
to have power over my own life
to have power and control over others
self-control
to get my own way
don't have to face being wrong
at least I know what to expect
revenge
access to people and things
for tough love
to get adoration

it's strong
to feel superior
state of being active (not passive)
to feel in charge
to get attention
to win
to get respect
manipulation
dominance
to punish others
to have no fear
don't have to feel
to enjoy being cruel
to vent rage
sadistic
greed
anger
hate
make others work
so I can be lazy
create order
feeling immortal
for fame
be a great leader

**In the corner labeled the
FEAR OF BEING A TYRANT:**
could be lonely
being punished
fear of making mistakes
fear of facing my power
I'd be unloved
responsible for consequences
fear of being hated
fear of being disapproved of
fear of not being accepted
isolated
fear of being unspiritual

hurting others
cruelty
being despised
fear of having no friends or family
bad karma
could be fatal
fear of feeling separate
fear of people not being honest
can't trust people
loss of love
being out of control

STEP FIVE — OFFER UP YOUR SQUARE

Now give the whole square back to spirit. Offer it up with a prayer, just like you did with the polarity processing and triangles techniques. It is important to remember at this point, after you have churned up all of this egoic stuff and feel as though you have emptied your cup, just to let it all go. You don't have to continue to analyze, fret, figure it out with your head, or be the one to fix the situation. Spirit does the work for you after you have made the unconscious conscious. Remember that all of the desires and fears are not real; they are not who you are. You are pure awareness, and these states just pass through you. You can rest and relax after your offering, knowing that you are releasing everything you have dug up. There is nothing more for you to do once you have made the four corners of the square conscious. You can trust that grace will come in and make the changes for you, bringing you more into wholeness, balance and healing, more into the knowledge of who you truly are—the Self.

STEP SIX — WAIT FOR GRACE

Just as with the opposites and triangle techniques, after you make your offering, remember to wait for grace. You can occupy your time by performing some simple, mundane activities, like tending the plants or taking a walk. You will get a shift from doing a square. Try to remain in your neutral witness and just be present and mindful, so that you can be conscious of and experience the shift. If you are sensitive, you may especially feel it in your body after doing a square. In fact, you may have already had an experience of feeling a shift in your body from doing polarities or triangles. But because squares take the process a step further, into the physical, you will be more likely to experience the shift physically, in addition to mentally and/or emotionally. You may also find new insights pouring in. You may find yourself saying, "Oh, I got it. I really got it!" Be open to new information coming in or a next step in your process being presented to you—from anyone and anywhere. Or as the layer of the process peels off, you may find that you begin to emote. In Chapter 14—Developing the Witness, we discuss in more detail a way to vent emotion from the place of the witness and to not make the emotion real. This is an excellent way to discharge old, stuck energy and is often a good sign that you have cleared something. If you don't feel the shift, that is okay. It is happening anyway. You can trust in that.

REVIEW
THE STEPS OF THE SQUARES TECHNIQUE
1. Pick a polarity
2. Draw and label a square
3. Make all four corners conscious
4. Apply data to the square
5. Offer up your square
6. Wait for grace

SUGGESTIONS FOR PUTTING THEORY INTO PRACTICE

1. Choose a polarity that is particularly charged for you. Do a square with it and offer it up.
2. Do a square on MANIPULATIVE and STRAIGHT FORWARD.
3. Do a square which includes the corner, the DESIRE TO SUFFER. Believe it or not, there is a part of us that loves our negative states, and we do not normally let ourselves see how much we love them. Can you work out what the corners of this square would be? (Remember the role of the victim, which we usually keep hidden in the unconscious.)
4. Here are some other polarities. Label the corners of the squares for these and think about how you play out each corner. Are they conscious corners or unconscious?
   Honest and dishonest
   Pleasure and pain
   Loss and gain
   Light and dark
   Security and insecurity
   Active and passive
   Over-reactive and non-reactive

TESTIMONIAL • LEARNING SQUARES

Six months ago I had liquidated my belongings and moved to Santa Fe, guided to come with very few things and a lot of faith. The Museum of New Mexico gave me a position doing archaeology, and friends invited me to stay with them until I found my feet. The work was fascinating, but the wages were low and the hours long. Despite this, life felt very full.

I was in doubt of ever affording my own place or of being supported in Santa Fe *on my own*. Everyone knows that there are no affordable houses or decent part-time jobs in Santa Fe! I imagined myself in a housing situation with several roommates, perhaps bagging groceries somewhere on the weekends, or asking my parents for money, which I didn't want to do.

One Sunday shortly after the move, I was feeling particularly frustrated, depressed and hopeless about the situation. The emotions were quite intense and persistently nagging away at me. I sat with my friends at the dining table for an hour or two using squares to look at the issues around my fear and desire to *make it on my own*. It was rough surf, looking at deep-seated separation and vulnerability issues. One particularly difficult square for me was about abandonment. The opposite side was about feeling cherished, and I got a big shift. Later that very same day I was guided to go for a drive and pick up a newspaper (a rarity for me in those days). I felt a shakiness and sense of surrender because of the changes taking place as a result of the square. My physical body felt trembly and vulnerable, but somehow there was also a new sense of innocence, joy and openness.

Although I had never found a job via the classifieds, I was drawn to look. Miraculously, there was an ad that read: "Small spiritual organization seeks part-time books and tapes manager." Yes!

My next stop was the rental board at a local whole-foods haven. There was a white index card that read: "Immediate sublet, downtown Santa Fe casita (cheap!)" Yes!

So, within 24 hours of learning squares, I had apparently cleared enough consciousness that I was given my next step. Grace provided me with the bonus of a house I could afford and part-time work that suited me! I see now that because I had become clearer inwardly, my outside world suddenly reflected that level of clarity to me.

As soon as you concern yourself with the "good" and "bad" of your fellows, you create an opening in your heart for [separation] to enter. Testing, competing with, and criticizing others weaken and defeat you.

—Morihei Ueshiba

TWELVE

THE DEEPER
POWER OF PROCESSING

So now that you have all the basic tools for processing—the polarities, triangles and squares—you are prepared to move more deeply into advanced processing. How you use the tools is completely up to you. There are no rules. You can adapt them and use them in whatever way most benefits you. As you clear shadow, you will develop your discernment, and your inner guidance will show you how best to apply the methods.

In this chapter we discuss some ways to help you deepen your experience of using the Marriage of Spirit methods and share with you a little bit of what to expect after you process. The topics are:

- Finding a theme to your story
- Finding all the right opposites
- Offering up positive *and* negative
- Writing your additional insights
- Finding the key square
- Following the thread of continuity
- Noticing the shift and speeding up your evolution
- Experiencing a simulation
- Ascension and the raising of consciousness.

You may want to wait a few days, or a week, and read this chapter after you have had some time to try out the techniques and get comfortable with them. Or, if you are inspired to continue right away, that is fine, too.

FINDING A THEME TO YOUR STORY

In the beginning as you familiarize yourself with processing, you will find the opposites technique very helpful in defining your issues. It is an excellent idea when you have finished your list and have found the opposites to go back through the list to try to find a general theme for it. Find the pair or pairs of opposites that seem to best encapsulate your process or that have the biggest charge on them for you. Write these words at the top of your journal page next to the date, so in the future you can track where your processing has taken you. Doing this allows you to see how the onion layers have peeled off over time and to gain a larger perspective on the unfoldment of your awakening process.

For example, Paul of the freeway incident decided the key to this particular story was the CONTROL - OUT OF CONTROL polarity, because most of the behaviors and emotions in his story, like *anger*, came from a place of being upset that he had no control over the situation. He wrote these words in large letters at the top of his journal entry next to the date. Now whenever he does a process about *control* issues, he can always go back and refer to this old list he created, to help fill in any missing pieces.

Usually the themes you will use to title your page are very basic polarities which are a part of any person's personality. They run very deeply in everyone—themes like VICTIM - TYRANT or APPROVAL - DISAPPROVAL or MASCULINE - FEMININE. It helps to be on the lookout for these deeply rooted structures as you investigate your own patterning.

FINDING ALL THE RIGHT OPPOSITES

When doing the polarity work, it is important to take your time in finding all the right opposites. You want to feel your way into each word as deeply as you can. Each word is a vibration and is a state of consciousness. If you can't find an opposite to a word, it is best to meditate on it and pray for help, rather than skimming over it superficially. Sometimes this extra effort will give you your biggest breakthroughs.

Not being able to find an opposite is a clue that this state is deeply buried in the unconscious. When an opposite is hidden in that way, it means that you probably act unconsciously in instances involving that polarity; it indicates you are being run by egoic patterning—like a computer program. It is an area where you probably tend *to get your buttons pushed*.

Paul's example is a good one for this. If you recall, one of the words on his list was *indignation*. He could not think of any word that would fit as an opposite for it. When he meditated on it for a while, he realized it was an unconscious area for him. He knew that this was a good indicator that he is probably a bit unbalanced in this area. In his inner probing, he realized that he felt trapped by this issue of feeling indignant, of feeling angry when treated unfairly. After meditating on what the opposite to indignation is and feeling into it for several minutes unsuccessfully, he finally gave up trying to think of a word. Instead, he got out his dictionary of synonyms and antonyms to look it up. There was a list of over a dozen words as opposites to *indignant*, out of which he chose *imperturbability*, which means *unshakable calmness*. That word resonated very clearly and held the exact opposite vibration for him. In fact, as soon as he read the word, he reported that he felt an immediate mental shift take place.

Paul also said that before he wrote about the story, when it was just floating around in his head, he didn't see how he was feeling indignant. It wasn't until he wrote the story and got stuck at finding its opposite that he actually saw his feelings of indignation and anger at believing he was right and she was wrong. He didn't realize he had such a charge on this particular feeling. He realized there were many, many instances throughout his life in which he ended up feeling indignant—angry and victimized by apparently unjust circumstances—and each time, his reaction of blame and rage and powerlessness in the face of life's cruelty was like an old broken record repeating itself. In finding the opposite unconscious side, some kind of magical shift happened for him, which allowed him to let go of the intensity of the situation and to not make it so real. If he had glossed over the incident as too insignificant to process and if he had not taken the time to find the right opposite for all the words on his list, he would never have had such a big breakthrough.

OFFERING UP POSITIVE *AND* NEGATIVE

It is important to offer up both sides of the polarity, not just the negative side. You will only get a shift if you offer up both negative and positive.

For example, let's say you are living out one side of a situation, like *the victim*. The other side, the oppressor, is in the unconscious and is being acted out for you by some petty tyrant, like your boss. You think, "Oh, I've had enough of being a powerless victim. I want change. I want to be powerful. I want to be the boss." Unless you ask to be released from *both* sides, the victim *and* the oppressor, the change you will get is a flip to the other side of the polarity. You will find yourself somehow living out an experience of the oppressor next. Either that, or you will find that some other oppressor shows up to pester you.

> *The secret is that you find the opposite side*
> *because that is the hidden side. As long as there*
> *is a piece hidden, the polarity will not integrate.*

It is better to offer both sides at once, the victim and the oppressor. Then there is no need to do the flip-flopping, which keeps us locked into ego. It is very difficult to shift if we address only one side of a situation. With this work, we are offering the negative and the positive side of the situation. Both! We don't say, "Well, I'm more than happy to get rid of the negative, but I want to keep the positive." That is attraction and repulsion.

There are many teachings that emphasize being positive all of the time. And that is fine if we are willing to or desiring to stay in the separate state, where we are still conscious and unconscious. Trying to be positive all the time is a good beginning, especially if our conditioning has taught us to be negative a lot. If the ego were a deck of cards, the technique of trying to think and feel positive all the time would be a bit like reshuffling the deck to try to get a better hand. But if we are seeking to ascend, we have to address both sides, negative and positive. *We have to be willing to detach from both sides.* We cannot hold on to the positive and try to get rid of the negative. Doing that keeps us locked into the separate system because we seek with the conscious mind to have only positive experiences. The attraction and repulsion traps us.

WRITING YOUR ADDITIONAL INSIGHTS

After you make your offering of positive *and* negative and while you are waiting for grace, you may find that you have insights into your process. It is important to keep them in your journal, as they are a gift to you to help you get clear and to come into balance. It is the unconscious becoming conscious, and it is very important to acknowledge that and to be grateful. The insights are a direct result of your offering and of the onion layer peeling off. This is the grace coming in.

No matter how insignificant you think your process is, you can still have profound insights to write about if you look deeply enough. For example, here are the insights that Paul wrote about after offering up his list of opposites and while he waited for grace. For such an apparently trivial episode, look how deeply he was able to unravel a major egoic pattern in his life.

> *I really realized that self-righteous indignation is a major issue that I have to work on. It was ironic that just a few days ago I was talking to a friend about a pattern I have of being indignant. And the fact that that feeling of indignation would come up again in this freeway incident a few days later was an indicator for me that I really need to look at it and process it. I see that I've always thought it was perfectly fine to feel indignant at times when I feel I'm right and someone else is wrong. I see that sometimes I feel so sure I am right, that there is no question about it, no allowing in of anything else. It's like there are good guys and bad guys, and that's it. God is on my side. I deserve to feel indignant when I'm right!*
>
> *It can get very subtle, too. Like for example, I see I get into this mode by holding onto opinions and belief systems. In this case it was really obvious because my button got pushed by someone else having control of the freeway, not me. And I wanted control of the freeway. It was a power struggle. So it played out blatantly on the freeway with cars. But I see that I do this in other arenas in my life. Like, for example, when I believe I know what is right for someone else, or for the world even.*

I'm really comfortable when I'm in control because I know everything. It's part of feeling safe and secure when I'm right. Everything's fine. So, the controller in me gets self-righteous and indignant when control is taken away. I can see that the opposite, <u>imperturbability—unshakable calmness</u>—holds a key for me. I need to move more in that direction of not caring so much whether I am in control or right all the time. Then I'm not so bothered, hurt, angry and personally affected in these kinds of incidents. I'm not so attached. I could have just relaxed on the freeway, and said, "Okay, so I'll be a few minutes late." No, instead it was this huge thing for me. It felt awful to be so self-absorbed and deeply affected by such a silly little thing. It feels really good to let all that go and to give it back to God.

I also see how important it was for me to have just a little shred of a witness available during the incident. That witness part of me knew the whole thing was a set-up so that I would learn something about my process! So, when I asked, "What was this teaching me?", I got this really big piece. <u>I saw the part of me that needs to be in control and then is indignant when I'm not in control.</u> Of course the whole list of words is important, but especially the control issue and the feeling indignant. It is about wanting things my way. I can see how it really holds me back in so many areas of my life, in subtle ways—and not so subtle ways, like on the freeway!

I am just realizing now how amazing this whole incident is. When I first wrote it down, I thought, "How insignificant. What a silly little story to process. It's not a big drama or anything." And yet, it highlighted my whole process of the last few months! This thread has run through all my issues of the last few months. It wasn't a random thing. If I hadn't processed it, I never would have seen this big piece of the puzzle.

FINDING THE KEY SQUARE

One of the most powerful ways to deepen the level of breakthrough experience you have with your processing is to do the key square. In other words as you process an issue that is keeping you off-balance, there may be any number of squares you could do to help resolve the situation. But finding the best square, using just the right polarity, is the key to having the most significant breakthrough. It takes practice to learn to do this, but it is an intuitive skill that does come with time. You can begin by praying for your intuition to develop. Your intuition also develops naturally as you do the processing, and you are able to feel into the process more deeply to find the perfect square. In the beginning you will find that doing a square on your theme polarity will be an excellent way to start, as Paul did with CONTROL - OUT OF CONTROL. But with practice, you will be able to sleuth out intuitively the one polarity that gets right to the root of the issue, which will save you a lot of time with your processing. You will find that as your intuition develops, you are able to navigate more easily the maze of your egoic patterning, zoom in on the knot in consciousness which holds the problem in place, and untie it.

FOLLOWING THE THREAD OF CONTINUITY

Usually grace will provide you with a thread of continuity through your processing that will lead you to have deeper and deeper insights. The more you follow the thread and the more rigorously you examine your issues, the bigger the breakthrough you will have. The thread leads you to freedom. So it is important to be persistent with a process and to take it deeper and deeper.

In practical terms here is how this might look. Following the thread of continuity relies heavily on intuition. You begin at one end of the thread by simply doing the polarity processing technique. Once you have offered up your list of opposites and have written about your insights, you may find that you are guided to do more processing. For example, by following the thread of your intuition, you may feel moved to do a square and a triangle on your theme polarity. This may lead you further along the thread of continuity to do more polarities, squares or triangles and then on to a major breakthrough in self-understanding. For example, you may find that your physical health improves, or that you are given an opportunity to release some old pent-up emotions, or that you heal a rift between you and an old friend.

To effect maximum change, you want to follow the thread to where you can say, "This is totally beyond me, God. I am locked into this mess, and I don't know what to do. Bail me out *now*! I give this situation back to you, because I don't really know what to do with it any more. Take it. Please. And balance it out for me. I feel like a juggler, trying to hold my life together with all of these pieces flying. And I can't stand it any more." Then, you will feel absolutely finished with the pattern and ready to surrender. Basically, change is what you are asking for, and it is always given.

All you have to do is ask, and it is given.

You just need to make sure you ask for something very specific. If you have got this list of things that you cannot deal with any more, you have worked with the squares and triangles, you have found the missing piece of the puzzle, the unconscious side, which completes it, and if you are fully surrendered, then you are ripe for change.

Here is Paul's example of how he followed his thread of continuity. After he had offered up his list of opposites and had written about those insights, he chose to do a square on CONTROL and OUT OF CONTROL. It was a big enough issue for him that he decided to spend a couple of hours daily on the square until he felt complete. He really probed deeply for three days and felt like he had followed the thread as far as it would lead him. After he offered up the square, he had another major breakthrough. His healing took the form of a dream. Here is his journal entry about his further experience:

Within a couple of days of offering up the square, I had one of the most profound dreams of my life. It was very long and detailed, but I will try to provide a synopsis here. I saw a beautiful unicorn freely galloping on a pristine white-sand beach.

I was with a spirit guide, who was on my right side watching everything unfold with me. Then a spaceship beamed up the unicorn in a ray of light. I got really, really upset and was complaining to my guide about the situation, asking, "How could they do that to that poor, helpless unicorn? They did that totally against its will. How dare they!" My guide just humored me and told me to be quiet and watch.

Next, we were on the spaceship, and I was the unicorn. Yet I was also separate and me, too. Many, many lovely light beings were there, running the ship, working very busily and in perfect harmony with each other. I noticed they all were very neutral, very smooth emotionally, and very loving. Their mission was to perform beneficial services for the Earth. When I complained to them about the poor unicorn, taken without being asked, abducted and not in control, I said indignantly, "Give me one good reason why I should allow you to keep the unicorn!" At that point all the beings on the ship stopped dead still and looked at me. There was a pregnant pause, and then one of them said, "Would saving your planet be good enough reason?" They explained to me that the unicorn was performing a service, too, in its surrender and neutrality.

Then, I went on some amazing adventures on board the ship, including being shown in-depth information about the reality of my being. At the end of the dream, the beings told and showed me in great detail the story of the Holy Grail, which is one of my favorites. Only one knight of all of them, with all of their noble virtues, was able to bring home the grail. That was Percival, and it was because of his purity, which was the virtue above all other virtues. I was told that I am Percival. Of course I told them that they had the wrong person, and I began to disclose all my faults to them. But they said none of that mattered; that it was just ego, just a temporary costume. And then I was told that I had to go back and save the Earth! I didn't want to leave them, but reluctantly I found myself being sent back.

Then I woke up in a completely altered state, feeling like I had actually been aboard a spaceship. I know something miraculous happened during the dream state, which hasn't fully unraveled and revealed itself to me yet. It is really clear to me that doing the squares and triangles were significant steps in my insights and breakthroughs of the past few weeks. I can feel I am letting go of much of the unbalanced energy around feeling indignant when I (the small, limited self) am not in control. I am moving much more into the heart states of surrender, detachment, neutrality and purity.

Noticing the Shift and Speeding Up Your Evolution

In addition to writing about your insights, it is very important to remain mindful and aware while the grace comes in and the shifting occurs. If you can notice and acknowledge the shift, you will find your processing becomes much more empowering, and your progress accelerates. Shifts come in many forms, and it helps to be able to recognize the various aspects.

Sometimes the shift is so subtle that you do not quite notice it, but other times, it will be so dramatic that something will change instantly in your life. Processing can have the effect of realigning the subtle body and physical body. You may even feel muscles, bones or joints in the body reposition and adjust. Or, the phone may ring, and the very person who was involved in the drama you have been processing will be on the line offering a solution or new situation.

That shifting of the energy is instantaneous as you offer it up. Sometimes the energy shifts as soon as you find the right opposite to a certain theme word in your story, even before you make an offering, as was the case with Paul's example. This is because you are working with mental energy, which moves more quickly than physical energy.

Processing like this can circumvent having to live out situations
in the physical plane over a period of months or years.

You can create more growth faster by using the mental techniques rather than by living it out in the physical. If you are on a fast track with your evolution, this is helpful.

We are built so that we feel only one side of a pair of opposites. We cannot access the missing side of us, the unconscious, on a feeling level; we can access it only intellectually. However, when you have done this polarity work for a while, the veil between conscious and unconscious begins to dissolve. For example you may find yourself being happy and sad at the same time. That is really quite bizarre at first. Feeling both sides of a polarity in this way may make you laugh. You laugh because you feel and see the two sides at once. When you see both sides, the realization pulls your awareness into the middle between the two sides, the neutral place, away from being stuck on one side of the polarity. When you see that, you are free! It is magical. If you have never tried it, it can be a powerful, miraculous moment.

Over the years of working with many people, I have also become aware of a very strange phenomenon. After processing an issue, shifts happen in quite amazing ways, and yet sometimes people don't see them! Very often it takes a friend or guide to point them out, even when it has been a dramatic shift. I attribute this phenomenon to the nature of human consciousness, which is to be aware of itself at any given time and to think that it has always been that way. Once we shift, we often don't remember how we used to think and feel. It is extremely helpful to stay in the witness and keep track of the big picture as well as the current process, watching the unfoldment of balancing and awakening over time. Keeping a good journal helps with this.

Many times when I work with people, they are starting out in a really bad state of mind. We do a list of polarities, we offer them up, and we sit around for a few moments. Then, five minutes later they are as chirpy and as cheerful as can be. Then, they will look at me and say,

"Oh, nothing has happened!" They do not even realize that one minute they were in a bad mood, the next minute they are actually feeling better, and that that was a result of the process we just did. We are so used to our consciousness moving from one state to another that unless we have practiced a bit, we are not able to see that the change took place because we did the list. The shift still happens anyway, though, even if we don't see it.

As we touched on in Section One, here is an example of the many I have encountered like this over the years. I worked with a woman once, helping her process some of her issues around money. I will call her Samantha. She said she was broke all the time. We discovered that Samantha had a lot of erroneous concepts, like if you are spiritual, you shouldn't have any money. So I suggested some squares and other processing she might do, which she was very excited about. In a follow-up phone call, she told me about many new insights she was having and how much the process was rolling right along. A couple of months later, one of my assistants reported to me she had spoken with Samantha on the phone. She said Samantha told her she was very depressed because nothing was changing in her life. She still didn't have any money. When the assistant probed a bit, she said Samantha happened to mention that in the last couple of months (since the processing!) she had been promoted from being a part-time employee to being a full-time employee with full benefits. When the assistant pointed this fact out to her and suggested that this shift had happened as a direct result of her intense processing, Samantha became very reflective. After a few minutes, it dawned on her that indeed that had been the sequence of events. She acknowledged that yes, perhaps she was moving in the direction of having more abundance in her life. But somehow, she had not put the two together!

So, it helps enormously to become aware of the big picture. You build spiritual momentum this way. Try to track your shifts. The more you acknowledge them and are grateful, the more grace will come and visit you, showering you with gifts.

EXPERIENCING A SIMULATION

As you do this work, you will learn to become more and more aware, mindful and in your witness all the time. You will find that it is a very pleasant state of being, very centered, balanced, relaxed and joyful. From this place there is an easeful moving into greater and greater states of clarity as you pass through the veils of negative ego. It is especially helpful after the processing and shifting are complete to be aware of what we have come to call *simulations* or *set-ups*. Usually after you have finished your offering and have cleared an issue, you will be offered one of these. They are simply little tests of some kind to give you an opportunity to really pass through the veil completely.

What does this look like? It is certainly not something to get scared about! It is not like final exams at school; spirit is much more forgiving than that! Sometimes it is an immediate test, and other times the test comes within a day to a week. Usually, you find yourself presented with a situation that has the exact structure of the issue you just cleared. The window dressing, the surface content, may change, but the underlying message of the experience is exactly the same. It is a situation that causes a certain type of mental-emotional reaction in you.

Are you awake and in your neutral witness enough to notice that it is a set-up? You are being given a choice in that moment. Do you buy into the old conditioning, the limited personality patterning, or do you let it all go? Have you shifted enough not to have to repeat the same old stuff again? Are you in your neutrality and awake and clear enough in that moment to go through the same type of situation you used to go through without reacting in the same way? The challenge of the simulation is to move past our own limitations into a more expanded, balanced, and whole state. If you can, you release that old patterning for good. That layer does not come back again, ever! This is your well-earned *A+* on your test.

Here is a trick to help you get through the test. After the clearing, ask for grace to help you remain vigilantly in your neutral witness so that you are prepared for your test. When the set-up comes (the same old situation that used to trigger your pattern) and you see it, say to yourself and to spirit, "I am not this." Acknowledge that you are not these things of the world, these emotions, these thoughts, the old patterned personality. They are passing through you. This way you will *not* hook into them and will not react in the same old way.

Then, you say, "I am That." Remember, *That* is one of the names of God. You are saying, "I am pure awareness. I am consciousness." You may feel the same old emotions and think the same old thoughts in the moment of the simulation, but you do not identify with them. As pure awareness, you let them pass through and do not hook into them or make them real.

This technique comes from the system of *Advaita Vedanta*, a form of Jnana yoga. "I am not this. I am That," translates in Sanskrit roughly as, "*Neti neti. Tat twam asi.*" When being tested, you can say either the English or the Sanskrit version.

You also do not suppress or deny or avoid the experience as it unfolds.

Instead, you allow it to be what it is. You surrender to it, remaining unattached and unaffected by the drama of it all. It can be very challenging and seem very real, but it is just the personality play, the dance of the duality. It is important to remind yourself of that and to make these statements to the universe and to your higher self. Then, miraculously, the drama is over, the turmoil abates, and you have passed the test. You are clear. You are free.

There is a great scene in the movie *The Little Buddha*, the Bernardo Bertolucci movie with Keanu Reeves, where Siddhartha is meditating and gets presented with the test of his greatest desires and worst fears. (Don't worry! This is an extreme example. When you first start processing, you'll get simple, little tests.) Images of violent storms, ugly monsters and war parade themselves before Siddhartha, but by remaining meditatively in his neutral witness, he acknowledges that he is just being tested, that fear is just born of ego, and that none of it is real. He remains unattached. When each simulation completes, the holographic image fades away. When it is all over, he is enlightened. The whole movie is wonderful, but it is worth watching just for that one scene, which is a brilliant depiction of how this principle works.

ASCENSION AND THE RAISING OF CONSCIOUSNESS

Observe yourself for several days, and you will see how your attention and your energy fluctuate constantly as you are pulled by the negative and positive reactions to life. This flip-flopping is what we often describe as the roller coaster of life. On any given day we may go from feeling elated to depressed and back to elated again. As we do the processes, the swing to the extremes lessens.

But something else even more profound and unexpected also happens. Our new lows will be where our old highs used to be. The median between the two extremes changes through the raising of the vibration. This shift in vibration, resulting from the increased energy flow, is known as ascension (Fig. 12-1).

The median between our high and low states
shifts as we do the transformation work.

This chart shows that the overall vibration of one's whole system is being speeded up. In the long run, processing ourselves out of conditioned and unbalanced states is a way of speeding up the vibration. The imbalances that we hold slow down the vibration. Clearing them allows a re-connecting with our larger energy, our spirit, our life force and with life itself. As we reach a higher vibration, we gain enormous strength. This moves us in an accelerated way to the next level of whatever we are working on, like a springboard to the next shift, so that our ascension just keeps on developing.

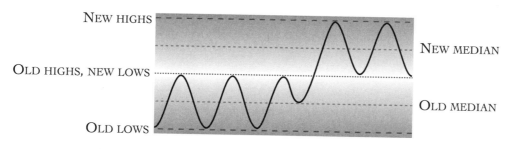

Fig. 12-1.

REVIEW
THE STEPS OF THE DEEPER POWER OF PROCESSING
1. Find a theme to your story
2. Find all the right opposites
3. Offer up positive *and* negative
4. Write your additional insights
5. Find the key square
6. Follow the thread of continuity
7. Notice the shift
8. Experience a simulation
   - Ask for grace to help you remain in the neutral witness
   - Say, "I am not this. I am That."

SUGGESTIONS FOR PUTTING THEORY INTO PRACTICE

1. Do a polarity processing story. After you make your list of opposites, find the theme polarity or polarities. Write it at the top of the page next to the date.
2. In making your list, if there is an opposite you cannot find or are not sure about, meditate on the word, feel your way into it, and see what you come up with. Also look up the word in a synonym-antonym dictionary or a thesaurus. Is there a word that resonates with you as the true opposite? Do you feel a shift or get any insights from doing this?
3. Do a triangle and a square on your theme polarity.
4. Review your list, triangle and square before making an offering. Are you able to offer up positive *and* negative? If not, write about it and pray to have a clearing.
5. After you make your offering, write about any additional insights.
6. Are you guided to do any other processing as a result of your offering? Follow the thread of continuity, and see where it leads you. Write about your experience.
7. Over the course of the next day or so, are you aware of grace coming in and of having any shifts? Write about your experience.
8. After you have had a shift, catch yourself in a simulation. Then do a journal entry about the test. Include answers to the following questions:
   a. How was the surface content different this time?
   b. How was the underlying structure the same?
   c. Where did you hold the witness strongly?
   d. Where did you react?
   e. Did you remember to say, "I am not this. I am That."?

TESTIMONIAL • THE ANGRY LAWYER

I work in a law office in Los Angeles. My direct boss is a woman attorney, and she in turn works for the head attorney, whom I will call Patrick. Patrick is what you might describe as a manipulative woman-hater. He has a real problem in that when any little thing is out of whack, he blows his stack and finds the nearest woman to blow up at. All of the women in our office were walking on egg shells around him so as not to tick him off. I observed him for about a year, watching him demean, insult and generally manipulate everyone to be afraid of him and wield the power he tries to hold over everyone. I have been practicing the Marriage of Spirit processing techniques for a few years, and so I spent a lot of time processing Patrick's personality and my reactions to him. I also processed many of the office dramas and blow-ups involving Patrick and his awful antics.

One day he was badgering my boss, whom I will call Henrietta, and had her to the point of near tears. I heard him screaming at her, and it hit me that no one was ever going to stand up to this man, and that he was going to continue doing this for as long as he could get away with it. I was at the point of quitting, but instead I just processed even harder, praying for a resolution and clarity. About a week later, spirit orchestrated a situation that was absolute perfection for me. Patrick was angry that something had not gotten done in the office. He called me in to his office because his own secretary was not around, and he obviously needed to vent on someone. So guess who? It was me. I stood in his office and spoke in a calm manner to him explaining that I had no idea why this particular thing was not done, and it seemed that the calmer I was, the more excited he got. At one point he stood up, his face as red as a beet, and began to scream obscenities at me.

It was at that moment that I knew spirit was supporting me, and I very calmly asked him not ever to speak to me like that, that if he wanted to discuss something, fine, but not in this manner. Well, he practically blew the roof right off of the building. I was frightened but did not budge. I knew that these were just words and could not hurt me. I also knew that I needed to stand my ground. He eventually threw me out of his office out of frustration. As calmly as I could muster up, I took myself into the ladies room and waited till the shaking stopped. Then I went back to my office. Within an hour he called me into his office again. He boyishly apologized, the best way he could. I did not say one word to him but simply nodded my head and returned to my work. It took about a week for the atmosphere to cool down, that is to say, till I was speaking to him again in a civil manner.

Now, this may not seem very monumental, but ever since that day, not only has the relationship changed between me and Patrick but between all of the women in the office and him. I believe that holding my ground with him and letting his anger pass through me rather than reacting to it allowed the charge that he puts on his power trips to fizzle out. I also believe that by doing my own processing, I became clear enough to not be compelled to react to him when he blew up at me. I was able to remain in my neutral witness and not to suppress my anger, but instead to let it pass right through me in the heat of the moment. He does not get angry very much anymore. Not only that, he tends to spend a lot of time in my office talking about his personal "stuff," and he has told me on more than one occasion that he feels like I am sort of his in-house psychologist. Ha, ha!! We are friends now, and I am in my heart with him. I attribute our new found friendship, our *merging*, to the fact that I processed his personality so much that I have *owned* his stuff as my own projections. I have owned my outside world as me. Remarkably, I have found that the gossip and chatter around the office regarding his behavior have subsided, and everyone feels better for it. I am still amazed to see that his behavior has changed because I processed myself and changed myself inwardly. I also feel that there was a merging of masculine/feminine consciousness in this office, better and easier for everyone to work in. For me, this is proof that I can change my outer reality by changing my inner consciousness.

The journey of a thousand miles begins with the first step.

— Lao Tsu

THIRTEEN

ADVENTURES IN TRANSFORMATION

Now that you have some more practice with applying the Marriage of Spirit principles and have experienced the aftereffects of processing, you are ready for an adventure in transformation. Here are some methods to help you dive a little deeper into the unconscious. This chapter includes:

- Ways to find the most hidden aspects of your pattern—your blind spots— using squares and a technique called mirroring
- Tips on some subtleties of triangles and squares
- A technique called double binds that helps to unravel the thorniest knots of the mind
- A look at overwhelm, doubt and meaninglessness, which will help to deflate the intensity of the potential process around these issues.

USING SQUARES TO FIND YOUR BLIND SPOTS

Doing squares helps you to start seeing your patterns pretty quickly. Squares really reveal situations where you often do not want to look, where you are choosing to keep a blind spot. Remember, you never experience all four corners at the same time, but you possibly *have* experienced each corner at one time or another. How much conscious awareness do you have of that? The whole point is to turn over the stone and look.

Sometimes you will find a corner
that reveals a whole pattern of avoidance,
and you will have a revelation.

You will realize that you are creating a push-pull of attraction and repulsion and are blocking aspects of your awareness from integrating. You are blocking your own ascension into wholeness. The push-pull associated with those states will not integrate until you have made all of the missing corners conscious. When you make them conscious, then the square integrates.

For example, if you find yourself in some sort of pain, and you do the square on PAIN and PLEASURE many, many times, along with other related squares, and you still don't feel a shift, you probably have a blind spot in one of the corners. You are probably not seeing the full extent to which you do the behavior of one of the corners. What can you do if this is the case?

If you cannot think of anything for a certain corner, then that corner is totally dead to you. You have buried it deeply in the unconscious. You have never let yourself see it. In this case, the first step is to pray for grace and ask spirit to show you the missing corner, which is holding the pattern in place because it is still unconscious.

Very often *other* people see how you do that corner, but you do not let yourself see it. The second step is to try processing with a friend or with a group of friends. It is incredibly helpful to process with other people who can help you see your blind spots. For example, in the PAIN - PLEASURE square maybe there is some aspect of the corner, the *desire for pain*, that you can't see but that someone else might be able to see for you.

There is a saying, "If we could see ourselves as others see us, what a revelation that would be." The opposite of that is our seeing our own faults in others. That is projection. So the third step is if you find a corner that you are having trouble with, try to see that corner in someone else. Then, see yourself in that person by owning the fact that we are all one, that we have a collective conscious and a collective unconscious. If we *really* own that, *believe* it, and *know* it in our hearts, it is possible to see ourselves in others and to fill in the corner. See your own unconscious all around you in everybody. If you continue drawing a blank in a corner of a square, for example if you cannot think of a single reason why *you* would *desire to be a tyrant*, you can ask yourself, "Why would *anyone* want to be a tyrant?" Figure out why Hitler wanted to be a tyrant. Look at the archetypes. Look at other people you have seen. Say to yourself, "Oh yes, my boss, mother, spouse, brother, or someone else is a real tyrant! Well, s/he wants power, s/he wants control, s/he wants to dominate." Write it down from any perspective that fills in the corner. It does not have to be from only your own perspective.

The fourth step is to continue your probing by asking the question, "Why?" repeatedly. As you write and explore each corner of a square, continue to ask yourself, "Why? Why do I desire or why am I attracted to _____? Why do I fear or repulse _____?" Have you ever considered, for example, why you desire happiness, or why you repulse sadness? It may seem quite obvious at a first glance, but it is not, actually. It is very important to probe deeply. You may want to take a few minutes and try this now with the square, *happy-sad*, before you continue reading.

Continue to ask yourself, "Why?" Meditate and ask inwardly to see what comes up for you. You may be surprised what you find below the surface, below what *appears* obvious. Some of the deeper motivations behind any of our desires are things like desiring to connect with God or with other people, or desiring to survive or exist. Some of the deeper fears may be things like fearing disconnection, separation or death.

Seeing how you live out all of the corners in detail and defining the patterns in the corners gives more insight and self-knowledge about *how* those patterns function. This leads to dropping them.

SQUARES ARE LOOPS IN CONSCIOUSNESS

The difference between processing a square in your journal and living out in the physical world the experiences associated with the desires and fears of the square is a time factor. It could take you a few minutes or hours to do the square. It could take you a decade or more to live out the square from a place of unconsciousness. In the course of life, people are living out squares all the time without knowing it. The reason we would choose to do the square is because our prime objective is to move our destiny forward on a fast path toward spiritual awakening in one lifetime, rather than to live unconsciously according to the turning of the cycles associated with the square, which could span many lifetimes and include a lot of suffering. And while living out the square in the physical may include interesting learning experiences, gradually building knowledge and awareness, it would delay our opportunity to reach clarity and the unified state. This is not a judgment of whether it is good or bad to live out the square in the physical world. Sometimes it is one's destiny to live out certain experiences physically, and other times it is not necessary. It is a soul's choice, and doing the square in a journal rather than living out a square in the physical is simply based on a different motive and intention for one's life—to clear attachments, rather than to fulfill egoic desires and to avoid fears.

Here is an example of how this works. We will use the square *wealthy-poor* to demonstrate the point. Let's say there is a man named Rob, whose patterning is such that he desires to become wealthy. He may spend years of his life striving and pedaling, so to speak, toward that goal. His desire to be wealthy is a major motivating factor in his life, and so his actions are always moving him in the direction of that corner of the square (Fig. 13-1).

Let's say he actually fulfills that desire to a high degree. For example, let's say after fifteen years he has a high-powered corporate job with a lot of success, power and prestige, and has accumulated several million dollars. Generally he is happy in his life, but somehow he does not feel completely fulfilled. Somehow what he thought he might find by pedaling toward that corner of desiring to be wealthy has not quite made him as happy and as fulfilled as he wants to be. This of course is the nature of ego. We pedal and pedal toward our desires, but ultimately they are not what fulfill us. It is only when we realize our true nature as Self that we find the ultimate fulfillment behind our desires.

So, Rob could spend the next twenty years or the rest of his life continuing to pedal toward that one corner, continuing to accumulate wealth ad infinitum, in order to try to fulfill that desire completely. But it will only be when he realizes consciously to some degree that perhaps he is not going to find complete inner fulfillment by accumulating more wealth, that he will change. Let's say he does realize this. It begins to dawn on him that the wealth is not the end-all. This would move his consciousness along the side of the square toward the repulsion of (or fear of) the wealth (Fig. 13-2).

This could look like a life change for Rob. Let's say he decides to leave his high-powered job and to move to the countryside in order to write a novel—something he has always longed for but that did not fit in with his primary motivation for wealth. Depending on how much of a change in consciousness Rob goes through, he may even begin to entertain thoughts that perhaps having no money might be easier than having to manage all the wealth he had accumulated over the years. He feels the

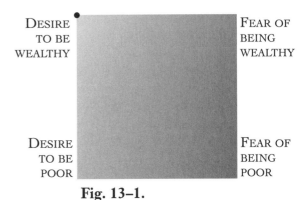

Fig. 13–1.

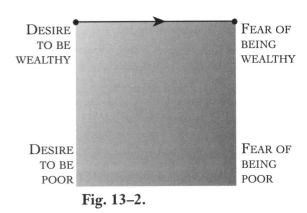

Fig. 13–2.

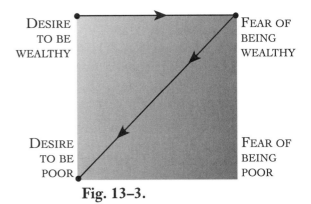

Fig. 13–3.

peace, quiet and stress-free life of not having the high-income job is better for him. Or perhaps he finds it a romantic notion that he is a jobless writer in the countryside who is earning no money. These thought forms would move his consciousness along the square toward the next corner, the desire to be poor (Fig. 13-3).

This phase may last for a few moments, a few weeks or a few years. The amount of time he spends in the corner, whether moments or years, is dependent on his patterning. He may even become the archetypal eccentric artist and live the rest of his life in that corner, contentedly having not much money. Let's say that at some point he realizes that pedaling toward that desire-to-be-poor corner also did not get him the fulfillment he was searching for. This would move him along the next side of the square to the repulsion of or fear of being poor (Fig. 13-4).

In fact, let's say Rob only lasts a few months in the desire-to-be-poor corner before he has a full-blown panic attack because he has no income. He believes he has done something absolutely foolish and crazy and zooms over to the fear-of-being-poor corner. This catapults him right into the desire to be wealthy corner again, and he is back where he started (Fig. 13-5).

So can you see the loop in consciousness represented by a square (Fig. 13-6)? It is actually a figure eight (Fig. 13-7).

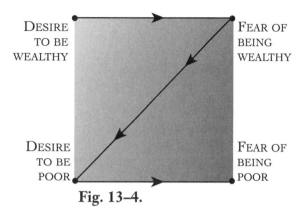

Fig. 13–4.

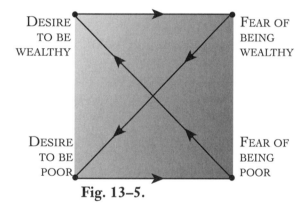

Fig. 13–5.

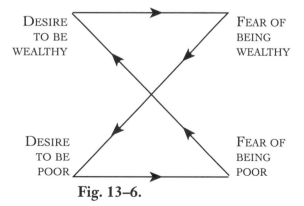

Fig. 13–6.

We go around and around unconsciously chasing desires and repulsing fears. Rob could spend the rest of his life chasing the same desires and repulsing the same fears. Like the figure eight the loop can repeat itself over and over, which is why we experience recurring lessons with just a change in scenery. In fact, when you turn the figure eight on its side, it is the mathematical symbol for infinity (Fig. 13-8)!

Of course the ego is not infinite. There is an end to the patterning, because it is finite. It is the beginning of the end when we begin to wake up, to become conscious of the desires and fears—the conditioned, programmed patterning—that motivate our behaviors, and to detach from them.

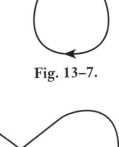

Fig. 13–7.

Granted, in our example, Rob probably gained enormous experience through living things out physically. Over the course of a few decades, he probably learned enormous lessons, had incredible joys and also experienced much suffering. And that is life in the unconscious state. It is an amazing, magical roller coaster ride. There is no judgment of good or bad in this. But when Rob tumbles to the fact that there is another way, that there is more to life than chasing desires and running from fears unconsciously, he will be able to shorten his path home enormously. By processing and by doing squares, he will

Fig. 13–8.

be able to move much more easefully and consciously through his experiences because he is clearer. In fact, we are able to experience more of life's richness when we are clearer.

Here is another scenario of how we move from corner to corner in a square. For instance let's say when Rob is in the desire-for-wealth corner, things are really going well for him and he is making a lot of money. The ego can become so expanded from feeling great and happy all the time that on some level it fears it is pushing its boundaries too far. It fears too much expansion and formlessness. The limited egoic patterning can only take so much expansion before it needs to contract. This is the ego fearing its own death. Remember that the walls of the ego are made of fear, and of course we would feel the fear when we push the egoic boundaries too far. So, Rob's inner saboteur may put the brakes on somehow, causing some problem in his business, so that the money stops flowing in. This is the contracting energy that begins to repulse the desire for wealth and move Rob along the side of the square toward the fear of wealth. The same thing would happen in the fear corners with the contracting energy. The ego can only contract so far before it fears its own death, and then it begins to expand again and move to a desire corner.

In our example with Rob, we have detailed out the movement of consciousness over several years. However, these loops in consciousness are often repeated daily, sometimes hourly, or even every few seconds, depending on what the polarity is that we are dealing with. If it is something we just tend to think about but not to act on, then we can traverse all four corners of a square in just a few moments. If these patterns are running by habit or unconsciously, generally we feel drained by them; they make us *spin* or feel *loopy*, and we lose our light. We keep trying and trying, searching in vain for what we think we desire, when in reality it is not what we really desire. We also keep repulsing, avoiding and denying the things we fear. Chasing the loop of the figure eight is designed to fail. It will never get us what we really want, which is to connect with our own inner core of divinity. Each time we strive to fulfill these polarized desires, we are settling for a facsimile of the real thing. When we avoid or repulse our fears, we are buying into the egoic programming, sweeping things under the rug, and stuffing them into the unconscious. Until we wake up to this fact, we are destined to repeat the limited program, desiring and fearing around this loop of the figure eight. The way out is simply by seeing it—by making the unconscious conscious and by offering it up to grace for true transformation.

At this point you may be wondering what it might look like when we clear the pattern associated with a square. Let's use Rob as an example. Since the wealthy-poor polarity was such a predominant theme in his destiny in the separate system, shifting it would probably mean a major life change for him. If Rob were to clear the pattern completely, including most of the patterns associated with wealthy-poor—like work-play, businessman-artist, for example—he would probably create a situation where he would have it all. This might mean he would create abundance in his life *and* live in the countryside *and* write his book. The either-or of the situation would disappear. We can create meaningful, fulfilling and lucrative work for ourselves when we are clear.

USING MIRRORING TECHNIQUES TO FIND YOUR BLIND SPOTS

In addition to doing squares, one very helpful tool you can use to help find your hidden, unconscious side is *mirroring*. If the person or the outer circumstance that feels unbalanced or that is bothering you persists, then you need to find what behavior or patterning in you is drawing the bothersome situation to you and is holding it all in place. Remember that your outside world is a reflection of a part of you, of your own unconscious.

The first step is to ask yourself these two questions:
1. How do I do the same bothersome behavior as the other person? Why?
2. How do I have an attachment to the opposite of the bothersome behavior? Why?

For example, if someone is angry with you, then ask yourself: 1) "How and why do I get angry at others? Do I outwardly express my anger toward others?" 2) "How and why do I do the opposite behavior? Do I stuff my anger?" Chances are that the angry person is mirroring to you some reflection of your own unbalanced dealings with anger.

Let's look at what the opposite behavior might be. One common pair of opposites that often is not considered here is: outwardly expressing anger versus stuffing/suppressing the anger. So, if the other person is expressing the anger outwardly, perhaps your answer to the second question would be that you do the opposite behavior by stuffing your anger and by rarely expressing it. By asking yourself the two questions, you may reveal your blind spot, which means you have made the unconscious conscious.

Here is another example. If someone is controlling you, then ask yourself, "How and why do I control?" Also ask, "How and why do I like to be out of control?" If you are manifesting someone or something that is controlling, chances are you have control issues yourself that need to be examined, addressed and cleared. When you discover the answers to these questions, then you have begun to unlock the door to freedom; you can make an offering of it and let it all go. Once you have discovered the answers, it is helpful to do a square about the behavior.

You can also use the technique in a circumstance that is bothering you and that does not involve another person. It is also a mirror of something inside you, some kind of pattern or behavior that you can examine and clear. For example, if you are having money problems, then it would be a good idea to examine your beliefs, attitudes and behaviors about money. If you feel the world is withholding money from you, use the simple two-question technique, and ask yourself, "How and why do I withhold from the world?" Also, "How and why do I over-extend?" How does your outer circumstance reflect the inner patterning? It would also be a good idea to do squares on whatever answers you come up with.

Sometimes behaviors or circumstances that are very charged for us and are being mirrored to us are so deeply buried in the unconscious, that there is no way we can remotely recognize them as a part of us, even using the mirroring technique. In that case, here's a little trick you can use.

Let's say for example you have a boss who is your petty tyrant. The first step is to ask yourself, "How and why am I a tyrant?" If you search and search inside yourself, but you just can't find any sign of a tyrant in there, right away you know you have buried your tyrant deeply in your unconscious. We do all have a tyrant, by the way; it is just that most of us don't see ourselves acting it out.

Sometimes all you have to do is catch the tiniest glimpse of how you run a hidden behavior. For example, if you really can't see how you are a tyrant in any aspect of your life, try to recall a time when you were continually wakened in the middle of the night by a buzzing mosquito. Did you get really mad and want to smash it to bits? This is the tyrant energy! Even that small glimpse of that kind of killer instinct is a start. If you can see it even that much, sometimes that is enough to free yourself.

Anyway, the next step then is to ask, "How do I do the opposite of the tyrant? Why?" The opposite could be, "by playing the role of the victim in general in my life," Again, doing a square about the behavior and its opposite helps. You will want to pray and ask to be shown your deeply buried behavior, like the tyrant for example, in order to complete the process. Obviously, this does not mean you will become a tyrant. It just means you will come to more of an understanding of that part of yourself; you will integrate it, have greater tolerance, forgiveness and compassion for it in you and in the outside world, and let the attraction-repulsion to it go. This is liberation.

FINDING THE GIVING AND RECEIVING ASPECTS OF SQUARES

Some polarities, usually verbs, have giving and receiving aspects. By finding the giving and receiving aspects, you find new qualities of a square, which helps you to expose your blind spots. Using this technique dovetails with using mirroring to find your blind spots.

Here are some examples of various giving and receiving polarities, which we will break out into squares. First, let's look at the polarity LOVE and HATE. One way of doing this square is: the desire to love and the fear of loving, the desire to hate and the fear of hating. This square is about giving love and hate.

But there are two different squares possible here. Another way of interpreting this polarity is *being* loved and *being* hated. In the second version of the square, the corners are: the desire to be loved and the fear of being loved, the desire to be hated and the fear of being hated. In this square love and hate are being received.

> *Some polarities can be made into two squares:*
> *one about doing something to the outside,*
> *and one about the outside doing something to you.*

Another example is with the polarity MISUNDERSTOOD and UNDERSTOOD. The receiving square looks like this: the desire to feel misunderstood, the fear of feeling misunderstood, the desire to feel understood, the fear of feeling understood.
The giving square is: the desire to misunderstand others, the fear of misunderstanding others, the desire to understand others, the fear of understanding others.

Here is how using this technique can help you find your blind spots, just as using mirroring does. Both methods help you to unhook yourself from uncomfortable dynamics with the outside by revealing the blind spot that holds it all in place. Here is an example.

I was counseling a woman once who was fed up with her twenty-year-old son because she said that for years he had been blaming her intensely for certain unhappy aspects of his childhood. She was unsuccessful at attempting to work it out with him and was very confused, disconsolate and frustrated about the whole thing. We talked about the situation at length, but with minimal results. I suggested she try doing a square on being blamed by her son, which she agreed to do. The opposite she used was being praised by her son. She looked at her desires and fears of both sides. Still, there was not much of a shift. When I mentioned to her that this was a receiving square and that perhaps she should also try doing the giving square, she felt as though that might be the answer. In fact as she did this other square, she started to see a whole pattern that had been totally blind to her and that was quite a revelation. The square was about blaming her son and praising her son. The corner on the desire to blame her son revealed to her that as a mother she had a lot of unexpressed, unresolved blame and resentment toward him for how much of her own life she had had to sacrifice for him.

Of course this was something she had never wanted to admit to herself because she loved her son and because she felt she was a very good mother for the most part. When she realized that her blaming him was the opposite, unconscious piece to his blaming her, her jaw nearly hit the floor, and she gasped in amazement. In that moment there was an enormous breakthrough in understanding that she was certain would cause a huge shift in their relationship.

Of course, her final realization was also the same realization she might have seen had she used the mirroring technique. That is, by asking herself the two simple questions, "How/why do I do the same bothersome behavior?" and "How/why do I do the opposite of the bothersome behavior?", she would have realized that she blamed her son just as he blamed her.

Both methods will help you reveal aspects of your pattern that you may not otherwise be able to see. Sometimes it is harder to see how we do the unpleasant thing to others, and therefore that is the very thing that holds the whole dynamic in place. Not being able to see how you blame others would hold in place the unpleasantness of having others blame you.

Sometimes it really helps to work out a particularly *hot* polarity in all the different possible combinations—the aspects of giving and receiving—so that you get a good look at all its hidden corners. You can do both squares—just to be sure you get a breakthrough. And you can also use the mirroring technique to complement the squares.

A Tip for Triangles — Finding the True Opposite *and* the Ascended Balance

When we are searching for the opposite to a particularly charged word, the natural temptation is to want to find the ascended balance rather than the true opposite. It is easy to make this mistake when first starting the processing work. Jumping ahead to the ascended balance word rather than finding the true opposite is only natural, as the tendency is to want to go to the place of the ascended balance right away. We see the one side of the polarity, know it is not in balance and go right for the balancing, instead of finding the hidden, unconscious opposite, which helps hold everything in place. So, it is best to find all three words—the ascended balance and *both* sides of the polarity. (This is a subtle distinction, and those of you who are good with words will find this to be like a fun word game. If you find this too challenging, don't worry about it and just skip this section. You will still get a shift.)

Here is an example. Say you are feeling deprived and decide to process it to clear it. You might feel like the opposite of the word *deprived* is *abundance* or *in the flow*. However, *abundance* and *in the flow* may be better used at the apex of the triangle. A better, truer opposite might be *spoiled*. Can you feel how *deprived* and *spoiled* have an equivalent but opposite vibration? Deprived implies that an authority figure outside of you (a parent, or God, maybe?) is denying you your due. And spoiled implies that the authority is giving you more than you really should have. Both are associated with the polarized world of right and wrong, powerful and powerless, inside and outside. *Abundance* and *in the flow* work best at the apex of the triangle. Those are ascended states that represent an alignment with higher truth. They imply you are living in a paradigm of knowing you always have exactly what you need, of trusting that your experience—whether one of pain or pleasure, of apparent lack or plenty—is perfect in every moment.

Remember, you'll still probably get a shift from using abundance as an opposite to deprived. This principle is a subtle distinction to help you refine your processing and get an even bigger breakthrough.

Here is another example. Say you have the word *control*, and you are looking for its opposite. At first you might want to use the word *surrender*. Surrender seems appropriate because it is a state of letting go of control. But perhaps better opposites might be *chaos* or *out-of-control*. Chaos implies the kind of haywire randomness that the small self fears as it struggles to be in control. *Surrender* might be better used as an ascended balance word, as it implies a balance between the two sides of *control* and *chaos*; we surrender our attachment to needing control or fearing chaos. Again, there is no right and wrong here; we are talking about subtle differences. It is up to you to find the words that work best for you.

Let's look at one more example. If you are looking for an opposite for the word *cynical*, you might be tempted to use the word *trust*. But perhaps trust is really what you are looking for as the ascended balance to your cynical attitude. A truer opposite to *cynical* is *gullible*, or *naive*. Cynical implies that you doubt everything, making you feel powerful and shrewd in a way. Gullible and naive imply that you believe everything, making you feel powerless and foolish. So, these make a better pair of opposites, as they are clearly polarized in an equivalent way. *Trust* as the ascended balance is the place where we don't need to be cynical or gullible, or feel powerful or powerless, but instead have faith in higher intelligence; we have the humility to recognize that our polarized attitudes can be balanced out by trusting in higher intelligence.

Again, these are subtle differences, but it is important to know that if you find the whole picture, the opposites and the ascended balance, then you have described all the levels; you have made the unconscious conscious, as well as seeing what will bring both sides into the oneness.

Understanding Double Binds

Double binds are a technique that complements the other processing techniques in a powerful way. They are one of the most important and powerful aspects of processing. A double bind is a paradox, a catch-22. In a double bind, we are damned if we do and damned if we don't.

When we uncover a double bind, we have discovered one of the underlying building blocks of the foundation of the ego. A double bind is a fundamental knot in consciousness that holds an aspect of the entire pattern in place. It is the paradox that we come up against as we move through the levels of consciousness. It is the ego's dilemma. By verbalizing the exact nature of the double bind, we see the inherent paradox in the nature of our dual system. By offering up the double bind and asking for release, we gain enormous freedom from egoic imprisonment.

Squares are full of double binds. In doing squares, we can see how one part of us desires one side of a polarity, and another part of us desires the exact opposite! And we can see how part of us desires something, and another part fears that very thing. How can we ever win with such conflicting interests? We can't. The ego is designed to fail in this way. It is designed to have you chase your own tail, repeating the same old patterns, the same old desires and fears, ad infinitum! Only the scenery changes.

Of course one of the ways out is by seeing how the game is played, by making the unconscious conscious. Double binds, twisted pieces of logic that they are, are especially helpful in freeing us when we make them conscious. They are a very deep layer of the pattern. When double binds become conscious, we are seeing a layer we don't usually get to see. Often, seeing them is a result of using the polarities, squares or triangles techniques—because we have peeled away some veils, and grace is revealing the knots that are below them.

We also uncover double binds in other processing situations, not just from doing squares. Sometimes after offering up a list of polarities, a double bind may just mysteriously pop into your head. Or perhaps you will wake up in the morning after processing one evening, and a double bind will be suddenly very clear to you. Or perhaps you can logically deduce the double bind after you have processed and have seen your patterns enough. Grace gives us these gifts of insight when we have cleared enough layers of ego and are ready to look at the root of the situation. We can also pray specifically to be shown the double bind(s) that hold(s) the situation in place. However we come to be aware of them, it is important to write them down and offer them up.

Here is an example of a double bind that we might find through grace or through logical deduction: "I can't trust God because when I have trusted in the past, bad experiences have happened to me. Yet until I learn to trust, bad experiences will continue to happen to me."

Realize that the double bind holds power not because it is true.
Rather, its power lies in the fact that some part of us believes it is true.

Often it is something we learned as children and have forgotten about. Simply seeing it, offering it up and asking for release from it, just like with the other techniques, is enough to free you from its power.

Here is another example: "I really want to let go of my poverty consciousness, because I see it is not benefiting me on my spiritual path. I want to have abundance in my life, but if I spend my time making money, then I won't have time for my spiritual path." When you see double binds like this, remember to write them down, verbatim. This is important because they can be confusing, twisted pieces of logic. By defining them in writing and offering them up, grace unravels the knot. Even draw a big box around it with arrows and exclamation points, and label it *DOUBLE BIND*. Always be watchful for these tricky paradoxes which usually underlie our most stuck places in consciousness.

SEEING THROUGH OVERWHELM

Some people feel daunted at the task of making so many lists and writing so many words. They say, "It just seems like the lists and squares would get longer and longer. It seems like to be thorough, almost any list or square would involve everything!" Sometimes they even quit the processing work because it seems so hopeless to take on such an apparently huge task. What they are up against is just *overwhelm*, which is a process in itself. So when you get to that point, you can process overwhelm. Its opposite is *coping*. You may want to do a square on this if it becomes an issue for you.

It is important to keep a perspective, to see the one tree right in front of you instead of trying to take on the whole forest. By just doing it a page at a time, you clear things. Eventually you will fill a notebook. Then, you start on your next notebook, one page at a time. Spirit will never give you more than you can handle. You just do one little process. When that's done, you feel a freedom. And then the next process will come in time, and you do that one, and you feel a freedom. You do actually reach the end of a process eventually.

Your pattern is not infinite.

You can finish completely with old, lousy stuff that keeps holding you back from life. It is a huge relief when you reach some major milestones in the dissolution work. If you feel so overwhelmed that you believe you will never have the time to really bring something to completion, just remind yourself that you are in the overwhelm process! And then simply take the next small step.

If you have a lot of processing to do, well, join the club. Everybody does. And, the best thing to do is just to proceed. Lao Tsu, in *The Way of Life*, said, "The journey of a thousand miles begins with the first step." So, with everything, not just processing, all you have to do to arrive at your destination is put one foot in front of the other.

Overwhelm is like a backdrop for a movie made in Hollywood. It sure looks real; that scenery seems vast and expansive and never-ending. But if you find the right razor blade, you can slice right through the canvas and walk through to the other side in an instant. Don't be fooled by it! One square or triangle or list of polarities could be the razor you are searching for.

SEEING THROUGH DOUBT

If you doubt that you are going to shift as a result of the processing, then *doubt* is a process in and of itself, and you can work through it. When you have developed a strong enough witness, you will be able to see that overwhelm and doubt are actually processes in them-selves, rather than thinking when you are in them that they are real. There is nothing to be overwhelmed by, and there is actually nothing to doubt or believe, either. You can do a square on *doubt* and *certainty*, or *doubt* and *belief*.

The rule of thumb is to neither believe nor disbelieve.

You may find that doubt comes up for you a lot, especially in the beginning. This is normal. It is because doubt is the first state at the top of the downward spiral. If you can catch doubt and name it as a process as soon as it arises, then you will find you don't have to go down the downward spiral. If you can remain in your neutral witness, you will see that doubt is not real. Doubt is just another process, an egoic state, an aspect of duality. Perhaps the ascended state is *wisdom* or *discernment*, and by remembering that, you may see through the illusion of doubt into the higher truth.

SEEING THROUGH MEANINGLESSNESS

Most people make meaninglessness real. It does not feel like an emotional vibration. So, when we get that far down the downward spiral, unless we have been doing the witnessing and processing work for a long time, we tend to really believe that life is meaningless. We forget that just last week or last month or last year everything was actually okay! This is why it is so important to develop a strong neutral witness. Keeping a good journal also helps with this so that you can refer back to the times when you were not in a deep process and you were seeing clearly. You have got to have some sort of reminder to yourself that meaninglessness is not real.

On the contrary, being in meaninglessness
usually means you are about to have a big breakthrough.

If you could but see the illusion of the emotional miasma, if you could see past the darkness of the meaninglessness cloud, you would pull yourself through to the other side with your faith. But it is like a great, thick fog that we get blinded by, numbed out into forgetfulness. It is important to give yourself a reality check in these moments. If all else fails, earmark this page and read this paragraph!

Since the death wish comes almost right after meaninglessness, if someone loses the witness and buys into meaninglessness, the person's life could be in danger. Closely associated states are things like numbness, purposelessness, hopelessness and worthlessness. Be on the lookout for these feelings. Because that is all they are—feelings, vibrations. They can all be processed away into the clear light of reality. When you emerge on the other side, you feel much lighter and more joyous and can hold much more light than before. As the saying goes, "You can only go as high as you are willing to go low." It is worth the journey into the darkness to experience the light on the other side. You can do a square on *meaninglessness* and *meaningfulness*. Or by finding the ascended state, which may be something like TRUTH, for you, or DHARMA, or GRATITUDE, then you can find your way out of meaninglessness.

The New Paradigm

The new paradigm of heart consciousness is the place where magic happens, where life unfolds easily and simply, like a red carpet in front of us. It is a system of flow as opposed to a system of rigidity. It is a heart-centered (fourth-chakra) way of being as opposed to a reliance on power, manipulation, domination and control. In the new paradigm there is very little clashing with other people's personalities or with life's situations. If dramas or power issues arise, we see them from the place of the witness, knowing that we are not the drama, that we are not the body, thoughts and emotions. We live in the neutral witness. While participating fully in the world, we can be completely present in each moment, loving life, having compassion and forgiveness for its pain and pleasure cycles. In this place, we do not desire or need to control life, circumstances or people. Instead of relying on our own, individual, separate power, we can surrender into the trust that we are perfectly cared for all the time, supported by the universe.

Although we may use different words to describe it, all spiritual traditions teach in some form about moving into the new paradigm. In one way or another, they all teach about the raising of one's consciousness or vibration, the movement of one's life or awareness into a more heart-centered way of being. Hinduism and Buddhism refer to the ascension of the kundalini energy in the body. In Christianity, Jesus taught about entering Heaven or the kingdom of God, which I don't believe was meant to be a place in the sky that you go when you die but rather more of an internal movement, an ascension in consciousness. I believe he was talking about focusing on the inner transformation, on moving one's awareness into the consciousness of the heart and into the luminous core of enlightenment within each one of us.

We move into this paradigm gradually as we do the inner processing work. We experience increasing degrees of this new way of living as the ego becomes clearer and clearer. Initially you have both feet in the world of duality. As you start to do the egoic clearing work, you move one foot into the new world, or maybe you will just test the waters with your big toe. Most people on the path of consciousness-raising are at various stages of having one foot in each world. Eventually, both feet will land in the new world. Many people are interested in processing just to the degree they need it to become happier people living more fulfilling, creative and abundant lives in the material world. This is fine and perfect for many people, and it is what their souls have chosen to experience this lifetime. Others, who have a burning desire to wake up and to become conscious of their own divine nature, will choose to take it further and to live fully with both feet firmly planted in the new paradigm.

An important aspect of moving into the new paradigm is learning to trust in the support of the universe to provide for us exactly what we need. It does not necessarily mean that we will get what we *want*, but rather we will get what we *need*. And spirit always knows what that is. As we move into the new paradigm, we bring in the support of the universe to take care of our needs. We learn to have faith in divine support; we ground on the invisible. As Jesus said in Matthew 6:33-34, "Seek ye first the kingdom of God… and all these things shall be added unto you." We find contentedness and detachment whether we are living in a palace or whether we are not sure where our next meal will be coming from.

This may sound like a fantasy world. The mind automatically doubts and projects fear onto the worst possible scenario in the future. "But how will *I* eat if *I* don't earn the money *myself*? What about *my* mortgage? What about providing for those who rely on *me*?" Me, me, I, I. The nature of ego is to doubt and to project worst case scenarios onto the future. Or, it will project its greatest desire onto the future, living in a fantasy world, hoping for its wants to be met.

Who is this *I* doing all of this surviving? Do we really have the arrogance to believe that we, in our limited state, have the power to control life, to know everything? There is an old joke which goes, "What is the easiest way to make God laugh?" The answer: "Tell God *your* plans."

The truth is that in our limited state we cannot know everything; we cannot control everything; we do not have the power to do everything. We cannot know the mind of God. But by processing the ego, by clearing the shadow, by making the unconscious conscious, we do move into the new paradigm of heart consciousness. It truly is an attainable goal: smooth, seamless, unbroken awareness of the unity of all things—even as we traverse the upward and downward spirals, amidst the roller coaster of life.

TAKE A LEAP OF FAITH — SKYWALKING

Over the years of doing this work with many, many people, we have coined a phrase for this aspect of moving into the new paradigm, which is one of the beginning stages of the awakening process. We call it *skywalking*. It is a major stepping stone on the path of Self-discovery and is about allowing grace to work in our lives. The level of trust and surrender that one moves into often feels like stepping off a cliff blindfolded, knowing (at first, just hoping!) that a pair of invisible hands is there to catch you. To illustrate the point, here is just one inspiring example of skywalking out of the hundreds of similar stories we have heard over the years.

We have a friend named Susan who lives in Los Angeles. She is an actress who is on a spiritual path, who is often out of work and so usually does not have much money. One day we received a call from her that she was having repeated strong feelings to come and visit us in Santa Fe. She felt as though she was ripe for some kind of breakthrough, some kind of special experience, and all she knew was that she felt very drawn to come to Santa Fe. The hitch was, though, that she didn't have any extra money to purchase a plane ticket. She had a credit card she could use, but she was very afraid of going into debt, because she had no extra income looming on the horizon. So, she kept resisting the feelings to come to Santa Fe.

This went on for months. During this time, she processed her money/debt issues and did her best to ignore her inner promptings. Until finally, the feeling was so strong and relentless that she just decided to take the plunge and put the $310 ticket on her credit card. She had processed enough to understand that spending the money was actually honoring her spiritual path, even though she did not know where the money would come from to pay the credit card company. Within three days after the purchase, she received a residual check in the mail from an old TV show she had done years previously, which had apparently aired as a re-run recently. The check was for approximately $310! She understood this to be confirmation that her skywalking was an accurate discerning of her highest path and that her trust had paid off. This is the magic of the new paradigm.

You probably have had some kind similar experience yourself at least once, even if not as dramatic, in which trust has paid off for you and in which you received a confirmation from spirit, but not until after you took the risk.

Usually the confirmation does not come until after you have taken the risk.

Skywalking is not about being flaky. It is not about just throwing caution to the wind and rushing into a risky situation because some part of you desires to. No, it is an act of power for which sober preparation is required. It is important to process yourself first, to look at the desires and fears around the issue in question, to get really clear before taking the risk and then to discern from a clear place if indeed spirit is guiding you to take the risk. It is not always possible to discern clearly, but by developing your intuition over time, you get good at it. It is best to start with small risks and then work up to bigger ones.

To give you a feeling for this, here is an example of being flaky as opposed to skywalking. You feel spirit may be asking you to stretch your budget a bit by making a large outlay of cash for something, for example to purchase a new car, to take some time off work, or to make a spiritual pilgrimage. But you are not sure if it is just a desire born of ego or if it is really in your highest good to do it. The flaky way to handle the situation might be to not balance the checkbook at all and just to do the thing after a quick process and a prayer, hoping a lot. If there is a heavy pattern of bouncing checks, of always being in credit card debt, of loathing keeping track of finances, or if there are deep childhood issues around feeling either deprived or spoiled with money, then it would be important to process those issues before attempting skywalking in this instance. Well-prepared skywalkers would first do a square on the desire and fear to do the thing, and the desire and fear to not do the thing. Then they might do some squares or polarities on related issues, like on having money and being broke. They might also want to examine their parental conditioning around money. Then, if the feelings to do the thing still persist, they might balance the checkbook to see just how much of a risk it really is. Then they might do some sober financial planning. They might also pray a lot and ask for strong guidance or signs from the universe. These are some examples of ways to prepare for skywalking.

Learning to skywalk is about letting go of neurotically needing to control your life yourself, of having to maintain your separate, individual, limited power. It is about building your discernment and trust muscles. Here are the steps:

- ◆ First you prepare with processing and prayer.
- ◆ Then you let go of attachments.

♦ Then you try to discern the appropriate course of action from the place of the witness (not from fear or fantasy).

♦ Then you act and have faith that you are loved and supported by the universe.

You may recognize where we got the name skywalking. In the movie *Star Wars*, the catchphrase, "May the Force be with you", sort of sums up the feeling of trusting in the invisible support of the Divine. And of course the main character who learned to do this so well is none other than—Luke Skywalker.

The new paradigm is a beautiful place to be. It is important you begin to recognize when you are in it, because then you will find it is easier to get back to it.

REVIEW

THE STEPS OF ADVENTURES IN TRANSFORMATION

1. Use squares to find your blind spots
   - ♦ Pray for grace and ask to be shown the hidden corner
   - ♦ Process with a friend or a group
   - ♦ See the hidden corner in someone else
   - ♦ Ask, "Why?" repeatedly
2. Use mirroring to find your blind spots
   - ♦ Ask, "How and why do I do the bothersome behavior?"
   - ♦ Ask, "How and why do I have an attachment to the opposite of the behavior?"
3. Find the giving and receiving aspects of squares
4. Find the true opposite and the ascended balance
5. Understand double binds
6. See through overwhelm, doubt and meaninglessness
7. Take a leap of faith—skywalking
   - ♦ Process and pray
   - ♦ Let go of attachments
   - ♦ Discern the highest course of action
   - ♦ Trust

SUGGESTIONS FOR PUTTING THEORY INTO PRACTICE

1. Do a square that you know you have trouble completing at least one corner of. Try all of the following techniques to see your blind spot. Write about your experience.
   - Pray for grace and ask to be shown.
   - Process with a friend or group.
   - See it in someone else.
   - Ask, "Why?" repeatedly.

2. Choose a bothersome person or circumstance in your life. Use mirroring to find your blind spots. Be sure to ask both questions: "How/why do I do the bothersome behavior?" and "How/why do I have an attachment to the opposite of the behavior?" Write about your experience.

3. Do squares on the giving and receiving aspects of:
   - Pleasure and pain
   - Like and dislike

4. Find the true opposite and the ascended balance for these words:
   - Manipulation
   - Anger
   - Avoidance
   - Shame
   - Guilt
   - Punishment
   - Fear
   - Worthlessness
   - Drudgery
   - Burden

5. Write a double bind in your journal. If you can't find one, pray to be shown one.

6. Do squares on:
   - Overwhelm and coping
   - Doubt and believing
   - Meaninglessness and meaningfulness

7. Take your next step in a skywalking adventure.
   - Process it
   - Pray about it
   - Let go of attachment to it
   - Practice discernment
   - Or actually take the leap of faith and do the thing

   Write about your experience.

Advanced Suggestions

1. Write a short biography of your mother and/or father, using lots of descriptive words, especially adjectives and adverbs. Include how you feel about her/him, if you like. Then use the processing methods on the story, underlining the key words, finding their opposites and offering the whole thing up. As you process, take the time to see how your parents' likes and dislikes affected you and still affect you. Try to find yourself in the story. Your parents are excellent mirrors for you. Do triangles and squares on the theme polarities.

2. Write short biographies on significant others in your life, for example: your spouse, your boss, your siblings, your petty tyrants, your past and present lovers. Use the processing methods with them, too. They are also significant mirrors of your own unconscious.

3. Do your own short biography and use the processing methods.

4. Can you find your core issue(s) (e.g., guilt, control, victim, approval)? Do a square and a triangle on your core issue.

TESTIMONIAL • DEADBEAT DAD

Several years ago, my daughter's grandfather died, and since her father was several years behind in his child-support payments, I decided to sue the grandfather's estate for the money.

After almost five years, the estate had not been settled, and that is when I learned how to do the Marriage of Spirit processing. I decided to process this situation. I was in great need of the money, and I hoped the processing would help me to resolve the issue.

I processed with a friend who had a lot of experience with the techniques. I talked to him about the hold up on the court and the money, and he wrote down all of the key theme words and phrases as I talked through my *story*. Then we did the opposites of all the theme words. And then we did squares on a lot of the theme polarities. I had many insights, covering a very wide range of issues, including how I felt about my deadbeat ex-husband, my feelings about men and being supported in general, my desire for and my repulsion to (this one was a surprise!) the money, and issues regarding the victim and tyrant. I saw many of my blind spots with my friend's help and discovered a lot about myself and about my projections onto the outside world (e.g., tyrants, and feeling unsupported by men and by God). These insights led to more polarities and squares.

Within a few days of the very first processing session, and after five years of waiting (!), the court issued a statement in our favor. The $14,000 was to be paid to my daughter. I was hooked on the Marriage of Spirit processing from that moment on.

Unfortunately, I was not quite finished with the situation. My daughter is disabled and had, at that time, become a ward of the state. Being a ward of the state, any money paid to her would go directly to the state. My ex-husband refused to put the check in my name so that I could give our daughter the money. I knew I still had some processing to do and some issues to clear!

Convinced of the power of processing and of changing my own inner consciousness in order to change the state of my outer world, I felt armed with powerful tools to resolve the circumstances. I processed with my friend again, and we worked on *having the check issued in my name*. I saw more about my concepts regarding men, money, support, and God, and worked through the next few layers of my *stuff*. We even found a lot of old stuff about my father and his beliefs about money. I had peeled off a lot of layers the first time to get that first shift, and I knew I would have to go even deeper to change my ex-husband's stubborn mind about this one.

I went home from that processing session and listened to the messages on my answering machine. To my total and utter astonishment, my lawyer had called about the exact time I had finished the processing session. He had left a message stating that my ex-husband had conceded and that the check would be issued in my name!

Needless to say, the immediacy and synchronicity of the changes during the whole episode convinced me of the power of processing, and I have not stopped doing it since. I am most grateful to Leslie for sharing the processing work with all of us.

You have to discover [your role or mission] and also the thing or things that oppose and do not allow it to flower.... In other words you have to know yourself, recognize your soul or psychic being. For that you must be absolutely sincere and impartial. You must observe yourself as if you were observing or criticizing a third person.... You should be like a mirror that reflects the truth and does not judge.

—The Sweet Mother of Pondicherry

FOURTEEN

DEVELOPING THE WITNESS

As we do the polarities, triangles and squares, we will strengthen our ability to remain in the witness at all times—while we work, while we play, even in very turbulent emotional situations. As the witness develops, we move into the clear light of reality and into a very joyful, expanded state of awareness.

In Chapter Six—The Witness we described in depth what the witness is, the principles behind witnessing and briefly introduced how to start witnessing. Just as a quick reminder, before we get into some further information about witnessing, here is a little summary of what the witness is and is not.

The witness practices neutrality and detachment. The witness does not take a position on either side of a pair of opposites. Being a witness is not about not having thoughts and emotional experiences anymore. Rather, it is about shifting your perspective of the thoughts and emotional experiences; it is about not *identifying* yourself with them. People sometimes fear that neutrality will be a rather boring, flat state where nothing much happens. This is not the case at all. We still experience thoughts and emotions. For example, pain and pleasure pass through us, and then they leave. But with a witness, we are unaffected by them. Even in experiencing them, we would not grab onto them. We would not say, "Oh, I'm having such pleasure. I am pleasure. I am a hedonist." Rather we would acknowledge, "Pleasure is passing through me, and I am pure awareness." When we embody the neutral witness, life is still very exciting. It is full of passionate, lovely experiences—births, deaths, triumphs, tragedies—yet we know none of it is real. We can let it pass through, not judging it, attaching to it or identifying with it. What is the neutral place, other than that part of us which does last forever? It is the one who is the witness, the one who watches life play through. That is the part of us that is eternal and changeless.

In this chapter we take a look at several important principles of witnessing and address ways to strengthen your witnessing capability. They are:

- ◆ Ask for a witness
- ◆ Simple suggestions to begin witnessing
- ◆ Meditating
- ◆ Processing supercharged and blocked emotions
- ◆ Not suppressing emotions
- ◆ Venting emotions, especially anger
- ◆ Speaking the truth of your inner feelings
- ◆ Changing old routines
- ◆ Processing with other people

ASK FOR A WITNESS

As we discussed in Chapter Six, the way to begin witnessing is simply to ask inwardly for the neutral witness to be instituted. You can start by praying for it to happen, by saying or writing in your journal daily affirmations that you want the witness to grow stronger. The more frequently you do this, the more grace will support you. Watch for judgment to come up, because it brings you out of the witness. When you see yourself doing judgment, process the judgments using polarities, squares and triangles. This applies when you see yourself identifying with your personality traits, too. Process them, and the witness develops as a natural by-product.

SIMPLE SUGGESTIONS TO BEGIN WITNESSING

Here are some simple suggestions to help you begin developing the witness:

- ◆ In key places at home and at work, place sticky notes that say things like, "Am I in my witness?" and "Remember the neutral witness." Write "witness" on the back of your hand. Get creative and have fun with this.
- ◆ Carry a small pocket notebook with you wherever you go, so that you can always make a note about things that pull you out of the witness or about areas where you are especially good at witnessing. Then later, you can journal about it.
- ◆ Make reciprocal pacts with friends that you will tell each other when you notice the other person has lost the witness.

MEDITATE

In order to develop a strong witness, it is very helpful to meditate daily. If you have been on a spiritual path, you know the truth of this. Meditating relaxes the body, stops the mind and helps you to let go into a very expanded state of awareness. You are able to detach and strengthen the neutral witness. For those of us who don't live in monasteries, meditating daily helps us keep our heads above water while being immersed in the world. It gives you energy, and when you have energy, you stay in your witness. Being tired means you fall back on automatic patterns. Meditating helps you find your balance when you have lost it. Even Western medicine has begun to acknowledge the benefits of meditation in that it reduces stress, lowers your blood pressure and improves your heart rate, just to name a few physical benefits.

I recommend at least two meditations a day: one when you wake up and one before bed. If you can do more, that is even better. Even twenty minutes here and there can be enough to keep you in your witness throughout the day.

If you have never meditated, there are plenty of places where you can learn. You can investigate these sources at any spiritual bookstore.

The processing work, coupled with meditation, is a terrific combination to help you strengthen your witness. In fact, I know of no better or faster way to clear the ego, to bring balance into your life and to wake up to who you truly are.

PROCESSING SUPERCHARGED AND BLOCKED EMOTIONS

As you do your processing work, you will find one of the greatest challenges you face is observing emotions from the place of the neutral witness. It is much easier to go into an emotional reaction, make the emotions real and completely forget everything about who you truly are—pure awareness through which emotion passes. When you get suddenly provoked and anger or betrayal or some other very volatile emotions arise, the normal reaction is to really get into it, to make a big drama out of it and to just dive into the juicy feelings. "To hell with witnesses…neutrality…spirit! I want my pound of flesh!!" As you continue to process, these supercharged programs, which run automatically, do weaken over time. It gets easier and easier to witness the feelings.

Another great challenge for many is just to get in touch with their feelings. Some people can be very blocked about what they are feeling. That is a very common pattern in most cultures, especially for men, but of course it applies to both genders. Usually when people first begin to learn the *unification of opposites* techniques, their stories will not have enough emotional content. But using the techniques helps people start to notice their emotions more. Then, even if they are only doing the polarities at the mental level, it will still have the effect, over time, of changing them, because they will start seeing their feelings more. Even if they are operating only at the *word game* level, some change will happen.

DON'T SUPPRESS EMOTIONS

The temptation to avoid in doing this work is suppressing your emotions. Many people mistake suppressing for detaching. The difference is that in detaching, you let the emotions pass through you. You enjoy them! If pleasure is there, enjoy it to the full, but when it leaves, let it go. It passes through. You don't need to cling to it and yearn for it be there all the time. When there is pain, feel it, give it full permission to be there completely, and it will pass, too. This is the trickiest part, because of course most people don't mind letting the pleasure pass through; it is the pain that we want to avoid! Pain is just a frequency. It may feel awful as it passes through you, but if you can ride out the storm, holding the neutral witness through it all, then you are freer in the end. Suppression means that you are actually cutting off the emotional body and pushing this emotional state into the unconscious. That is not a good idea. That just increases the sense of polarization and splits you even more.

So, doing this clearing work does not mean that you are not supposed to feel anything. You will still feel love, hate, pain and pleasure passing through you. Being neutral does not take away the feelings or the experience of life; it re-orients how you experience them. On the contrary, the emotions, feelings and experiences of life pass through you with a greater intensity when you are not attached to them, when you maintain an identity with the neutral witness, which actually becomes the higher self with time. You become more able to be fully present with them, to enjoy them for being an amazing and wondrous part of the human experience.

VENT EMOTIONS WITH A WITNESS

There are many processing methods or therapies that focus on venting and releasing emotions. Venting emotions means physically expressing whatever feelings arise in you and not suppressing them. For example, if during the processing session you remember as an infant how you felt traumatized by your mother for some reason and you feel like a two-year-old that wants to cry and throw a tantrum, then you express it. You sob, emote, throw your body on the floor and beat the rug with your fists.

This is an excellent way to discharge old, pent-up stuff, to become clear of emotional garbage that holds you back. If you choose to follow this path, I highly recommend that you develop a strong witness throughout the use of the venting technique. In fact, it is essential. Sometimes people can get caught up in the positive, charged feeling of catharsis that comes when venting emotion. It can bring with it a sense of apparent aliveness and exuberance. However, if there is not a very strong witness present while venting, catharsis has very little value. In fact reliving heavy emotions without a neutral witness present just deepens the groove that you cut for yourself in the first place. So, do vent, but remain vigilantly awake while doing it.

For example, just before venting, make an offering prayer to spirit, just as with the other techniques. Offer up your raging emotions and ask for detachment from identifying with them. Feel them, act them out, but let them pass through you, knowing you are not them.

Also, I highly recommend not venting *at* someone. Usually by doing this, you are just incurring karma, to use the Eastern terminology, the opposite of the goal. You want to complete your karmic debt, not add to it. Venting at someone and acting on feelings as though they are real means you invite future situations or lessons into your life in which you will need to relive and resolve those feelings and actions. As the Bible says, "…for whatever a man sows, that will he also reap." (Gal. 6:7) This is the law of karma. For example, you blame a co-worker or your therapist for something, and without a neutral witness present you explode in anger at the person, or covertly you seethe, grumble and despise the person for a week. At some point in the future, you will have someone blame you and get angry at you. However, the degree to which you are able to maintain a neutral witness in the face of volatile emotions is the degree to which you will not incur karma.

So, it is best to vent emotions like anger by beating your bed with a tennis racket, or by screaming into your pillow, or some other activity.

Vent and Detach from Anger

Many people say that no matter how much they process anger, they still find that they feel stuck with it and run by it. Anger is something that runs very, very deeply in everyone. Some are more successful at suppressing it. Others have a personality in which anger is very active in the conscious mind. But, anger is still an issue for everyone. Some people have more anger and some have less, depending on how much work they have done on themselves in one lifetime or another. With spiritual practice (in whatever discipline you feel drawn to), there is a lessening of anger.

You may have noticed that younger souls are often more prone to have anger spill out and to act out the anger than older souls. Younger souls are less developed souls. They have had fewer lifetimes of learning experience. Older souls have been around the block a few lifetimes and have accumulated a wealth of experience that has shown them where and how to be more circumspect in the choices they make in their daily lives. Older souls have learned that it is wiser to let anger pass through them and not to act it out. It is a good idea to let anger pass through you, rather than to identify with it. Remember that when you say, "I am angry," you are identifying that you are that thing. "I am the anger," is what you are saying. When you say it and think it like that, you actually become the anger, and then you have to act it out.

So, the process of detachment is one of the ways that spiritual practice teaches you to deal with anger. You do not suppress it. You simply allow the waves of anger to flow through you and do not have to act them out. Anger is just a frequency. Just as fear is just a frequency. Try examining your belief systems about anger. If you see that it is okay just to let anger be there and not to act it out, then you have awakened to a certain extent. If you see that anger can just pass through you because it is just another frequency, it will not even particularly ruffle your feathers when it goes through you. These are just degrees of learning to cope with anger.

Anger will always be there until the ego completely reorganizes, because it runs very deep in the system. Many of the veils that we experience that separate us from life and from the divine state are actually made of anger and fear. Anger and fear are very closely aligned to each other. They are very, very intense, volatile frequencies, which is why they upset us so much. It is not bad to feel anger. It is not necessarily good or bad. It is not necessary to put a judgment on anger at all. Anger, as I said, is just a frequency. If you understand that you are the eternal, changeless Self, then anger is just another aspect of life that passes through you. You do not have to make a big deal out of it.

It is important to come into balance with your attitudes about anger. Say for instance you have been someone who suppresses anger on a regular basis. You may spend quite a bit of time opening up the unconscious and letting that suppressed anger come to the surface. It is a way of getting to know yourself. You begin to see where it is that you have suppressed anger and what the sort of situations are that make you do that. Then, you begin changing them. It is not a good idea to suppress anything.

So, then the anger begins to show, and what do you do? Often it is very socially unacceptable, especially if people have known you as a fairly peaceable person—all of a sudden, you start acting out your anger, or they see a lot of anger coming out of you. You have to find ways to deal with it within your spiritual practice. And, it is best to find a way to vent anger in a harmless way. Have you seen the movie *Cabaret*? There is a wonderful scene where Liza Minelli and Michael York stand underneath a train overpass, screaming at the top of their lungs when the train passes overhead, and then they burst into laughter. You should try it. Or you scream into your pillow or beat your pillow or your bed with a tennis racket to vent the anger. You can get very creative at venting anger.

Anger is a highly magnetized, highly charged frequency, and it packs into the body in layers. So, once in a while, as you open up and the layers of the onion begin to dissolve, you have anger come through you. It has to be vented in a way that does not create more karma.

There was a man I worked with for a while who had a lot of suppressed anger to get rid of, so I suggested that he learn the martial arts by joining a karate school where they had a punching bag. Then when nobody was around, when the class was over, he would spend fifteen minutes punching the punching bag in the corner of the studio until he had completely cleared that volatile frequency out of his body.

The body then becomes relaxed and expanded. Anger has a way of creating a lot of contractions, a lot of tension in the muscles. You have to be able to vent it out. And, if you are venting it in a harmless way, then you are lessening the karmas. If you vent it by acting it out against someone, then you are creating new karmas. So, anger has got to be vented, and it is important that you do it in a harmless way. If dealing with anger seems to be more than you can handle on your own, it is best to find a good therapist to help you work through it. Often, having a guide is very helpful in this instance.

SPEAKING THE TRUTH OF YOUR INNER FEELINGS

After practicing the role of the witness for a while, you may find it is time to move into a more advanced level of witnessing. This includes being able to speak the truth of your inner feelings from your heart while remaining in your neutral witness. It is not as difficult as it sounds. Here are some guidelines and examples as to how to do this.

SPEAKING THE TRUTH OF YOUR INNER FEELINGS
STEP ONE — PROCESS YOURSELF FIRST

If you find yourself in a situation where you are feeling in conflict with someone, the best thing you can do is to process yourself first. The first plan of action is to go into your room with your notebook and process the conflict to see where *you* need to shift, where *your* hooks are, where *your* lesson is. By doing this, the other person's behavior usually changes because you have changed. As most of us have experienced, we don't usually create a win-win situation by telling the other person what is wrong with them and why they should change. However at a certain point after you have processed yourself deeply, there may come a time when you do need to speak to the other person about the situation. It is best not to do this until you feel very clear and in your heart with the person, otherwise you may cause more conflict, dig a deeper hole for yourself and create more karma. One processing session may not peel enough layers to do it. Sometimes it may take days or weeks or even months to get clear enough to be able to speak to the other person about the process. As you develop your inner discernment, you will know when it is time.

You may not always have the luxury of being able to process yourself first. During the initial conflict, you may have to say to the other person, "You have to excuse me, but I can't talk to you right now because I'm not in my heart with you." Then leave to go and process! Or if you are at work and saying that might not go over so well, you have to muddle through the best you can. Usually it is best to not say or do anything, but just make a mental note or a note in a pocket notebook about whatever the process is so you can process it later. When I had a 9-to-5 job, I used to keep a pocket notebook with me at all times for this very reason.

What is the benefit of speaking the truth of your inner feelings? When we speak untruth, a shadow is created, a veil that keeps us in separation. The purpose of this work is to extract ourselves from the separation, not to create more veils that will keep us trapped in the separate system, feeling isolated and alone and cut off.

The other option instead of revealing our inner truth is not to speak at all, to keep our feelings to ourselves, inside and hidden. Usually suppressing in this way leads to suffering, to creating shadows, occasionally to blowing up like a pressure cooker, and possibly to manifesting as ill physical health.

Most people have trouble speaking truth. It is not usually what we are taught as children, and so most people never learn how. For example, if you have the feeling of being drained of energy whenever you are around a particular friend or relative because they act like an emotional vacuum, would you be willing to say something to them about it? Often this kind of confrontation is very awkward and uncomfortable, and most people would prefer just to avoid the person rather than disclose the truth of their experience. As we learn to process our mental-emotional knots, speaking truth comes more easily with time. The flow of light and energy becomes clearer, and so the way we speak follows naturally along with this. For example in this instance, perhaps you could say to the person, "I feel like you must be in some kind of turbulent emotional state right now, because I'm feeling uncomfortable around you. Is there something you'd like to talk about?" At least this way you open the door to a healing and a deeper level of friendship.

For some who have learned to speak truthfully, the next step is to learn to speak the inner truth from the heart. It may be easy for them to voice their opinions and insights truthfully, but if it is done without heart, very often the effects may be detrimental to all involved. Even if their openness is well-intentioned, they may find that they are met with resistance or ill feelings if it is not from the heart.

How do we learn to speak the truth of our inner feelings from the heart? This is where the *unification of opposites* techniques come in very handy.

SPEAKING THE TRUTH OF YOUR INNER FEELINGS
STEP TWO—DISCERN YOUR TRUTH

The second step is to discern what the truth of your inner feelings is. With the processing comes great mental clarity, and along with that we get better and better at discerning our inner truth. We know when we are angry or upset or confused or hurt, instead of perhaps just ignoring all feelings, telling ourselves that how we feel or what is happening inside of us is not important. This tends to be the standard mode of operation for most people. Instead, as we process and do the journaling, we get very clear about the state of affairs of our inner world. The next step, speaking about it, is almost as vital.

SPEAKING THE TRUTH OF YOUR INNER FEELINGS
STEP THREE — SPEAK IT WHERE APPROPRIATE

The next step is to learn to speak the truth of our inner feelings where and when appropriate. We want to speak truth to create healings, to build bridges, to become of one heart and one mind with the other person—for example, letting your spouse know that you feel hurt by a comment, or letting your parent know you feel unheard. It is not a good idea to speak truth to get attention or revenge or for shock value or to indulge a selfish need to get something off your chest.

For most people, speaking about their inner feelings can bring up a lot of fear. Usually we fear the repercussions of it. Perhaps as children we got smacked for speaking out or were told, "Children should be seen and not heard." Or perhaps we were just ignored and learned by example that our opinions don't count. Very often we fear that what we need to say will hurt the other person. Whatever the reason, breaking through the wall of fear is a big step. The best way to break through the wall of fear is to pray for help. Ask for courage and grace. Most of the time, we don't break through the wall until we are pushed to the edge of our tolerance, until we feel so corralled by the limitation of our fear, which is actually the vibratory wall of the ego, that we are forced inwardly by our own discomfort to speak out. Usually we find that if we are very clear and can speak truthfully from the heart, the other person receives our news without a big drama or negative reaction. It is taken as it is given, with heart; and we find that our great fear was unfounded.

The irony of the whole situation around speaking the inner truth is that since we are all connected inwardly, at a certain level everyone knows exactly what we are feeling inside anyway! We think we are these separate, autonomous beings, and whatever is inside our heads is our own private domain which nobody can enter or see into. This is simply not true. As you do the clearing work and begin to wake up, you will see that you begin to become psychic. Sometimes you don't even need to be very psychic at all to know what someone is feeling or thinking because it is written all over the person's face. The person thinks they are hiding their feelings, but in reality everyone can see exactly what is going on inside. At this point the question becomes, "Why *not* speak your inner truth?!" Everyone involved usually feels a great sense of relief after the truth is spoken and the tension is broken.

SPEAKING THE TRUTH OF YOUR INNER FEELINGS
STEP FOUR — SPEAK IT FROM THE HEART

So, the next step is learning to speak from the heart. As we get clear inside by doing the processing work, we move into the heart naturally. We move from polarized, lower-chakra awareness into the consciousness of the fourth chakra and higher, into an acknowledgement that we are all one, even with people we are apparently in conflict with. Again, this happens only by processing ourselves first. It is not a good idea to enter into a discussion about the conflict until you have processed yourself first. Otherwise the tendency is to blame and project your own issues onto the other person. Best to see the other person's behavior as a mirror for yourself, as a reflection of your own unbalanced patterning, rather than blame. The other person probably has their own process involved in the conflict, too, but all you can do is process yourself. By doing this, you change, and then by default the other person will change their behavior toward you. Sometimes others don't change, but we are no longer triggered by them.

Here are some of the ways you will know if you are in your heart with someone, or at least moving in that direction. After you process, you will feel your awareness as a gentle, loving, easeful and numinous presence centered around the heart chakra, instead of as an agitated, heavy, uncomfortable, push-pull sensation in the lower chakras. There is a level of calmness, peace and clarity to your mental-emotional state. You will also have a certain degree of detachment to what the other person's reaction might be. Since you know you are in your own truth and intend no blame or harm toward the other person, you can let go, surrender and be unattached to the outcome of the discussion. You will also feel some degree of love, forgiveness and compassion toward the other person and the whole situation.

Waiting to talk with the other person until you have moved into the heart completely is not always possible. Sometimes it has to be a work in progress. We exercise our *heart muscles* in this way, and like a young child, we may fall down sometimes before we learn to walk steadily, and then to run. But eventually with practice we do become very good at the technique.

SPEAKING THE TRUTH OF YOUR INNER FEELINGS
STEP FIVE — FIND WHAT TO SAY TO OPEN THE
OTHER PERSON'S HEART

The next step is, if possible, try to find the thing you can say that will open up the other person's heart. Sometimes there is a common denominator to your process that can be the one key to unlock the door to the heart space. This may not always be an option, but here is an example. If you feel your spouse is not pulling his/her weight around the house, doing his/her fair share of the chores, you might find that you feel angry, resentful, abused and neglected. But perhaps underneath all of that, you might find the real trigger for you is that you feel *overwhelmed* by the messiness; you find it hard to cope with a sloppy house. So, you start by saying, "I am really having trouble with this because I feel overwhelmed by it. It's bringing up all kinds of strange emotional stuff that is uncomfortable, like anger and resentment. That makes me feel disconnected from you. Can we work out some kind of solution?" So, instead of unloading lots of data, details, surface content and huge amounts of emotion on the other person, you find the thing that will open the heart. You try to find the aspect of the process that will defuse the situation, rather than fan the flames. If you began by telling your spouse what a slob s/he is, that would not be very heartful and diplomatic.

Here is another of many examples I have experienced over the years of how this works. A friend of mine works in an office with three other associates. He would always complain to me about one of the coworkers, saying how she never pulled her weight. He always felt put upon because she was late, she didn't do the things she said she would do, she wouldn't do them in time or efficiently enough, she seemed to leave work early quite often, and he suspected she was not working her full amount of hours. He found all kinds of things to complain about, and yet he never said a word to her. He felt very comfortable complaining to me, but somehow he couldn't to her. He made excuses like: he didn't have enough proof to confront her, they were friends and so he didn't want to jeopardize their working relationship, her work was not bad enough to warrant a confrontation, and so forth.

Basically, he was just afraid of confrontation. So, finally he and I processed enough to where he felt he was in his heart with her and to where he felt he could speak his inner truth to her. Underneath the anger, frustration, resentment, blame and feelings of betrayal, we found that he really felt *unsupported* by her. This was the common denominator and felt like the piece that would open up her heart so that they could come to resolution. So he took big breaths, decided to plunge in and have the discussion. This was extremely difficult for him, as he loathed confrontation. He spoke his truth from his heart in each moment and explained how he felt. He did not tell her all of the things he perceived she was doing wrong. He simply said he felt unsupported and gave her a few examples as to why. He was amazed at the response. She was so happy he spoke up! She said that she had known for a long time that something was funny between them. At some level she knew there was a problem, but they couldn't resolve it until he was able to get it out in the open and heal the shadow of his unspoken feelings. She said the reason was that she was in a new relationship, felt very preoccupied and didn't feel present at work. She agreed to change because she valued their friendship and wanted to support him. They created a win-win working relationship.

CHANGE OLD ROUTINES

In developing a strong witness, it is necessary to break old patterns and routines. As long as you are acting by rote, there is no witness present. After you have processed and as your consciousness begins to shift, you may find yourself wanting to change aspects of your physical world. Of course the theme of this book is that first you change the inside by processing, and this helps to break the old patterns and routines. But when you have processed enough and you begin to wake up to the ways you run on automatic and are unconsciously stuck in old habits, it is time to physically act to change things. This helps provide a new environment where you are able to be more present, alive and aware, moment by moment—more in your witness.

You can begin changing old routines and getting the stuck energy moving in a very simple way. For example, get rid of old clothes that don't fit, that you don't wear anymore, or that are out of style. Give them to Goodwill or Salvation Army. Clean out your closets of other old things. They just remind you of old, stuck parts of yourself, anyway. They are the physical representation of stuck, old energy in you. Let them go. Plus, you will gain some good karma by giving the stuff to a charity or to someone else. It will help you to break your attachment to your possessions.

You can also clean your whole house. This is a spiritual trick that helps you purge the old, stuck energy. Try it, and you will see it is much easier to change yourself and to be fresh, alive and in the present moment with your new awareness and in your witness.

Next, get some nice new things. You don't have to be extravagant, and you don't even need much money to do this. How about a new haircut? Change you appearance. Start working out at the gym. Take a new route to work each day. Change your diet. Learn to do hatha yoga. Find unique ways to be fresh and new. You will see your witness move forward much more quickly if your physical world has some new life breathed into it, so you aren't so locked into old, grooved patterns.

So we are not talking about changing the trappings in an unconscious way, rearranging the furniture inside the prison, so to speak. It is important to remember first to process and to make the unconscious routines conscious. These suggestions are about the mystical practice of fluidity, of not being stuck in habitual behavior. Working on changing your physical world complements your work on changing your inner world—your energy and your patterning. Sometimes a physical act will be the very thing that helps you shift a pattern you have processed ad infinitum. Find fun and inspiring ways to change. It is all necessary to developing the witness.

Process with Other People

Processing with other people can be a really effective way to develop your witness and to see your blind spots because you can get objective viewpoints, instead of just your own. Your own viewpoint often will be quite narrow. You would not be having a problem with a polarity if you were not stuck on it, unable to see all aspects of it. Maybe in your community you can get some friends together to process. You do not even have to do it face-to-face. You can do it over the phone. You can even do it via e-mail! Create an agreement with other people about this work. "When I'm in a process, can I call you, and we'll process together?" You can even do group work with just one other person.

One way to do group work is decide on a square that everyone wants to work on together. It is usually easy to find a polarity that is particularly *hot* for at least a few people in the group. First, each person silently works alone on the first corner of the square for a while. Then, everyone shares answers with each other. Each person in turn reads aloud all the answers he or she found under the first corner of the square. Then, when everyone has finished sharing for the first corner, move on to the second corner, etc., until everyone has shared all their answers for all four corners. Then the group offers it up and waits for more information to come in. You can share that information with each other, too.

I know of many groups who get together weekly to do this kind of processing. They all have fun sharing their insights, helping each other with blind spots, and I see them progressing very fast with the clearing work.

If you are interested in participating in or starting a processing group in your area, please contact us at CoreLight. We may be able to help get you started. It is a wonderful way to do the egoic clearing work.

REVIEW
THE STEPS OF WITNESSING

1. Ask for a witness
2. Simple suggestions
   - Sticky notes
   - Carry a pocket notebook with you wherever you go
   - Make reciprocal pacts with friends to help each other witness
3. Meditate
4. Process supercharged and blocked emotions
5. Don't suppress emotions
6. Vent emotions with a witness
7. Vent and detach from anger
8. Speak the truth of your inner feelings
   - Process yourself first
   - Discern your truth
   - Speak it where appropriate
   - Speak it from your heart
   - Find what to say to open the other person's heart
9. Change old routines
10. Process with other people

SUGGESTIONS FOR PUTTING THEORY INTO PRACTICE

1. Place sticky notes around your house and in your car that say things like, "Am I in my witness?"

2. Carry a small pocket notebook with you wherever you go, so that you can always make a note about things that pull you out of the witness or about areas where you are especially good at witnessing. Then later, you can journal about it.

3. Make a reciprocal pact with a friend that you will tell each other when you notice the other person has lost the witness.

4. Rent a movie, or go to the movies. Keep a notebook in your lap. Try to stay in your witness the whole time. When you catch yourself losing the witness, make a note of it. Later, write about where you were pulled out of your witness and why. What did your mind do during that time?

5. Try venting once a day for a whole week. Try different methods of venting. For example, with anger: scream into your pillow, beat the bed with a tennis racket, throw a tantrum on your bed when nobody is around to hear you. Write about your experience.

6. Catch yourself once being in fear of speaking the truth. Write about it.

7. Speak one truth of your inner feelings to someone, even if a small one. Write about the experience. Where were you in your witness and in your heart, and where were you not?

8. Do at least two of the following:
   ◆ clean your home
   ◆ give away old clothes and other things
   ◆ change your appearance (e.g., a new haircut)
   ◆ drive a different route to work every day for a week.

9. Take two hours and do something that you would not normally do (e.g., go bowling, visit a museum, make a painting). Be in your witness during the whole adventure. Write about it later.

10. Learn to meditate. If you know how already, increase your meditation time. Write about your experience. Did it help you to maintain your neutral witness each day?

11. Form your own weekly squares processing group. Choose a polarity each week that the group agrees is relevant and do a square on it.

12. Call us at CoreLight to find or start a processing group in your area.

TESTIMONIAL • ORDER IN THE COURT

I work in a law office. We are the attorneys for plaintiffs in very big medical malpractice cases. Most of these cases involve people who have been mistreated and are extremely injured or possibly a spouse who has lost a husband or wife through a wrongful death. These people are usually in very depressed states and very vulnerable. When they come to us, they also have their depositions taken, which is a very difficult process for them to go through in their fragile and emotional state, because attorneys ask them probing and intense questions, sometimes simulating the extreme pressure of a courtroom. One day I was talking to one of the clients before her deposition, early in the morning. She was worried and frightened. She had already been through two sessions of depositions on two previous days, and because there were so many defendants (nine in all, which means nine different attorneys asking her questions), they needed a third session to try and complete her deposition.

She was a wreck, and the two times before this, she was in tears by the middle of the day. We talked for awhile, and I began to relate to her some of the tools I use with the Marriage of Spirit processing. One very important one is to be in touch with the neutral witness. I suggested that instead of reacting to their manipulating barrage of questioning, she should try to look at the whole picture like she was looking at a movie and like these are all of the players in the movie. I suggested that when something struck her and when she was beginning to feel attacked, to breathe deeply and watch it all pass through her. It is not real. It is just fear. I did not want to get into it too deeply because I felt she would not understand and possibly start to be put off. So, I kept it really simple. Well, she went in there like a new woman, confident and grounded.

Not only did she make a great witness that day, but they were through with her by 1:00 in the afternoon. Furthermore, when she came out of the room, she was beaming instead of crying. I was so happy for her. My boss noticed the difference, and now she lets me meet with our clients about 30 minutes before their depositions just to talk and relax together. I am grateful to Spirit for allowing this knowledge to come through me to help these people in an environment where it is needed so badly.

The ego's greatest triumph is to inveigle us into believing
its best interests are our best interests, and even into
identifying our very survival with its own. This is a savage
irony, considering that ego and its grasping are at the root
of all our suffering. Yet ego is so convincing, and we have
been its dupe for so long, that the thought that we might
ever become egoless terrifies us.

—Sogyal Rinpoche

THE DAILY REALITIES OF PROCESSING

This chapter includes some ways to further develop your processing skills and to make the most of the skills presented in previous chapters. We will take a look at some of the day-to-day realities of processing, including the importance of:

- ◆ Keeping track of your progress
- ◆ Witnessing bodily side effects of processing
- ◆ Witnessing re-wiring and re-circuiting
- ◆ Respecting others' process of integration.

I also want to share with you some ways that friends of mine have become really inventive with adapting the Marriage of Spirit techniques—in their work and in teaching them to others.

KEEPING TRACK OF YOUR PROGRESS

Each time you integrate polarities, you are creating little mini-enlightenments or unifications of the once-divided awareness. As you clear the patterning in those areas, limitation is replaced with awakeness. Working bit by bit with the different parts of a pattern, you gain awakening by degrees. Witnessing your progress as you move through the awakenings is important.

It seems as though there has to be some sort of spectacular revelation of progress before most people are willing to really see and accept what is happening to them. This does not negate the other small awakenings. A spectacular, experiential confirmation comes mostly as a result of a cumulative effect of the work; it is often given by grace to encourage you to accept your progress.

A phenomenon that I have noticed with this work is that sometimes people have trouble recognizing growth because they accommodate to the shifts of awareness so quietly and quickly. For example, I was working with a young man who was having trouble with his work environment. It seemed as though he always got really tyrannical bosses and would end up quitting. He learned the processing principles and applied them to his job situation, processing the tyrant-victim polarity.

After a few months he landed a new job. In a conversation with his mother, she expressed to me that she felt he was dubious about whether the processing had worked. I asked her whether he had created another tyrannical boss. She replied that he had not, but that his new boss had a tyrannical boss over her. I noted to her that the processing must have worked because he did not have a tyrannical boss and that this time he was in the position of observing someone else have the problem. It seemed to me that he then got the chance to observe the victim position objectively, without having to play that role himself. This was a sure sign that he had cleared some level of his tyrant issues. In the meantime his process had evolved to another stage so naturally that he did not quite notice it. Strange as it may seem, not noticing the shifts is quite common.

If the shifts come too gradually, you may lose track of the small incremental changes that eventually add up to a bigger and more obvious change. It is a funny thing about consciousness. Since most people do not have a witness, they are not able to see their progress. Not only do they not have the capacity to see where they are at any given moment, but they forget where they have come from. Usually the place we find ourselves at any given moment is perceived to be the place where we have always been. This is not the case at all. Awareness is cycling up and down and from side to side all the time, as we have seen in our explorations so far.

One of the problems is that we have trouble seeing the big picture and tracking the cycles of daily shifting. Mostly this is because we are too distracted, have no witness, and we forget. But it is also that we do not have enough right-brain function (holistic seeing, able to conceptualize the big picture) to synthesize our circumstances, especially in the Western world, which seems to operate mainly from the left brain (linear, logical, sequential, detail-oriented). I cannot stress enough the importance of holding the big picture as well as focusing on the details. Both are important in waking up.

There are several things you can do to overcome this dilemma and to help you witness your progress:

- ◆ Choose to work at a fairly fast pace so that there is definite, discernable progress. You are the one to set the pace with spirit; you can always ask for things to speed up or slow down.
- ◆ Keep a journal of your shifts, as it serves as a mirror for you. It is encouraging to see your progress mirrored back to you over time. Without that seeing, you may just drift along and mistake the flip-flopping of polarities for progress.

◆ Ask someone for objective feedback about your progress and have the person be your mirror. It is often easier for a close friend or a teacher to see the shifts you make. For example, perhaps a friend can tell you if you are easier to get along with in certain kinds of situations and if you are less reactive in circumstances that used to push your buttons.

I find I am able to track someone's progress by watching the changes that happen in the light body. Even if we do not speak often and if I see them only once in awhile, I can compare the before and after. The changes to the light body appear as an intensifying of the fullness of light and shine.

As we process over time, the light body becomes less a patchwork of dark and light and more solidly filled with light. Eventually, the light body has the look of solid light and is very aligned along its axis, very straight. The person begins to visibly glow through the skin, no matter how old he or she is. The axis, or core within the light body, becomes like a glowing pillar of light. Correspondingly, the posture, strength and overall health of the physical body improve enormously.

Life will become discernibly smoother over time with the processing work. Eventually, bursting through a dam of perception, change is realized, and you see you are different. The connection to presence becomes more and more tangible as you become more unified. You begin to see clearly that you are waking up, even though you may not be all the way there. It is also important to remember that although there are major milestones along the way which show you how far you have come, it is the small daily successes in integration that add up to progress.

WITNESSING BODILY SIDE EFFECTS OF PROCESSING

As you do the processes, you will find that your body goes through shifts, which are important to witness. If you have shifted a major block, symptoms often manifest which appear to resemble illness for brief periods. Sometimes you may have to go to bed for a couple of days if a really big shift takes place. Do not be alarmed by any of this. Some of the difficult symptoms could look like this:

◆ Flu-like achiness in the muscles
◆ Fever
◆ Diarrhea
◆ Constipation
◆ Sleeplessness
◆ Needing more than usual amounts of sleep
◆ Dizziness and fuzziness

- ◆ Fatigue and lack of motivation
- ◆ Hot flashes
- ◆ Sudden acne or rashes erupting, particularly along the body's meridian lines.

The more enjoyable effects could look like this:
- ◆ Tremendous amounts of energy and stamina
- ◆ Needing less sleep than ever before
- ◆ A luminous glow to the skin
- ◆ A feeling of lightness, buoyancy and joy
- ◆ Feelings of effervescence and expandedness
- ◆ Creative ideas coming faster than you know what to do with
- ◆ Health and strength as never before.

We all go through phases of experiencing the above with any kind of transformational work. This is pretty normal. When we experience the temporary negative effects, usually there is an intuitive knowing that the symptoms are associated with the work, and this helps us not to get alarmed. As you cycle through rapid change, expect to pass through many of these symptoms at one time or another. Never assume you will be stuck in any one of them for long. If it seems you are, you will need to process why you are stuck. Or use your discernment and seek medical assistance if you feel it is necessary. When you experience the positive effects of processing, enjoy them!

WITNESSING RE-WIRING AND RE-CIRCUITING

As you work on yourself, the body eventually enters a period of health, freedom and strength that is unparalleled. As you learn to manage your energy and to live impeccably, the light body becomes stronger. As you process and clear the mental-emotional beliefs, ideas of lack and limitation and all the attachments, which form constricting overlays on the light body and the physical body, the physical body feels lighter, safer, and freer.

The symptoms mentioned above are relatively short-lived. They are usually a signal that you are being re-wired. Just as an old house needs a new electrical system when it is renovated, so the body needs to be re-circuited after a big shift has taken place. The re-wiring usually only takes a few days and seldom is strenuous enough to make you stay in bed, although that will happen occasionally. Relax. Witness the feelings. Enjoy some rest time. You will be better than ever when it is over. If this does not happen easily, then there are issues in the way that need to be processed. In time you will be able to see them all and clear them.

If you have deep-seated physical problems born of *samsara* (past life tendencies), they might take awhile to clear, but you *will* get to them eventually. *Samsara* is the Sanskrit term for the tendencies which are carried forward from another life and repeated in this lifetime. These old-new patterns of belief give rise to ways of thinking that are limiting to your life's expression and which block you from growing and awakening into new, clear perceptions of truth. As you do your spiritual practice, the body improves enormously, basking in the light of the cleared mental and emotional bodies.

RESPECTING OTHERS' PROCESS OF INTEGRATION

We are entering a time when the state of enlightenment, or spiritual awakening, will become much more commonplace. You or your best friend could become enlightened. Certainly if you are on a spiritual path, then there is a good chance that you will soon know someone who is already enlightened or well into the process of waking up.

This, in itself, raises new and interesting possibilities for dramas. How will you cope if your best friend becomes enlightened? Especially if you have been on the path for years, and it is the desired and coveted goal. We must remember that many beings are moving into this phase now. We must accept this phenomena and avoid competing with others who are awakening into these levels.

Most people at a personality level are so accustomed to competing with others that these unusual circumstances are making it absolutely necessary to clear the personality. It is important to develop new levels of respect and acceptance for our peers, and it seems imperative that we support one another with our clearing work. In fact it has become increasingly clear that this mass awakening is a collective effort and that we are being presented with the unprecedented possibility of waking up together, as groups. Enlightenment was once so rare. Now there is the possibility of it happening to each of us and to many of those around us. As large groups do the work of processing their patterns, the veils of conditioning will clear in the archetypes of Western society and divine presence will become a tangible resource available to all. When this happens, all will be at peace and in cooperation with life rather than in resistance to it.

These new energies entering awareness are asking you to cooperate with others who are seeking the same goals. Assisting each other as fellow seekers in this work is appropriate now. In the near future you will be asked to assist the many others who are going through changes.

It is important to respect others' paths by not judging them and by clearing your own patterning instead. When we are not clear ourselves, it is hypocritical to try to *fix* others. As Jesus said (Matthew 7:3-5): "Why do you look at the speck in your brother's eye, but do not consider the plank in your own eye? Or how can you say to your brother, 'Let me remove the speck from your eye'; and look, a plank is in your own eye? Hypocrite! First remove the plank from your own eye, and then you will see clearly to remove the speck from your brother's eye."

You must be very accepting of the fact that everyone is unfolding at different speeds and often in different ways. Everyone passes through the different stages of integration in their own time and in their own way. As you proceed in this work, you will see that enlightenment comes in gradually. There are many degrees of enlightenment. You cannot necessarily know where people are on the journey, and you must respect their development.

GETTING CREATIVE WITH THE TOOLS

You can really get creative with the processing techniques. Over the many years of teaching the methods, I have watched my friends take the principles and apply them to their own fields of work. For example, a psychologist with a background in theater and performing arts has applied the polarity work to her psychodrama classes. She actually has people act out both sides of a polarity, perhaps from childhood scenarios or from more recent dramas. She will have them act out their role and their antagonist's role (maybe a parent or a boss) so that they can physicalize both sides of the drama, both sides of their own consciousness! I have watched her facilitate some of my own classes with this method, and it creates very powerful transformation.

One friend of mine has a background in emotional release therapy. In his therapy groups, he will have the group process a square. They designate each of the four corners of the square to correspond to the four corners of the room. Then people go to one corner of the room at a time and from the place of the witness feel the emotions in that corner of the square. When they have finished all four corners, they make an offering and let it go. The groups report powerful shifting happening.

Another friend of mine who was the manager of 500 employees at a state government office, liked the squares technique so much that he taught everyone how to do them at a staff meeting! When I learned about this, I was a bit shocked. But several months later, when I checked in with him about how things were going with his little experiment, he said that many people had really taken to the squares. He said as a regular weekly occurrence, he would overhear people processing together at work! After some time, he reported higher productivity in his department, and he noticed that people in general became happier and more light-hearted. He said that he noticed a sense of buoyancy around the office that he had never felt before.

Others have used the Marriage of Spirit in teaching art therapy classes, in working with the dying and in leading many kinds of workshops, from the practical to the esoteric.

If you are interested in attending a Marriage of Spirit seminar, which we offer from time to time in various cities around the world, please contact the CoreLight office.

In gratitude for the gift of the techniques I was given by my spiritual guides, I have felt inspired to share the information. So, I invite you to be creative with them. If you find the principles helpful, please apply them in whatever way you see fit and share them with people you know. The information is freely given, with a lot of love. I hope you find as much grace and receive as many gifts as I have by taking the Marriage of Spirit to heart.

REVIEW
THE DAILY REALITIES OF PROCESSING

1. Keep track of your progress
   - Work at a fairly fast pace
   - Keep a journal of your shifts
   - Get feedback from a friend
2. Witness side effects of processing on the body
3. Witness re-wiring and re-circuiting
4. Respect others' process of integration
5. Get creative with the tools

SUGGESTIONS FOR PUTTING THEORY INTO PRACTICE

1. Consider making a commitment to spirit to speed up the pace of your processing.
2. For one month keep track of your overall progress by writing in your journal and getting feedback from a friend. Can you notice progress in any specific areas of your patterning?
3. The next time you feel any symptoms of physical illness, ask inwardly if they are related to your current process. Witness them, knowing they are temporary and not real, and write about your insights.
4. The next time you feel extraordinarily joyful or exuberant, or full of energy or creativity, ask inwardly if the feelings are related to a breakthrough in your current process. Enjoy them and write about your insights.
5. Next time you experience a shift from processing, go into a meditation and try to feel the re-wiring happening in your physical body and along the body's meridians. Write about your experience.
6. Do one supportive thing for a friend who is also on the path of Self-discovery. If you find there is any part of you that in some way is not respecting your friend's process (e.g., resentment, competitiveness, jealousy), witness it and use the polarities, squares and triangles techniques to clear yourself.
7. Can you think of a creative way to bring the Marriage of Spirit techniques into your own line of work or home life?
8. Contact us at CoreLight to inquire about attending a Marriage of Spirit seminar.

TESTIMONIAL ◆
THE STORY OF THE STALKER

Strange things were afoot. Heinous debates raged over an anti-
gay ballot measure to officially declare homosexuality
"immoral, unnatural, and perverse" in the Oregon state char-
ter. Divisiveness reigned. For nine months every front lawn had
a sign for or against the measure, including mine (against).

Meanwhile, anonymous nocturnal visitations wrecked my domestic
peace. It was several weeks before I told the police and my closest friends
what was happening. I was in total denial until the night I heard a ladder on
my bedroom window and found myself unable to speak to the 911 operator
for want of breath.

The presumed source of this phenomenon became known as *the stalker*.
In vain, police and friends tried to help me discover who was culpable. No
amount of sleuthing or vigilance offered a clue or viable solution. I became
a sleep deprivation case. Both dramas (the ballot measure and the stalker)
became intertwined in my mind and emotions. I felt rage at the unknown
forces of collective hate manifesting in the state and at the specific terror-
ism directed at me in my home. Yet I felt totally to blame within.

Eventually the ballot measure was defeated by a slim margin, but the
stalker's activities were not to be curtailed by any such democratic process.
Regardless of my new motion-sensitive floodlights and recently rented,
140-pound Rottweiler companion trained to kill, the rap-a-tap-tapping
continued. I kept stuffing all the feeling as best I could, hoping the fear and
pain of powerlessness and helplessness would go away if I ignored them. I
told myself I was safe with my huge dog and got a couple of decent nights'
sleep. I was beating this thing, I thought.

One evening Baron (my dog) and I were sprawled out before the fire,
me with a book, him with a bone. I took care that all the shades were pulled
tight. One shade, however, was raised just a tad by a catch on the sill. I
started with fear when I noticed this and reproached myself for an
unfounded paranoia. A few moments later my eyes nervously darted to
inspect the spot again. There were two eyes staring in at me! The look that
met my gaze sent a violent shudder through my body. Baron had not heard
a thing.

I called my brother in Los Angeles. I was desperate. On the phone I
cried, told him the whole story, and asked for his advice and help. He has

since told me that he had been waiting for a few years for the opportunity to tell me about the Marriage of Spirit processing techniques. He had tried to tell me once before, but I had met him with what he tells me now was a stony, skeptical, and self-righteous resistance. Moi?

Anyway, we both sensed I was desperate enough to surrender my reason long enough to let something new in, something beyond reason. What little *reason* I had left was on its way out by this point anyway. In short, I felt I had nothing left to lose. He proceeded to tell me about the principles and techniques of the Marriage of Spirit. I opened my heart to it, and we processed right away. I made lists of words and their opposites about my drama with the stalker and with the Oregon anti-gay ballot measure. The lists included everything I was thinking and feeling. They included my opinions about liberality, which I prided myself on, and conservatism, which I was repulsed by. Some of the main themes of my list were the polarities of: victim-rebel, victim-tyrant, and rebel-tyrant.

In my desperation, I agreed to accept that this *stalker* was merely acting out for me projections of my own unconscious mind. He was mirroring to me the split-off, projected-out pieces of me. I was stalking myself! I prayed to be able to own the stalker as a part of me. I also agreed to look deeply at the anger and indignation the ballot measure had inspired, all of which I had swept under the rug and stuffed into the unconscious. I had projected it all outside, would not look at it and would not acknowledge it at the time.

We processed for about an hour on the phone before I felt a shift. I did not know quite what had happened to me, but I could tell that some aspect of my consciousness had changed somehow. I felt slightly clearer, although how so was a bit vague. To my amazement, but not to his, after that phone call, I never heard or saw anything of the mysterious stalker again. I have been a processor ever since and grow increasingly grateful for the techniques. Not only have I not experienced gross and dramatic traumas like the stalker story, but over time my life and my consciousness have become much smoother and more joyful.

My Commitment to You

Dissolving the veils of ego and becoming very transparent with life and with those around you brings in the transcendental light, which is the energy of unconditional love, unity, wisdom and vitality. It is called transcendental because it is transcendent to, or beyond, the conditioned personality or ego. As you do the processing and clear the knotted parts of the conditioned personality, you begin to see more of your luminous, true nature, which is present but transcendent to your old, everyday states. Over time you become less dense and more able to hold light in your mind, your heart, and in your physical body. As you process, there are magical moments when the curtain of illusion parts and a much more expanded vision of existence and of your true self is revealed. When you are full of light, it becomes easy to be completely present with life, giving every moment your full attention and receiving fullness from life in return.

Time taken to clear the ego and to discover the depths of your soul is never misspent. Life becomes immeasurably better when you work on yourself. Self-discovery leads you to the riches and depth of the greatest treasure trove there is—your true self. My commitment to you is that you will realize your wholeness by reading and using the Marriage of Spirit teachings.

REFERENCES

Assagioli, M.D., Roberto. *Psychosynthesis, A Collection of Basic Writings*. Wellingborough, UK: Turnstone Press, Limited, 1984.

Awakening Osiris. Translated by Normandi Ellis. Grand Rapids: Phanes Press, 1988.

Bhagavad Gita, The Song Of God. Translated by Swami Prabhavananda and Christopher Isherwood. Hollywood: Vedanta Press, 1987.

Casteneda, Carlos. *Tales of Power*. New York: Simon and Schuster, 1974.

The Collected Works of C.J. Jung, No. 6: Psychological Types. Edited by Michael Fordham and R.F. Hull. Princeton: Princeton University Press, 1971.

The Collected Works of C. J. Jung, No. 9: Archetypes and the Collective Unconscious. Edited by Michael Fordham and Herbert Read. Princeton: Princeton University Press, 1968.

The Collected Works of C.J. Jung, No. 13: Alchemical Studies. Edited by Adler Gerhard and Herbert Read. Princeton: Princeton University Press, 1983.

Courtenay, Bryce. *The Power of One*. New York: Random House, 1989.

Dharma, Krishna. *Ramayana*. Los Angeles: Torchlight Publishing, Inc., 1998.

Eliade, Mircea. *Yoga, Immortality and Freedom*. Princeton: Princeton University Press, 1973.

Fromm, Eric. *The Art of Loving*. New York: Harper, 1956.

How To Know God, The Yoga Aphorisms of Patanjali. Translated by Swami Prabhavananda and Christopher Isherwood. Hollywood: Vedanta Press, 1983.

Hua Hu Ching: The Unknown Teachings of Lao Tzu. New York: Harper Collins Publishers, 1992.

Houston, Jean. *The Passion of Isis and Osiris, A Union of Two Souls*. New York: Random House, 1995.

Janov, Arthur. *The Primal Scream, Primal Therapy: The Cure For Neurosis*. New York: Dell Publishing Company, Inc., 1970.

Johari, Harish. *Chakras, Energy Centers of Information*. Rochester, NY: Destiny Books, 1987.

Keyes, Ken. *The Hundredth Monkey*. Coos Bay, OR: Vision Books, 1986.

The Life of Milarepa. Translated by Lobsang P. Lhalungpa. Boulder, CO: Shambhala Publications, Inc., 1984.

M. *The Gospel of Sri Ramakrishna*. Translated by Swami Nikhilananda. Forward by Aldous Huxley. New York: Ramakrishna-Vivekananda Center, 1977.

Man The Artist, His Creative Imagination. Edited by Sir Gerald Barry, Dr. J. Bronowski, James Fisher and Sir Julian Huxley. Designed by Hans Erni. London: Macdonald and Company Ltd., 1964.

Matt, Daniel C. *The Essential Kabbalah: The Heart of Jewish Mysticism*. Edison, New Jersey: Castle Books. 1997.

Mayotte, Ricky Alan. *The Complete Jesus*. South Royalton, UK: Steerforth Press, L.C., 1997.

Mookerhjee, Ajit. *Kundalini - The Arousal of the Inner Energy*. New York: Destiny Books, 1982.

The Nag Hammadi Library in English. Edited by James M. Robinson. San Francisco: Harper and Row, 1988.

Perls, Fritz. *In and Out of the Garbage Pail*. Lafayette, CA: Real People Press, 1969.

Purce, Jill. *The Mystic Spiral, Journey of the Soul*. New York: Thames and Hudson, 1997.

Ram Dass. *Remember, Now Be Here, Be Here Now*. San Cristobal, New Mexico: Hanuman Foundation, 1978.

Redfield, James. *The Celestine Prophecy: An Adventure*. New York: Warner Books, 1993.

Shankara's Crest Jewel of Discrimination. Translated by Swami Prabhavananda and Christopher Isherwood. Hollywood: Vedanta Press, 1978.

Shlain, Leonard. *Art and Physics, Parallel Visions In Art, Space and Light*. New York: William Morrow and Company, 1991.

Sogyal Rinpoche. *The Tibetan Book of Living and Dying*. New York: Harper Collins Publishers, 1994.

Tibetan Yoga and Secret Doctrines. Arranged and Edited by W.Y. Evans-Wentz. Oxford, UK: Oxford University Press, 1981.

The Upanishads. Translated by Swami Prabhavananda and Frederick Manchester. Hollywood: Vedanta Press, 1996.

Witteveen, Dr. H. J. *Universal Sufism*. Rockport, MA: Element Books. 1997

The Yoga of Delight, Wonder and Astonishment. Translated by Jaidava Singh. Albany: State University of New York Press, 1991.

Yogananda, Paramahansa. *Autobiography of a Yogi*. Los Angeles: Self-Realization Fellowship, 1990.

GLOSSARY

ananda—bliss; joy; a type of *samadhi* in which awareness experiences the unity of the Divine, primarily through the deeper levels of the awakened heart.

archetypes—larger-than-life personalities which have become role models, or events which have become familiar constructs, impacting collective consciousness in different cultures throughout history. In the West we have been most influenced by the biblical and Greco-Roman archetypes.

ascension—the raising of the vibration of the mind-body system, in which awareness perceives from a more expanded vantage point.

Atman—the inner, divine God-consciousness present within each of us.

bi-polar—two magnetic poles, the negative and positive.

brain, left and right—the human brain comprises two hemispheres, and they perceive differently. The left is linear, logical and sequential, and the right is holographic and synthesizes large amounts of diverse pieces of information. The left brain is usually associated with the masculine, and the right with the feminine.

chakras—energy centers; swirling vortices of energy in the subtle body, reflecting different levels of attention and supporting and upholding physical form.

collective consciousness— a repository of information and thought-forms accessed by everyone in a group; a mass agreement. The full spectrum of shared knowledge of all humanity—both conscious and unconscious.

core—an English word for the *shushumna*. Core energy is found in the nucleus of each cell.

detachment—letting go of egoic desires or needs for and dependency on the transitory things of the material world—on the unreal, on the illusion.

darshan—a gathering to share spiritual lore and to receive divine blessings.

dharma—spiritual truth; religious duty; the way of truth; spiritual destiny; natural law.

double helix—an interlocking ascending and descending spiral. A double-helix makes up the electromagnetic field of the subtle body, termed the *ida* and *pingala*; also found in the DNA of each cell.

duality, dualities (pl.)—divided in two; the term for describing our world, reflecting its nature of opposites.

ego—the separate self; the false identity; the conditioned personality which perceives itself as separate from the whole.

enlightenment—an all-encompassing perception of non-separation. It is the awareness that we are all one, interconnected on a mental, emotional, physical and spiritual level, contained by and directly extended from the Oneness of cohesive essence that gives rise to the universe and existence itself.

eternality—referring to the changeless, timeless, immortal nature of God.

fourth chakra—the heart chakra; the energy center corresponding to the area of the physical heart.

grace—a force of divine love, healing and support which flows to us when we invoke it or pray for it.

grounding—the ability that people have to steady and balance themselves by mentally, emotionally or physically holding onto something, such as: an idea, a physical possession, another person, an occupation, the earth.

ground of being—the essence which, though unseen, supports life.

higher self—the Atman, the inner God-consciousness.

humility—non-judgment of oneself and others; a state of non-rebelliousness; non-willfulness; a state of acceptance; a state of quiescence in the mind and emotions; a state of not identifying with ego.

ida—the passive, descending flow of energy and awareness in the subtle body; associated with the feminine.

impeccable, impeccability—a subtle state of order; the ability to use energy in a balanced, perfect and economical way.

Jnana yoga—the yogic practice of inquiring into the nature of ourselves, including the personality and all spiritual levels of awareness, with the intention of seeing the truth of our being. (see also *yoga*).

karma—consciousness or action. Consciousness gives rise to action, reflecting the fact that action has a cause and an effect and that we have to face the consequences of our actions.

koan—a paradoxical statement; or idea reflecting a paradox; by being unexplainable through logic or language, it stimulates deep inner shifts of awareness.

kundalini—energy; life force; fire of life; *Shakti*.

light body—the subtle-physical body which is formed of light and energy; aura.

lineage—a succession of teachers and students coming from a common spiritual teacher.

Maya—the principle of appearance; illusion; marvelous power of creation.

metaphysics—the study of that which is subtly perceived beyond the physical.

mystic—one who studies the mystery of life, the metaphysical.

neti neti—Sanskrit, "not this, not this." Meaning, "not the illusion of life" but rather the ultimate reality. Coupled with "*Tat twam asi*," or, "I am That," it is an affirmation of one's divine state. A term used in the practice of *Jnana yoga*.

neutral observer, neutral witness—that part of us which is able to perceive without judgment the conditioned personality being acted out.

persona—energy patterns which have formed a matrix, having particular characteristics, and which have developed their own sense of identity. Often several personas are contained within one individual's sense of personal identity.

pingala—the active, upward energy flow in the subtle body usually associated with the masculine energy.

polarity—the opposition formed by negatively and positively charged attributes.

processing—our method of working with limited, blocked and rigidly structured awareness, in order to free and restore its naturally fluid state.

projection—one's unconscious ability to push away energies which one does not like or want to be directly associated with.

rebirthing—a method of dissolving egoic patterns using special breathing techniques. It facilitates emotional release and insight into past experiences, including the traumatic.

reconciliation (or unification) of opposites—the method of processing polarities to bring about balance. Joining the opposites to create a third, ascended state.

samsara—aggregates of awareness from past lives which have been stored in the soul and are carried forward to influence the personality in the current life.

samsaric—of *samsara*.

samadhi—an unusually balanced state of awareness without negative or positive bias. A person in *samadhi* is holding a state of unity consciousness, emanating truth and effulgence.

self—associated with one's sense of oneself as the personality. Yet the self is really the superconscious Self in disguise.

Self, the—the authentic, eternal, immortal beingness that we all are; God.

Self-discovery—the practice and inquiry into the Self, or God; the spiritual path of awakening.

self-inquiry—the practice of looking at consciousness, whether patterned or liberated.

Self-realization—experiencing and permanently actualizing direct knowledge of the Self, or God, making this more real than the apparent "realness" of the world.

shadow—one of the descriptions given to the unconscious side of the ego

Shakti—the creative force of light which gives rise to the world; divine energy, usually symbolized by the feminine.

Shiva—the supreme; one of the names of God. One of the Hindu trinity with *Vishnu* and *Brahma*.

shushumna—in the subtle body, corresponding to the spine, it forms the body's axis or center. It is the mysterious internal presence of non-dual consciousness.

sixth chakra—in the center of the forehead, just slightly above the eyebrows; third eye.

squares—a method of polarity processing which allows views into the unconscious.

subtle body/bodies—non-physical body/bodies, e.g., see "light body".

superconscious—awareness beyond and more all-encompassing than the limited personality.

synchronicity—an aligning of energies and events with such perfect timing so as to make them appear miraculous or coincidental.

Tantra—a practice or a pathway to enlightenment using the reconciliation of opposites.

tat twam asi—Sanskrit, meaning "I am That," in which "That" is one of the names of God. When repeated in the face of illusory situations, it is an affirmation of our true divine state and leads to a deepening of Self-realization.

third chakra—the chakra at the solar plexus; the center for the energies reflecting power and powerlessness.

third eye—the chakra or energy center located in the center of the forehead between the eyebrows; the center of wisdom; the center for the neutral observer; sixth chakra.

triangles—a method of the reconciliation of opposites which brings our attention into the heart and upper chakras.

unification (or reconciliation) of opposites—the method of processing polarities to bring about balance. Joining the opposites to create a third, ascended state.

unity consciousness—the superconscious or divine state of awareness where all dualities have resolved into wholeness.

Upanishads, the—a collection of ancient scriptures forming the last part of the *Vedas*.

warrior spirit—a spiritual state of great strength and courage attained by a seeker who has faced limitations and has transcended them. One who has faced the enemy within.

wheel of karma—without an understanding of the nature of cause and effect, we will continue to perform actions which trap us in physical existence. This turning cycle resembles a wheel.

Veda—knowledge; wisdom; the sacred scriptures of the Hindu religion. (see "*Upanishads, the*")

Vedanta—the name of the different schools of philosophy founded on the teachings of *the Upanishads*. The central question of the *vedantic* schools concerns the nature of the Self or *Brahman*.

yang— in the Chinese Taoist schools of thought, the yang energy is the active, expressive, extroverted, masculine energy.

yin—in the Chinese Taoist schools of thought, the yin energy is the passive, receptive, introspective, feminine energy.

yoga—union or yoke; the path to unity consciousness, to the experience of oneness with all that is.

Zen—The enigmatic state of unity with all that is.

About the Authors and CoreLight

Leslie Temple-Thurston graduated from the University of Witwatersrand, Johannesburg, South Africa with a degree in fine arts. In the mid-1970s, she moved to Los Angeles with her family. Here she deepened her studies of ancient wisdom through meditation and by exploring the works of the new spiritual psychologies. In 1988, she began presenting her Marriage of Spirit seminars and meditation/discussion events. Today she continues to offer events worldwide and is dedicated to working closely with groups of people who are committed to transformation and spiritual awakening. Leslie lives in Santa Fe, New Mexico. *The Marriage of Spirit* is her first book.

Brad Laughlin is the Executive Director of the non-profit organization, CoreLight, which presents the Marriage of Spirit seminars and other transformational, meditative events worldwide. He has a BS degree from Duke University and has been involved with this work for over ten years, helping to develop the Marriage of Spirit techniques. He lives in Santa Fe, New Mexico.

CoreLight is a community of people worldwide who are connected by their commitment to spiritual awakening and to fostering inner and outer peace in the world. Our name, CoreLight, refers to the luminous core of enlightenment within each one of us. We first gathered in Los Angeles in 1990 to support the work and teachings of Leslie Temple-Thurston and are now a non-profit organization.

Leslie's teachings flow from the blessings she has received on her own spiritual path. They are a unique and eclectic blend of different traditions, and their roots are based in universal truth. One aspect of her work is her transmission of healing and transforming energy, known in the East as shakti, given at all of her events to each person present, during periods of meditation and discussion. The effects of the transmission are profound and enduring. Leslie also works with energy at a collective level to help foster peace in the world.

CoreLight offers ongoing courses (Spiritual Warrior Training and Teacher Training), darshans, retreats and other events worldwide. We have audio tapes of Leslie's teachings on an extensive range of topics, all of which are available by catalog and via our website.

To receive more information about Leslie, an event calendar, information about ongoing courses or a catalog of audio tapes, please visit our webite or contact us:

CoreLight's Main Office:
223 North Guadalupe Street, PMB 275
Santa Fe, NM 87501-1850, USA
Local Phone: (505) 989-3552
Toll free (U.S. and Canada): (888) 989-3552
Fax: (505) 989-1074
Email: info@corelight.org
Website: www.corelight.org
or www.marriageofspirit.com

CoreLight Tapes & Books:
Local Phone: (505) 984-1045
Toll Free (U.S. and Canada): (888) 301-9282
Fax: (505) 984-1639
Email: ganesh@corelight.org

The Marriage of Spirit **is distributed by:**
Blessingway Books, Inc.
(800) 716-2953

Why is it when we talk to God
we're said to be praying,
but when God talks to us
we're schizophrenic?
—Lily Tomlin